Garden City Elementary School

Donated to the Garden City Elementary School

Dec. 19, 1975

By The Twilighter Extention Club

Mary Smithmier "President"

Garden City Elementary School

DEDICATED TO:

Mrs. H. K. (Epsy) Johnson, a HOMEMAKER whose vision and appreciation of the arts, has made the 'Dream' of TREASURE TRAILS a reality. Her earnest devotion is reflected through every page of this cultural contribution to America's heritage and beauty.

EPSY JOHNSON
TREASURE TRAILS Founder.
Editor,
Coordinator

BUILDERS OF AMERICA
1776-1976...

Every builder has a plan,
A pattern of some kind.
It may be on paper,
Or imprinted on the mind.
He may build with wood or stone,
Maybe wool or clay to mold—
No matter what the substance,
Precision is his goal.

All peoples of America
Are builders of varied arts—
They're shaping human structures
That grow as each imparts.
As the pattern is daily woven,
It brings the secret on display:
"The only thing you keep—
Is what you give away."

Epsy Johnson

Epsy Johnson
Rt. 5, Box 2
Laurel, Ms. 39440

NATIONAL EXTENSION HOMEMAKERS COUNCIL

OFFICERS:

President—
Mrs. Martin Muchow
Route 4, Box 164
Sioux Falls, South Dakota 57101
Telephone 605/528-6284

Vice-President—
Mrs. Richard Agness
Route 1, Box 129
Bunker Hill, Indiana 46914

Secretary—
Mrs. Paul L. Fletcher
Route 7, Box 516
Kinston, North Carolina 28501

Treasurer—
Mrs. Stuart H. Griffin
Route 2, Box 234
Vale, Oregon 97918

DIRECTORS:

Central—
Mrs. Bernard Brown
Route 2
Owensville, Missouri 65066

Eastern—
Mrs. Herbert Wydom
16 Nylan Road
Brockton, Massachusetts 02401

Southern—
Mrs. Don Weinkauf
1225 East 18th Street
Tulsa, Oklahoma 74120

Western—
Mrs. Ralph Geffe
6507 Butte Street
Boise, Idaho 83704

EDUCATION:
CHAIRMEN:

Citizenship—
Mrs. Norris Givens, Sr.
713 East Market Street
Georgetown, Delaware 19947

Cultural Arts—
Mrs. Mack Hudson
Cross Roads Farm
Route 1
Benson, North Carolina 27504

Family Life—
Mrs. Ellsworth Marshall
Route 3, Box 310
Cambridge, Maryland 21613

Health—
Mrs. John Hage
609 Belden Street
Lewistown, Montana 59457

International—
Mrs. Earl Friedly
Route 4
Georgetown, Kentucky 40324

Public Information &
National Notes Editor—
Mrs. A. E. Corey
Route 1, Box 189C
Crestview, Florida 32536

Safety—
Mrs. Lewis Edmundson
Box 128
Walsenburg, Colorado 81089

Subscriptions Manager—
Mrs. Jon Woody
Route 4
Lebanon, Indiana 46052

ACWW Representative—
Mrs. Corodon S. Fuller
7 Howard Street
Foxboro, Massachusetts 02035

AD HOC COMMITTEE:

Treasure Trails of the U.S.A.—
Mrs. H. K. Johnson, Coordinator
Route 5, Box 2
Laurel, Mississippi 39440

Advisor—
Dr. Opal H. Mann
Assistant Administrator
Home Economics—Extension Service
U.S.D.A.
Washington, D.C. 20250

treasure trails
in the
U.S.A.

Copyright © 1975 by
The National Extension Homemakers Council
Mrs. Martin Muchow, President
Sioux Falls, South Dakota
Mfg. in the United States of America
All Rights Reserved
1st Printing

NORTH PLAINS PRESS
1216 S. Main St.
Aberdeen, S.D. 57401

Printed in U.S.A.

FOREWORD

Since the early Nineteen hundreds, when the first Home Demonstration Clubs were organized, women from all walks of life in the United States have banded together in an educational organization now known as the National Extension Homemakers Council.

In 1972, the idea was conceived by Epsy Johnson, while she was serving as National Cultural Arts Chairman, to begin making records of all the historical interest areas in each state that are least known about. The idea became a dream, and a project of our Organization. With each Homemaker group, through their State Cultural Arts Chairman, searching out hidden treasures, gathering the data, doing research, donating time and effort, and with proper coordination, we could compile the information into one national publication—by 1976.

This "dream" of the Extension Homemakers has now become a reality—this book! TREASURE TRAILS IN THE U.S.A. is the contribution of 600,000 Homemakers all over the United States. We invite you to enjoy the beauty and heritage of our great Country, and to this end have prepared this book of maps with pertinent information.

The aim is to help you travel through any state, finding points of interest to your own enjoyment and enlightenment. It does not intend to limit your enjoyment to only the things in its pages, but to whet your appetite to further explore the treasured trails of our beautiful Nation. Organization of the book, convenience of size, legibility and proposed cost made elimination of much data necessary.

This book is our way of saying: "Thank you, America, for the rich heritage that has been passed on to us."—And now, we want to leave our marks behind for others to enjoy.

As you revel in the pages to follow, re-live the eras of the past with pride and look forward to the future with dignity.

The UNITED STATES OF AMERICA—a land that we have helped to build, love, defend—and shall preserve. God bless America!

Mrs. Martin Muchow
President—NEHC

THE WHITE HOUSE

March, 1975

Mrs. Martin Muchow, President
NATIONAL EXTENSION HOMEMAKERS COUNCIL
Route Four, Box 164
Sioux Falls, South Dakota 57101

Dear Mrs. Muchow:

May I congratulate the National Extension Homemakers Council on its interesting and useful contribution to our Nation's upcoming Bicentennial. Your book, TREASURE TRAILS OF THE UNITED STATES, is sure to be an educational and well-read guide to our great country.

The rural heritage of the Council provides you with a special viewpoint and background to enable you to compile a book like this. I'm certain Americans everywhere will be grateful that you have shared your knowledge with us.

Again, congratulations to you and your 600,000 members for the job you have done.

Sincerely,

Betty Ford

CONTENTS

	Pages
ALABAMA	1-4
ALASKA	5-8
ARIZONA	9-12
ARKANSAS	13-16
CALIFORNIA	17-20
COLORADO	21-24
CONNECTICUT	25-28
DELAWARE	29-32
DISTRICT OF COLUMBIA	33-36
FLORIDA	37-40
GEORGIA	41-44
HAWAII	45-48
IDAHO	49-52
ILLINOIS	53-56
INDIANA	57-60
IOWA	61-64
KANSAS	65-68
KENTUCKY	69-72
LOUISIANA	73-76
MAINE	77-80
MARYLAND	81-84
MASSACHUSETTS	85-88
MICHIGAN	89-92
MINNESOTA	93-96
MISSISSIPPI	97-100
MISSOURI	101-104
MONTANA	105-108
NEBRASKA	109-112
50 STATE FLAGS	113-116
NEVADA	117-120
NEW HAMPSHIRE	121-124
NEW JERSEY	125-128
NEW MEXICO	129-132
NEW YORK	133-136
NORTH CAROLINA	137-140
NORTH DAKOTA	141-144
OHIO	145-148
OKLAHOMA	149-152
OREGON	153-156
PENNSYLVANIA	157-160
PUERTO RICO	161-164
RHODE ISLAND	165-168
SOUTH CAROLINA	169-172
SOUTH DAKOTA	173-176
TENNESSEE	177-180
TEXAS	181-184
UTAH	185-188
VERMONT	189-192
VIRGINIA	193-196
WASHINGTON	197-200
WEST VIRGINIA	201-204
WISCONSIN	205-208
WYOMING	209-212
STATE NICKNAMES & MEANINGS	214-215
BICENTENNIAL FESTIVITIES	216-217

DEPARTMENT OF AGRICULTURE
OFFICE OF THE SECRETARY
WASHINGTON, D.C. 20250

March 12, 1975

Mrs. Martin Muchow
President
National Extension Homemakers Council
Route 4, Box 164
Sioux Fall, South Dakota 57101

Dear Mrs. Muchow:

This nation is a vast storehouse of unheralded historic sites and areas that are a part of our rich heritage.

The decision of the National Extension Homemakers Council to seek out, research, and publish information about these little-known areas and sites is one for which it should be commended.

Your book, "Treasure Trails of the United States," pulls together this information and makes it available to all Americans. You have made a significant contribution to our national well being. This contribution is especially timely because of our upcoming Bicentennial.

May I congratulate you and the members of the Council for this appropriate and meaningful contribution to American life.

Cordially yours,

Earl L. Butz

EARL L. BUTZ
Secretary

EARL L. BUTZ
Secretary of Agriculture
of the United States

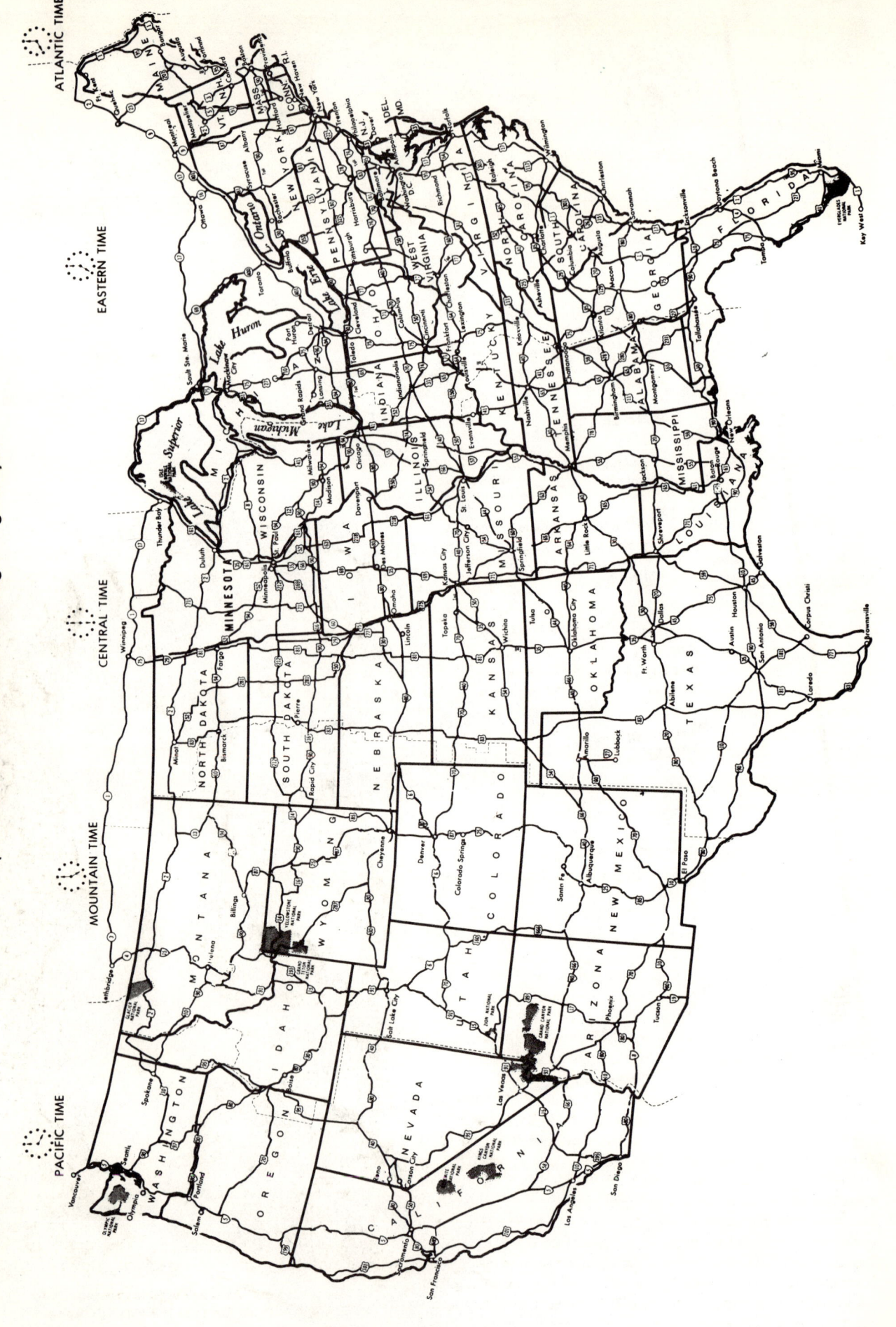

MOTTO: We Dare Defend Our Rights
STATE BIRD: Yellowhammer
STATE FLOWER: Camellia

ALABAMA
Admitted to the Union in 1819

FOR FURTHER INFORMATION WRITE:

- U.S. Forest Service
  P.O. Box 40
  Montgomery, Alabama 36101

- Fishing and Hunting
  Department of Conservation
  Montgomery, Alabama 36101

- L. Warren Mosely, Jr.
  Alabama Travel Council
  Montgomery, Alabama 36101

Alabama has been inhabited for more than 8,000 years. Hernando DeSoto was the first white man to enter Alabama. He claimed it for Spain. Alabama was the home of the great Creek Indian Nation. Along with the Cherokee, Chickasaw, and Choctaw they were known as the Civilized Tribes. They engaged themselves in hunting, fishing and farming.

In 1702 the French established the first permanent white settlement in Alabama, located at Mobile Bay. Great Britain gained possession of Alabama in 1763. At the end of the Revolutionary War it was made part of the Mississippi Territory. The Alabama Territory was established in 1817 and in 1819 Alabama became the 22nd state in the Union. Montgomery was the first capital of the Confederacy with Jefferson Davis as its president.

Agriculture was the major economy in the state until the late 1930's and 40's when the great industrial development began.

Alabama is divided into 67 counties. South Alabama on the Gulf Coast is semi-tropical, Central Alabama is rolling prairie and north Alabama is the foothills of Appalachia. The average temperature is 65.8 degrees and the rainfall is 53.3 inches. An estimated 10 percent of the nation's natural resources is located in this state. Two of every three acres in Alabama is covered with "Green Gold" . . . trees. Alabama also leads the nation in navigable waterways with 2,092 miles.

Alabama has a population of 3,444,000 with 41.6 percent residing in the rural areas and 58.4 percent in urban areas. Birmingham is the largest city, Mobile, Huntsville, and Montgomery follow.

Birmingham is often called "Pittsburgh of the South" because of its large iron and steel production. Huntsville has become the Rocket Capital of the nation. Here the rockets that carried men into space and to the moon were researched and developed. Other industries are lumber, pulp, and paper, cotton, textiles, and apparel, plus livestock production, rubber products and tires, and aluminum processing.

Noccalula Falls, in Gadsden, Alabama, is a breath-taking one hundred foot plunge from a limestone ledge.

treasure trails / page 1

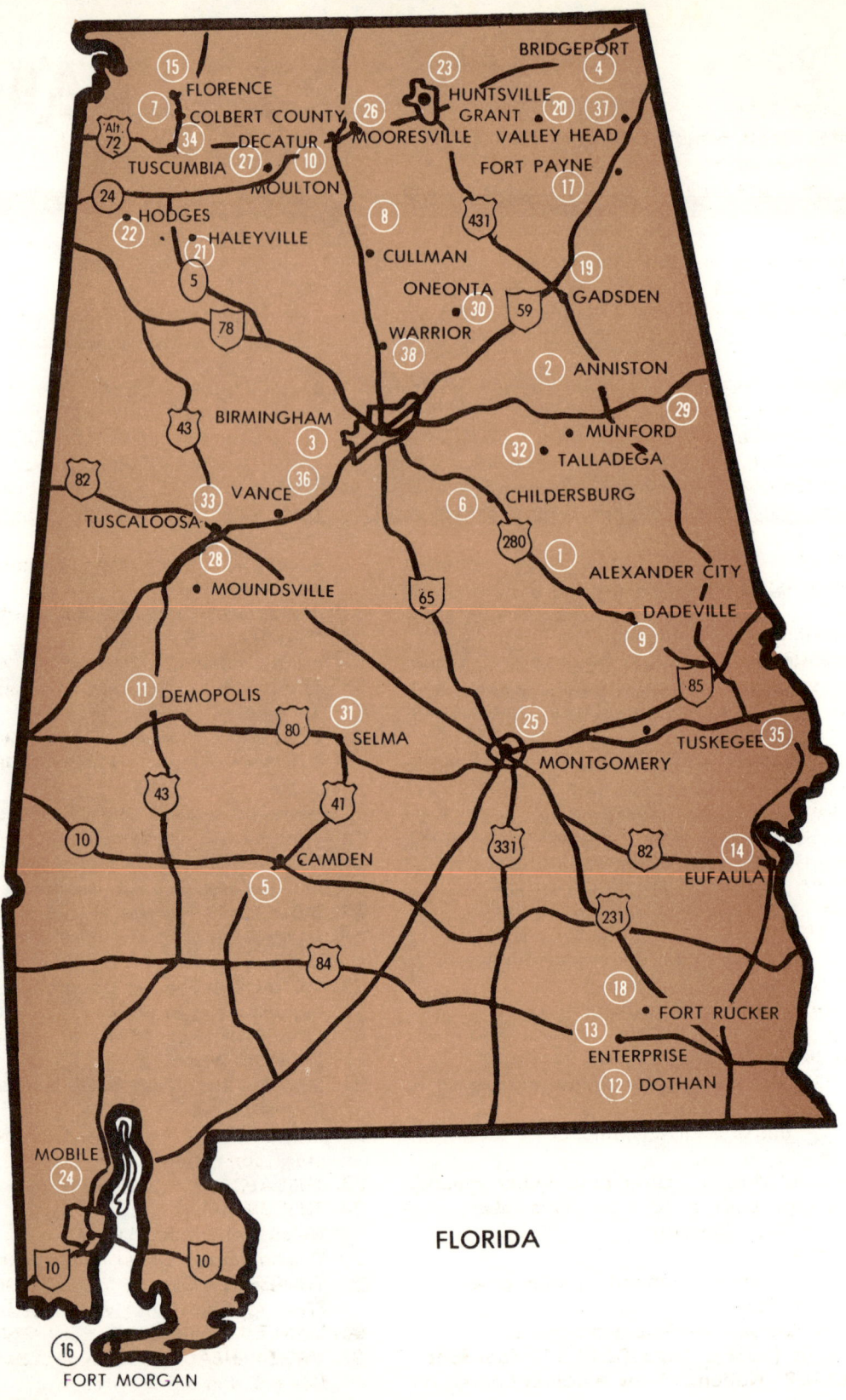

Key:
① relates to number 1 on the following page.

page 2 / treasure trails

ALABAMA POINTS OF INTEREST

1. ALEXANDER CITY
   Horseshoe Bend National Military Park, site of bloody battles of Horseshoe Bend;
   Wind Creek State Park, Lake Martin, private camp grounds
2. ANNISTON
   Regar Museum of Natural History;
   The church of St. Michael and All Angels, considered one of the most beautiful churches in America
3. BIRMINGHAM
   Vulcan Statue, largest iron statue cast;
   Museum of Art, Holy Land antiques;
   Arlington Antebellum Home and Gardens;
   Birmingham Zoo, largest zoo in southeast;
   Botanical Gardens, Japanese teahouse;
   Festival of Arts, oldest continuous arts festival in America
4. BRIDGEPORT - Site of Russel Cave National Monument, home of nomads
5. CAMDEN - White Columns (The Starr Home), magnificent 19 room mansion
6. CHILDERSBURG - Kymulga Onyx Cave, oldest recorded cave in America
7. COLBERT COUNTY - The Oaks, antebellum architecture
8. CULLMAN - Hurricane Creek Park, swinging bridges
9. DADEVILLE
   Battle of Horseshoe Bend Amusement, General Andrew Jackson defeated Creek Indians;
   Still Waters, dedicated as wildlife refuge
10. DECATUR - Point Mallard, aquatic center
11. DEMOPOLIS
    Bluff Hall, overlooks the Tennessee-Tombigbee at Demopolis;
    Gaineswood, three architectural styles
12. DOTHAN - National Peanut Festival and Fair, annually in the fall
13. ENTERPRISE - Boll Weevil Monument, monument to the insect
14. EUFAULA - Site of Shorter Mansion
15. FLORENCE
    Indian Mound Museum, ceremonial Indian mound;
    Pope's Tavern, built in 1811 by slave labor
16. FORT MORGAN - Museum
17. FORT PAYNE
    Manitou Cave, once inhabited by aborigines;
    Canyon Land Park;
    Little River Canyon (DeSoto State Park);
    DeSoto Falls (DeSoto State Park) 110 foot falls
18. FORT RUCKER - National Army Aviation Center, air craft display
19. GADSDEN - Noccalula Falls, pioneer village
20. GRANT - Cathedral Caverns
21. HALEYVILLE - Natural Bridge, longest natural bridge east of Rockies
22. HODGES - Rock Bridge Canyon, sub-tropical plants and Indian caves
23. HUNTSVILLE - Alabama Space and Rocket Center, tours of NASA available
24. MOBILE
    Bellingraph Gardens, gardens and home;
    Cathedral of the Immaculate Conception, minor basilica;
    Battleship USS Alabama, World War II Submarine;
    Dauphin Island, old military fort;
    Longs Gardens, old antebellum home and garden;
    Malbis Greek Orthodox Church, Malbis Plantation;
    Azalea Trail, 35-mile floral lined trail;
    Blessing of the Shrimp Flee, Bayou La Batre (held in late summer);
    America's Junior Miss Pageant (held in mid-March);
    Mardi Gras (held five days before Lent)
25. MONTGOMERY
    State Capital, also first capital of the Confederacy;
    White Houses of the Confederacy, home of Jefferson Davis;
    Governor's Mansion, Greek Revival Mansion;
    Ordeman Shaw House, Italianate style of architecture;
    Alabama State Chamber of Commerce Building (Teague House), historic mansion
26. MOORESVILLE - Mooresville Post Office, first incorporated town in Alabama
27. MOULTON - Pioneer House Museum
28. MOUNDSVILLE - Mount State Monument, Indian relics
29. MUNFORD - Cheaha Mountain (Cheaha State Park) highest point in state
30. ONEONTA - Horse Pens 40, natural stone corral on Chandler Mountain
31. SELMA - Sturdivant Hall, designed by a cousin of Robert E. Lee
32. TALLADEGA - Alabama International Speedway, stock car racing
33. TUSCALOOSA - Gorgas Home, antebullum home
34. TUSCUMBIA
    Helen Keller's Birthplace;
    Wilson Dam, highest single lock in the world
35. TUSKEGEE - George Washington Carver Museum (Tuskegee Institute) works of Dr. Carver
36. VANCE - Eama Scenic Rock Gardens
37. VALLEY HEAD - Sequoyah Cave, colored calcite flowers and stalagmites
38. WARRIOR - Rickwood Caverns, stalagmites

treasure trails / page 3

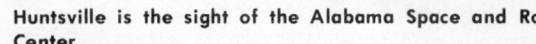
Huntsville is the sight of the Alabama Space and Rocket Center.

The First White House of the Confederacy, located across from the State Capitol, in Montgomery, Alabama, was the home of Jefferson Davis.

Photographs furnished by Alabama Bureau of Publicity and Information

The Vulcan Statue, Birmingham, Alabama, is the world's largest iron cast statue.

The famous and beautiful Ave Maria Grotto at St. Bernard near Cullman, Alabama, represents the life's work of a devoted monk, Brother Joseph.

page 4 / treasure trails

MOTTO: North To The Future
STATE BIRD: Alaska Willow Ptarmigan
STATE FLOWER: The Wild Native Forget-Me-Not

ALASKA
Admitted to the Union in 1959

FOR FURTHER INFORMATION WRITE:

- U.S. Department of Agriculture
  Forest Service
  Box 1628
  Juneau, Alaska 99801

- State of Alaska
  Department of Fish and Game
  Subport Building
  Juneau, Alaska 99801

- State Division of Tourism; Guy Russo, Director
  Department of Economic Development Pouch E
  Juneau, Alaska 99801

- U.S. Department of Interior
  Fish and Wildlife Service
  Bureau of Sport Fisheries and Wildlife
  6917 Seward Highway
  Anchorage, Alaska 99502

Alaska, known as "The Great State," contains 586,400 square miles, and is as large as Texas, California and Montana combined. Alaska was officially proclaimed a state on January 3, 1959. The 1970 population was 302,647; a gain of 3.1 percent since 1960.

Since early man migrated across the Bering land bridge 10,000 and more years ago and began fishing and hunting in the coastal waters, Alaska's resources have played an important part in populating the 49th state.

The Eskimos who occupy the area along the western and northern coasts, the Bering Sea and the Arctic Ocean, have long harvested their livelihood from the sea. In southeastern interior and southcentral Alaska live the Indians who obtained their needs from the land animals, the land itself and the rivers. In southwestern Alaska, along the peninsula and the Aleutian Chain, live the Aleuts who originally derived their livelihood primarily from the sea.

Shortly after the first European contracts were made in Alaska, the quest for fur started bringing in the first of non-native influences.

The first sizeable influx of people occurred during the gold rush at the turn of the century. Most of these miners left Alaska after the gold played out, but those that remained helped to establish many of the population centers of today.

The second large influx of people arrived in Alaska with the military in 1940 and the construction that occurred up to 1950. The post-war homestead program was influential in bringing many families to settle in Alaska. During the late 1960's and early 1970's, the potential development of petroleum fields in Alaska also influenced the population.

The abundant sea life, the furs, the gold, the strategic military location of the state, and the oil have all played an important part in the size and make-up of Alaska's population.

This tiny tot, in Fairbanks, finds one of the many large and delicious cabbages produced due to the long summer days.

treasure trails / page 5

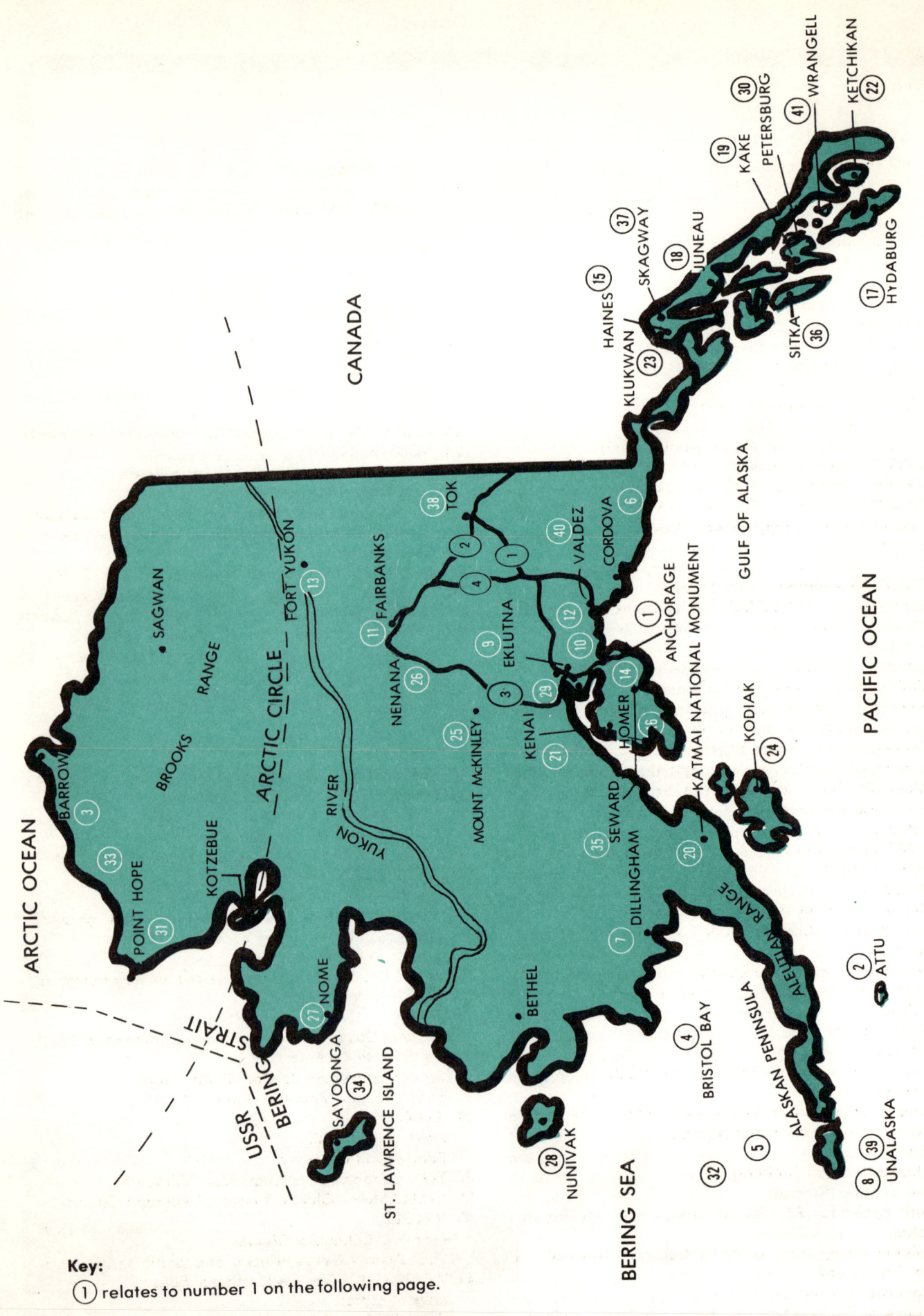

page 6 / treasure trails

ALASKA POINTS OF INTEREST

1. ANCHORAGE
   Sleeping Lady Mountain;
   Earthquake Park;
   Mount Alyeska;
   Fort Richardson;
   Wildlife Photo Safaris;
   Transportation Museum;
   Eskimo Dancers;
   Oil Platform Tours (Cooks Inlet);
   Site of first major gold rush (1887)
2. ATTU - Aleutian Grass Basket Weavers
3. BARROW
   Home of the Midnight Sun;
   Eskimo Village - Blanket Toss;
   Baleen Baskets (made of whale bone)
4. BRISTOL BAY - Alaska's leading salmon fishing
5. CHAIN - Beach combing for Japanese floats
6. CORDOVA - Crab, shrimp and salmon canneries;
   The Morgan - Guggenheim "Iron Trail"
7. DILLINGHAM - Home of Walrus Island
8. DUTCH HARBOR - Base of fighting in World War II
9. EKLUTNA - Indian Burial Houses
10. ELMENDORF AIR FORCE BASE - Site of Emperor Hirohito's meeting with President Nixon
11. FAIRBANKS
    Silver Fox Mine - operating hard rock mine;
    Gold Dredges, and gold panning;
    Midnight Sun Baseball Game, played without artificial lighting at midnight;
    Eskimo Indian World Olympics (last week July);
    Robert Service Poetry Readings, Malamute Saloon;
    Musk Ox Farms and Quivitut Garments;
    Sled Dog Kennels;
    Eskimo Village
12. FORT RICHARDSON - Japanese mass burial
13. FORT YUKON
    Athabascan Indian bead work;
    Dog races (sled dogs)
14. GIRDWOOD - Glacial Walk (walk on glacier)
15. HAINES
    Bald Eagle Council Grounds;
    Chilkat Dancers at Port Chilkoot
16. HOMER
    Homer Split;
    Octopus;
    Site of the first railroad built in Alaska
17. HYDABURG
    Totem Parks (also at Setka, Ketchikan & Klawack);
    Home of Alaska's Haida Indians
18. JUNEAU
    Alaskan capitol building;
    Mendenhall Glacier;
    Rent-a-Lake for $5 - Forest Service Shelters "Fly in Lakes";
    Salmon Derby (also at Ketchikan and Seward);
    Ice Cap Tours;
    Governor's Mansion;
    House of Wickershem (home of territorial judge);
    State Museum
19. KAKE - Site of world's largest totem pole
20. KATMAI NATIONAL MONUMENT - Land of Ten Thousands Smokes (an active volcano)
21. KENAI
    Trumpeter swans;
    Dall Sheep and mountain goats;
    Russian shrine;
    Canoe trails;
    Moose Pass
22. KETCHIKAN
    Alaska's wood pulp mill (also at Ketka);
    Rain Forest
23. KLUKWAN - Chilkat (goat hair and cedar) blankets
24. KODIAK ISLAND
    Home of famous Kodiak Brown Bears;
    First town built in Alaska;
    "Cry of Wild Ram" - Play of the founding of Baranofs Russian Colony in Alaska;
    Crab Festival
25. MOUNT McKINLEY and National Park
26. NENANA
    Site of driving of Golden Spike by President Harding on completion of Alaska's railroad;
    Tripol Day "Ice Classic" - breaking of river ice
27. NOME - Site of snow machine races
28. NUNIVAK - Musk Ox Island
29. PALMER
    Alaskan State Fair;
    Malanuska Valley Farms
30. PETERSBURG - Sourdough fishing
31. POINT HOPE - Whaling community
32. PRIBILOFS (St. Paul and St. George)
    Fur seal and Murre (bird) rookeries
33. PRUDHOE BAY - North slope of oil fields
34. SAVOONGA - Walrus Carnival
35. SEWARD
    Mount Marathon Race - Alaska's most grueling cross country climbing race;
    Stellar Sea Lion Rookery;
    Jessie Lee Mansion Home - Alaska's flag designer;
    Fish weir (fish ladder)
36. SITKA
    Baranof Castle - Site of purchase of Alaska in 1867;
    Centennial Center;
    Mount Edgcumbo (sister of Mt. Fuje);
    First Alaskan Pioneer Home
37. SKAGWAY
    Days of '98 Trail;
    Soapy Smith's Grave
38. TOK - Tanacross (Athabascan Village)
39. UNALASKA - Oldest Russian Orthodox Church
40. VALDEZ
    Ferry to Columbia Glacier;
    Tital Area - Geese, ducks and arctic terns
41. WRANGELL - City under three flags;
    Garnet cliffs;
    Chief Shakes Ceremonial House

Southeast Alaska Indian Community House, near Ketchikan, reminds visitors of the Indian's way of life.

Hikers descend into the Valley of Ten Thousand Smokes, a portion of Katmai National Monument on the Alaskan Peninsula.

Two boatmen inspect an iceberg near the massive Mendenhall Glacier near Juneau.

Alaskan Eskimo games are suited to a small, confined space of the home during long, cold winters.

page 8 / treasure trails

STATE MOTTO: God Enriches
STATE BIRD: Cactus Wren
STATE FLOWER: Blossoms of Saguaro Cactus

ARIZONA
Admitted to the Union in 1912

FOR FURTHER INFORMATION WRITE:

- U.S. Fish and Game Department
  2222 West Greenway
  Phoenix, Arizona 85007

- State Liaison Officer
  U.S. Travel Service
  1645 West Jefferson
  Phoenix, Arizona 85007

- Arizona Economic, Planning and Development Corp.
  1645 West Jefferson
  Phoenix, Arizona 85007

The lure of gold and silver first brought people to Arizona in the early 1700's. Popularly known as the Grand Canyon State, Arizona finally became a state in 1912, after many years of being a corridor between Texas and California for fleeing bandits, renegade soldiers and marauding Indians. After the Jesuit and Franciscan Priests built missions, more people came to live off the land. There were many missions built by the priests, who were the first people to bring a different culture to "New Spain" as Arizona was first called in those years. Some of these missions still remain standing. Padre Kino was probably the most influential person who had traveled through Arizona. Among others he founded San Xavier Del Bac, "white dove of the desert", a mission outpost. The mission, over 200 years old, still is in continuous use.

Arizona has made remarkable progress in the last one hundred years. Crops of alfalfa, cotton, oranges, dates, grapes and other winter crops are grown.

The Arizona mountains and plains contain large deposits of ore. Some of the mines have been worked for more than three hundred years.

Arizona's natural resources are ample supplies of copper, lead, tungsten, zinc and many others.

Boasting more sunshine than any other state in the Union, Arizona averages 292 sunny days each year. The atmosphere is dry, and the temperature occasionally goes over the 100-degree mark. Because of this, Arizona attracts many winter visitors. The tourist industry is very active.

The first teachers in what is now Arizona were the Jesuit missionaries from Mexico, but this has progressed throughout the years to a progressive educational system. The University of Arizona is located in Tucson and there are state colleges throughout the state.

Arizona's "first families" the Indians, number more than 95,000. The Navajo is the largest group.

Visitors to Southern Arizona should allow time to enjoy the excitement of walking the streets of Old Tucson.

treasure trails / page 9

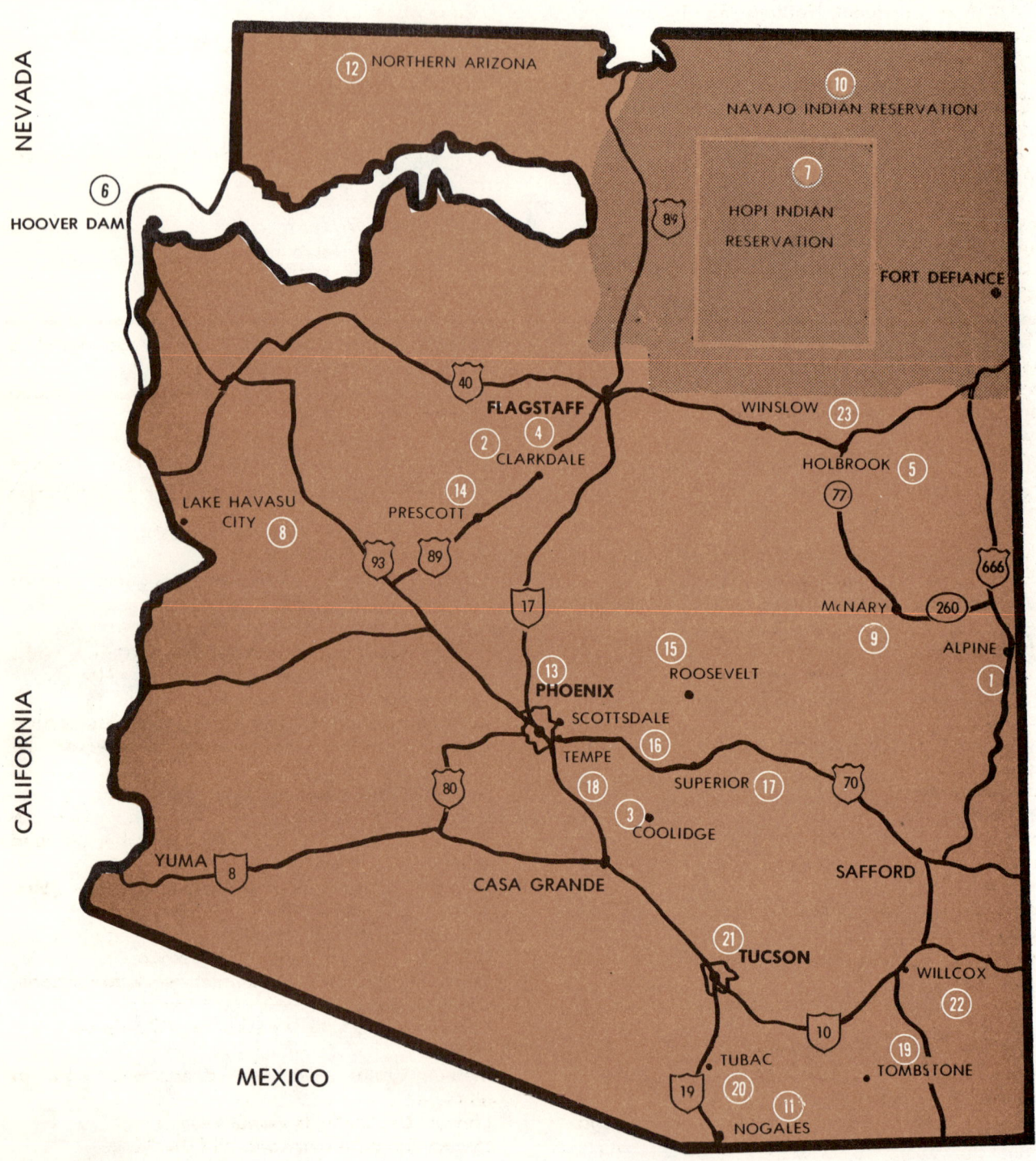

Key:
① relates to number 1 on the following page.

page 10 / treasure trails / Arizona

ARIZONA POINTS OF INTEREST

1. ALPINE - Alpine divide, altitude 8,540 feet, on highway 666, also referred to as Coronado Trail.
2. CLARKDALE - Tuzigoot National Monument, Pre-Columbian ruin
3. COOLIDGE
   Casa Grande Ruins National Monument, 800-year-old Indian watchtower;
   Sacaton, tribal headquarters for Pima Indian basket makers
4. FLAGSTAFF
   Grand Canyon, world's greatest natural wonder, elevation 6,876 feet;
   Sunset Crater, volcanic crater;
   Montezuma Castle National Monument, prehistoric Indian cliff dwellings;
   Walnut Canyon, remains of 200 Prehistoric cliff dwellings;
   Wupatki National Monument, 12th century ruins;
   Oak Creek Canyon, scenic route;
   Navajo National Monument, villages from 1300 A.D.;
   Humphreys Peak, Arizona's highest peak;
   Museum of Northern Arizona, Indian exhibits
5. HOLBROOK
   Petrified Forest National Park;
   Painted Desert (along Hiway 66)
6. HOOVER DAM - highest dam in U.S.
7. HOPI INDIAN RESERVATION - Hopi Villages, famous snake dances (late in August)
8. LAKE HAVASU CITY - Site of London Bridge
9. McNARY - Lumbering Site (train trip)
10. NAVAJO INDIAN RESERVATION - Fort Defiance
11. NOGALES
    Tumacacori Mission National Monument, historic mission;
    Gateway to Mexico
12. NORTHERN ARIZONA
    Pipe Springs, historic Mormon Fort;
    Glen Canyon Bridge and Dam, 1,500 feet long
13. PHOENIX
    Pueblo Grande, ruins from 1200 A.D.;
    Capitol building;
    Civic Center (Central Ave. & McDowell Rd.);
    Phoenix Art Museum;
    Arizona Museum, Pre-historic, and Territorial;
    Desert Botanical Garden;
    Heard Museum, Indian artifacts;
    Arizona Mineral Museum (State Fairgrounds), complete ore display;
    Arizona History Room (First Avenue and Washington), authentic display of early Arizona;
    Arizona State Capitol, building, museum, and Jay Oatus paintings.
14. PRESCOTT - First territorial capital of Arizona;
    Sharlot Hall Museum;
    Smoki Museum;
    Old Governors Mansion
15. ROOSEVELT
    Tonto Natural Bridge, formed by wind and water;
    Apache Trail;
    Roosevelt Lake and Dam;
    Fish Creek Canyon;
    Tonto National Monument;
    prehistoric cliff dwellings
16. SCOTTSDALE
    Wax Museum;
    Taliesin West, home of Frank Lloyd Wright's Architectural School
17. SUPERIOR - Southwestern Arboretum, 10,000 species of plant life
18. TEMPE - Charles Trumbull Hayden Library
19. TOMBSTONE - Colorful Arizona boom town, site of O.K. Corral (gunfight between Earp Brothers and Clantons)
20. TUBAC - Arizona settlement (1750)
21. TUCSON
    Saguaro National Monument, Saguaro Cactus (Bloom in April and May);
    Colossal Cave;
    Picacho Peak State Park, Civil War Battle Grounds;
    San Xavier Del Bac Mission, built in 1700;
    Arizona Sonora Desert Museum;
    Kitt Peak National Observatory, sun observatory;
    Mount Hopkins Observatory, conducted by Smithsonian Institute
    Arizona State Museum, anthropology;
    University of Arizona Art Museum, works of Samuel H. Kress, C. Leonard Gallacher III, and others;
    Fremont House, restored historical home (Mrs. Nixon spoke here);
22. Fort Lowell Military Museum
    WILLCOX - Cattle Capitol of Arizona;
    Chiricahua National Monument—rock formations;
    Old Fort Bowie;
    Cochise Stronghold, Apache chief's hide-out
23. WINSLOW
    Meteor Crater, 600 feet deep, one mile in diameter;
    Canyon De Chelly National Monument;
    Navajo Indian stronghold, cliff dwellings

Many interesting displays await visitors at Kitt Peak National Observatory atop the Baboquivari Mountains.

One of the more famous missions of the West is San Xavier del Bac near Tucson.

Arizona's Grand Canyon is one of the world's splendors. This national park is viewed by more than two million visitors a year.

Arizona visitors enjoy luxurious accommodations combined with "Old Paint" style western atmosphere at famous guest ranches.

page 12 / treasure trails

STATE MOTTO: The People Rule
STATE BIRD: Mockingbird
STATE FLOWER: Apple Blossom

ARKANSAS
Admitted to the Union in 1836

FOR FURTHER INFORMATION WRITE:

- Mr. Lou Oberste
  Travel Director
  Arkansas Department of Parks and Tourism
  149 State Capitol
  Little Rock, Arkansas 72201

- Ozark - St. Francis National Forest Headquarters
  Russellville, Arkansas 72801

- Arkansas Game and Fish Commission
  Game and Fish Building
  Capitol Hall
  Little Rock, Arkansas 72201

- Ouachita National Forest Headquarters
  Hot Springs National Park
  Hot Springs, Arkansas 71901

Arkansas, the smallest state west of the Mississippi, is a state of contrast of terrain. From the highlands of the Ozark and Ouachita Mountains to the Delta and Gulf Coastal Plains, Arkansas offers a wide variety of scenery.

All roads seem to lead to Little Rock, the geographic center of the state and the only city in the nation with three state capitols.

Arkansas is noted for its preservation of mountain folklore, music, arts, and crafts. The Ozark Folk Cultural Center at Mountain View is the hub of activities for folk heritage. Near Mountain View is the Blanchard Springs Cavern, the largest living cave in the United States.

Agriculture is the number one industry in the state. Arkansas ranks first among all states in the production of rice and broilers, and third in cotton. Another major crop is soybeans with more than four million acres in production. Beef cattle, dairy, and forestry are other major sources of income.

Arkansas has a rich historical background. Among the earliest inhabitants were the Folsom people. After this group came the Bluff Dwellers and the mound-building Indians. When the white men arrived in Arkansas, the major Indian tribes were Osages, Caddoes, and Quapaws.

Arkansas has the diamond mines, horse races, and camp sites second to none.

Arkansas has the diamond mines, horse races, and camp sites second to none. Arkansas officially adopted the popular name "The Wonder State" in 1923 because of the variety of mineral wealth, its health-giving hot springs, and its many natural resources. Mercury plus an abundance of oil, natural gas, coal and limestone are present in Arkansas.

Processing the sorghum harvest is an historic part of the Ozark Frontier Trail Folk Festival and Craft Show.

treasure trails / page 13

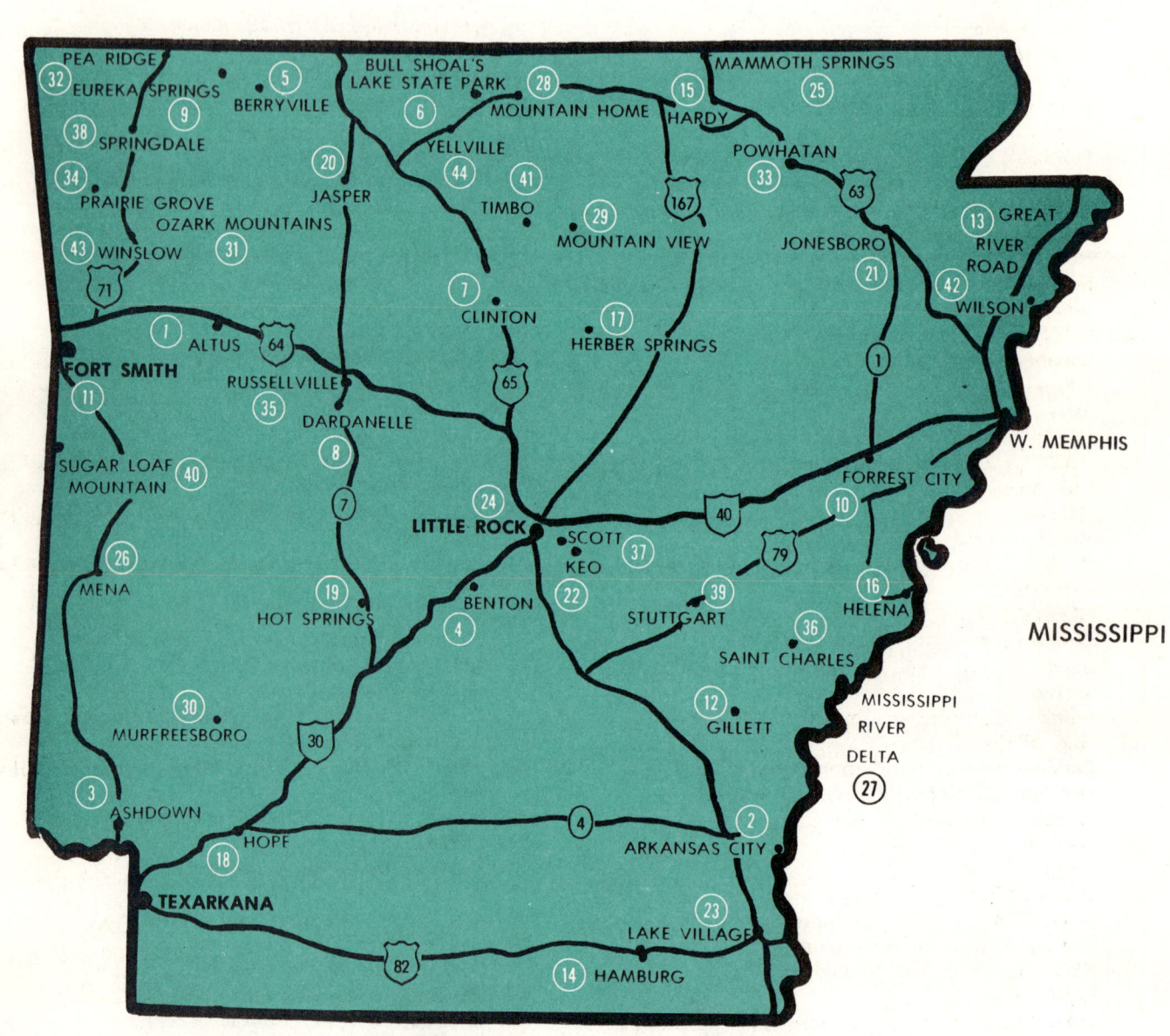

Key:
① relates to number 1 on the following page.

page 14 / treasure trails / Arkansas

ARKANSAS POINTS OF INTEREST

1. ALTUS - Wine capital of the South
2. ARKANSAS CITY - De Soto's landing
3. ASHDOWN - Top Bass producing lake
4. BENTON - Aluminum capital
5. BERRYVILLE - Sanders Gun Museum
6. BULL SHOAL'S LAKE STATE PARK
7. CLINTON - Natural Bridge
8. DARDANELLE - Lake Dardanelle, reservoir;
   Dardanelle Rock, Indian meeting place
9. EUREKA SPRINGS
   Passion Play;
   Christ of the Ozarks Statue, seven story figure of Christ;
   Blue Springs, natural spring producing 38,000,000 gallons of water daily
10. FORREST CITY - Village Creek State Park
11. FORT SMITH
    Judge Parker Courtroom and National Historic Site, location for "Hanging Judge Parker";
    Mount Magazine, tallest in mid-America;
    Butterfield Stage Route, home of notorious Belle Starr and daughter;
12. GILLETT - Arkansas Post National Memorial, oldest European settlement
13. GREAT RIVER ROAD - Scenic highway along Mississippi River
14. HAMBURG - Armadillo Festival (August)
15. HARDY - Arkansas Traveler Folk Theater, Ozark folk musical
16. HELENA
    Antebellum Architecture;
    Phillips County Museum, Indian artifacts and Edison exhibits
17. HERBER SPRINGS
    Ozark Foothills Arts and Crafts Show;
    Seven Springs Park, city park with seven medicinal springs
18. HOPE - Watermelon Capital of the World
19. HOT SPRINGS
    Oaklawn Race Track, thoroughbred racing;
    Hot Springs National Park, 47 springs;
    Ouachita National Forest
20. JASPER
    Dogpatch U.S.A.;
    Diamond Cave, recreation area and camping
21. JONESBORO - Arkansas State University Museum, history of eastern Arkansas
22. KEO - Toltec Indian Mounds
23. LAKE VILLAGE
    Lake Chicot State Park, largest natural lake in Arkansas;
    Colonel Charles A. Lindbergh Monument
24. LITTLE ROCK
    State Capitol;
    Historical State House;
    Arkansas Art Center and Museum of Natural History;
    MacArthur Park, birthplace of General Douglass MacArthur;
    River Museum;
    War Museum;
    War Memorial Zoo;
    Wye Mountain, seven acres of daffodils, spring attraction;
    Quapaw Quarters, Historical collection of antebellum and Victorian homes
25. MAMMOTH SPRINGS - largest spring in the U.S. producing over 200,000,000 gallons of water in 24 hours
26. MENA - Talimena Drive - 55 mile drive through Stair Mountains
27. MISSISSIPPI RIVER DELTA
28. MOUNTAIN HOME - Norfork National Fish Hatchery, trout hatchery
29. MOUNTAIN VIEW
    Blanchard Springs Cavern, largest living cave in the United States;
    Ozark Folk Cultural Center;
    Ozark Folk Festival and Craft Show;
    Rackensack Folklore Society;
    Wolf House, white man's first house
30. MURFREESBORO
    Crater of Diamonds State Park, only diamond mine in North America;
    Indian burial grounds
31. OZARK MOUNTAINS
32. PEA RIDGE - Pea Ridge National Military Park, site of civil war battle
33. POWHATAN - Powhatan Courthouse, a national historical site
34. PRAIRIE GROVE - Prairie Grove Battlefield, civil war battle
35. RUSSELLVILLE
    Arkansas State Highway 7, one of America's ten most scenic routes;
    Ozark National Forest;
    Dwight Mission, first white settlement west of Mississippi River
36. SAINT CHARLES - White River National Wildlife Refuge
37. SCOTT - Dortch Plantation Museum
38. SPRINGDALE
    Poultry Capital of America;
    Beaver Lake;
    War Eagle Mills Arts and Crafts Show
39. STUTTGART
    Duck Capital of the World;
    World's largest rice mill
40. SUGAR LOAF MOUNTAIN
41. TIMBO - Old Timey Craft Fair
42. WILSON
    Wilson Plantation, largest cotton field in the world;
    Hampson Museum and State Park, collection of Indian artifacts
43. WINSLOW - Devils Den State Park, mountainous wilderness state park
44. YELLVILLE - Buffalo River National Recreation Area, wilderness area

A lone and silent cannon stands in the battlefield of Pea Ridge, it can be seen in the Pea Ridge National Military Park in Northwest Arkansas.

Arkansas' First State Capitol, an elegant structure, reflects the tradition of the South.

One of the interesting historical sites in Arkansas is "Hanging" Judge Parker Court Room. The authentic court room is located at Fort Smith.

It was from this historic point that the vast Louisiana Purchase land was surveyed.

Cane from the sorghum harvest is ground at the colorful Ozark Frontier Trail Folk Festival and Craft Show at Heber Springs, Arkansas each fall.

Photographs furnished by Arkansas Department of Parks & Tour

MOTTO: A World Within A State
STATE BIRD: California Valley Quail
STATE FLOWER: Golden Poppy

CALIFORNIA
Admitted to the Union in 1850

FOR FURTHER INFORMATION WRITE:

- California Chamber of Commerce
  455 Capitol Mall
  Sacramento, California 95814

- National Park Service
  U.S. Department of the Interior
  450 Golden Gate Avenue
  San Francisco, California 94102

- California Division of Highways
  1120 N. Street
  Sacramento, California 95814

California, nicknamed the golden state, gets its name from the golden sunshine, sandy deserts, orange groves, and from the gold fields that are among the richest in the world.

In size California ranks third in the union, and is bordered by Oregon, Nevada, Arizona, Mexico and the great Pacific Ocean. The length is approximately 770 miles and the width varies from 150 miles to 589 miles. Its capitol is Sacramento.

California history began with the building of Carmel mission by Father Junipero Seraa in 1770. John Marshall found gold at Sutter's Mill in 1848 and then the world found California. After gold came incredibly richer strikes: cattle and real estate, farming and citrus, oil and aero-space, education and entertainment ... the movies. Hollywood set a style for the nation and the world.

California's tourist attractions are known all over the world, and the tourist industry is very important to California's economy.

About one-third of California's total area is used for growing crops or for pasturing livestock. Farming of livestock, vegetables, and fruit is what California is all about.

Until 1845, the white population of California numbered about five thousand people. These were chiefly Spanish and Mexican cattle raisers. By 1849, the gold seekers had increased the population to more than 92,000. By 1860 there were nearly 380,000 persons in the state. As the railroads were built thousands of Chinese coolies were imported to help. Most remained to work within the state. Between 1920 and 1930 the population grew 65.7 percent and it continues to be one of the most populas states in the union.

"Welcome Pardner" is the friendly hello that greets visitors to California's Mother Lode gold country where traces of the wild west have been preserved.

treasure trails / page 17

Key:
① relates to number 1 on the following page.

page 18 / treasure trails / California

CALIFORNIA POINTS OF INTEREST

1. ANAHEIM - Disneyland
2. BEVERLY HILLS - Homes of Movie Stars
3. BUENA PARK
   Movieland Wax Museum;
   Alligator Farm and Knott's Berry Farm
4. CARMEL
   Scenic Drive on Highway 101;
   Big Sur;
   San Carlos Borromeo del Rio Mission
5. COLOMA - Site of gold discovery
   James Marshall Historical Monument;
6. DEATH VALLEY - Death Valley National Monument, lowest elevation in U.S.
7. EUREKA
   Indian Island;
   Sequoia Park and Zoo
8. IMPERIAL VALLEY - Agricultural Area, world's largest irrigation project
9. INDIO - Date Capital
10. LA JOLLA
    La Jolla Caves, seven sea-sculptured caverns;
    Scripps Institute of Oceanography
11. LAKE TAHOE - resort area
12. LONG BEACH - Queen Mary, featuring Jacque Cousteau's Livina Sea
13. LOS ANGELES
    Opera and Art centers;
    Home of Douglas Aircraft Co. and Boeing Aircraft Co.;
14. MONTEREY
    Presidio guarding Monterey Bay;
    Old Custom House;
    Stevenson House
15. NAPA - Silverado Museum, a rare collection of Robert Louis Stevenson's possessions
16. PALM SPRINGS - Salton Sea, Wildlife National Refuge
17. PALOS VERDES - Marine land of the Pacific, animal show
18. PASADENA - Rose Parade (annually on New Year's Day)
19. PETRIFIED FOREST
20. PISMO BEACH
    Clam Capital of the world;
    Vandenberg Air Force Base
21. PLACERVILLE - Historical gold mining town, home of J. M. Studebaker
22. SACRAMENTO
    Capitol Building;
    Sutters Fort Historical Monument;
    Indian Museum
23. SAN CLEMENTE - Summer home of President Nixon
24. SAN DIEGO
    Mission San Diego DeAlcala, Mother Mission;
    Santa Ysabel Mission, Indian burial ground;
    San Diego Old Town, site of original settlement;
    Museum of Man and Natural History;
    San Diego Zoo, one of world's largest
    Cleveland National Forest (west of San Diego);
    Elsinore Lake State Park (west and north of San Diego)
25. SAN FRANCISCO
    Golden Gate and Oakland Bay Bridges;
    Muir Woods National Monument;
    Mount Tamalpais State Park;
    San Luis Obispo;
    San Rafael, 1817 Franciscan Mission (north of San Francisco);
    Fort Ross, Historical outpost of Russian Empire (State Park);
    Chinatown;
    Cable Cars
26. SAN JUAN CAPISTRANO - Spanish Mission
27. SAN SIMEON - Home of famous Hearst Castle, $50 million worth of art objects
28. SANTA CATALINA ISLAND
29. SANTA ROSA - Home of Luther Burbank, famous gardens and church made from single redwood
30. SEQUOIA NATIONAL FOREST
    Ash Mountain, 1,200 kinds of trees and shrubs, plants and flowers, wildlife;
    General Sherman Tree
31. SHASTA NATIONAL FOREST
    Shasta Lake;
    Mount Shasta
32. SONOMA - Buena-Vista Vineyards, oldest winery in U.S. founded in 1857
33. VAN DAMME STATE PARK - Pygmy Forest
34. YOSEMITE NATIONAL PARK
    Bridalveil Falls;
    Yosemite Valley, Cathedral Spires;
    Yosemite Falls;
    Yosemite Mountain Lagger Steam Train
35. WEAVERVILLE - gold rush town
36. WILLITS
    Fort Bragg;
    Fort Humbolt State Historical Monument and Gardens

treasure trails / page 19

The old buildings at Bodie, now preserved as a state historic park, draw thousands of visitors annually to this genuine California gold-mining ghost town.

The richest and most powerful in California, old Santa Barbara mission was reconstructed after the earthquake of 1925.

Touring the Napa Valley wineries, just a short drive north of San Francisco, is a favorite pastime of visitors and local residents alike.

The black-hulled, three-masted lumber schooner, C. A. Thayer, is one of the four ships in the San Francisco Maritime State Historic Park.

page 20 / treasure trails

Photographs furnished by California Office of Tourism.

STATE MOTTO: Nothing Without Providence (or Deity)
STATE BIRD: Lark Bunting
STATE FLOWER: The White And Lavender Columbine

COLORADO

Admitted to the Union in 1876

FOR FURTHER INFORMATION WRITE:

- Colorado Division of Wildlife
  6060 Broadway
  Denver, Colorado 80216

- Mr. Hal Haney
  Commerce and Development Division
  Travel Development Section
  State Capitol Annex
  Denver, Colorado 80202

Colorado Territory, created in 1861, was admitted to statehood on August 1, 1876, one hundred years after the Declaration of Independence, and thus became the "Centennial State." Prior to 1861 Colorado's area was part of Kansas, Missouri and Louisiana. Originally, it was the domain of prehistoric Indians, basket makers and cliff dwellers.

Colorado is an almost perfect rectangle situated near the center of the western half of the continental United States. It's the eighth largest of the 50 states in area, covering 104,247 square miles. More than one-third of the land is owned by the Federal Government and allocated to National forests, parks, monuments, historic sites and recreation areas, military reservations, and Indian reservations and the public domain. Colorado is the highest state in the Union. Its elevation ranges from 3,350 feet to 14,431 feet. The eastern half of Colorado has flat high plains and broad rolling prairies gradually rising westward to the foothills and high Rocky Mountain ranges that bisect the state. The Colorado River with headquarters west of the Continental Divide flows east to Missouri, southeast to Mississippi and south to the Gulf of Mexico.

The eastern half of Colorado has grazing lands, both irrigated and dry farming lands, and outcroppings of sandstone, limestone, siltstone and shale. The subsurface resources include oil, gas and coal. Much of the oil, coal, the largest oil shale reserve and molybdenum supply in the country, and numerous other minerals. Grazing lands and fertile farming and fruit growing areas also are important resources.

Bear Lake—Rocky Mountain National Park

treasure trails / page 21

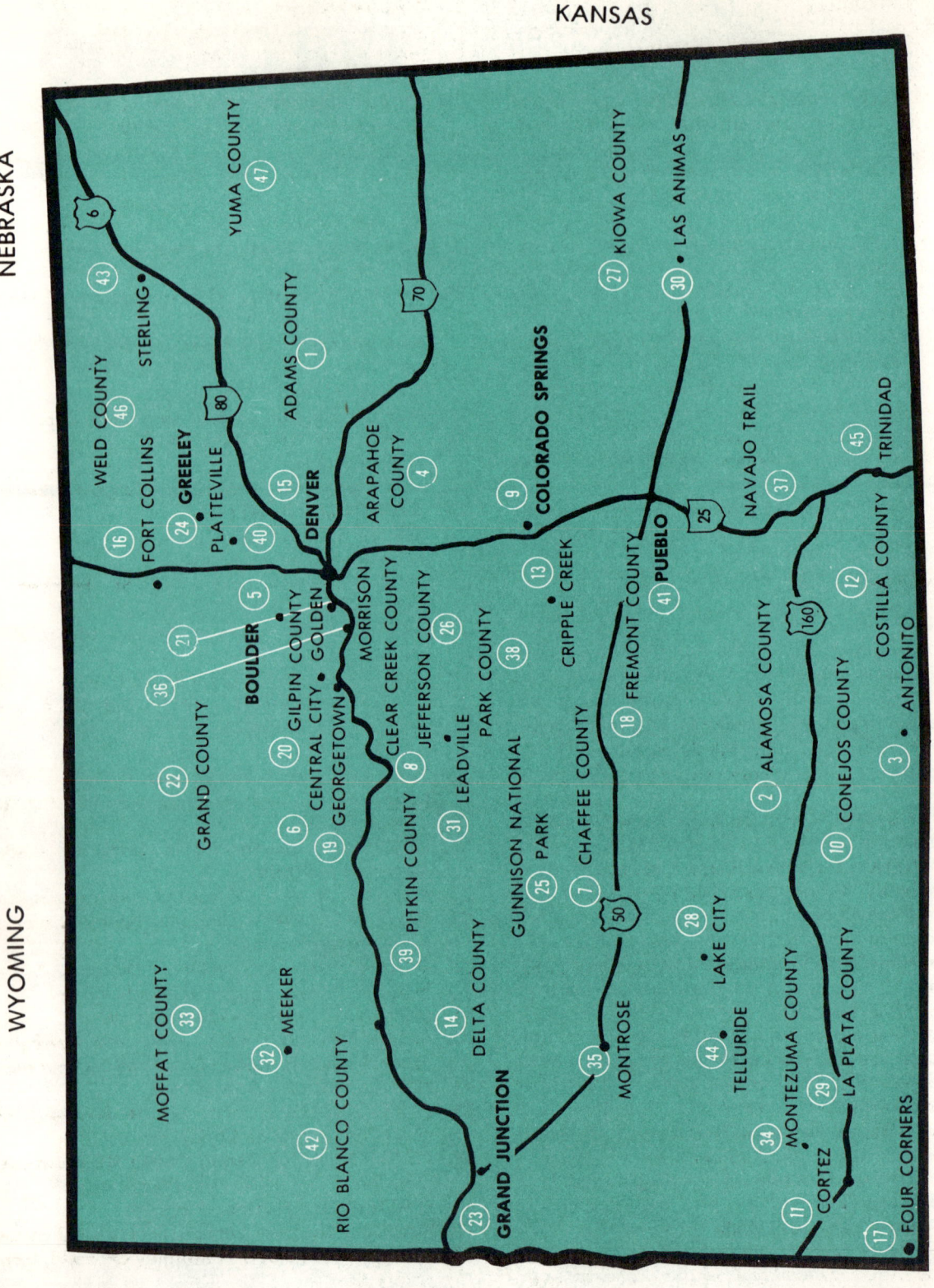

Key:
① relates to number 1 on the following page.

page 22 / treasure trails / Colorado

COLORADO POINTS OF INTEREST

1. ADAMS COUNTY - Colorado Railroad Museum, historical exhibits
2. ALAMOSA COUNTY - Great Sand Dunes, National Monument
3. ANTONITO
   Conejos Church - First church, 1858;
   Antonito to Chama Railroad, rides over Cumbes Pass
4. ARAPAHOE COUNTY - Commanche Crossing, historic railroad site
5. BOULDER
   Valmont Presbyterian Church, oldest active Protestant Church;
   Ryssby Church, used for Swedish festivals;
   First schoolhouse, 1860
6. CENTRAL CITY - Historical boom town, opera house, historical monument
7. CHAFFEE COUNTY - Marshall Pass Railroad Drive
8. CLEAR CREEK COUNTY
   Hamill House, historical museum;
   Mount Evans Highway, highest in U.S. (14,262 feet)
9. COLORADO SPRINGS
   Garden of the Gods, Red sandstone formations;
   Pikes Peak, toll road to summit (14,110 feet);
   Cave of the Winds;
   Cliff dwellings;
   Santa Claus' North Pole;
   Seven Falls;
   Will Rogers Shrine;
   Helen Hunt Memorial;
   U.S. Air Force Academy, open to public
10. CONEJOS COUNTY - Pike Stockade State Historical Monument, site of Captain Pike's capture
11. CORTEZ - Summit Lake, National Landmark, state fishing area
12. COSTILLA COUNTY - Fort Garland State Museum, restored fort
13. CRIPPLE CREEK - Early day historic district
14. DELTA COUNTY - Grand Mesa, 200 lakes on largest flat-topped mountain
15. DENVER
    Colorado State Capitol, Colorado gray granite, gold leaf dome;
    Colorado State Museum;
    Denver Art Museum;
    Denver Zoo, foreign, domestic animals;
    Denver Museum of Natural History;
    Brown Palace, historic hotel;
    Evans-Byers Home, National landmark;
    Four Mile House, National landmark;
    Governor's Mansion, National landmark;
    Saint Elizabeth's Church;
    United States Mint, tours daily
16. FORT COLLINS - Lindenmeir Railroad Museum
17. FOUR CORNERS - Only point in U.S. where four states meet
18. FREMONT COUNTY
    Royal Gorge, highest suspension bridge (1,055 feet)
    Buckskin Joe, reconstructed mining camp;
    Phantom Canyon, scenic drive
19. GEORGETOWN
    Chimney Rock, Archeological site;
    Museum;
    Historic district;
    Ore processing mill, dam;
    Lebanon and Everett Mine Tunnels;
    Hotel de Paris
20. GILPIN COUNTY - Central City Opera House, Summer opera and play festival
21. GOLDEN
    Mount Vernon House Museum;
    Coors Brewery, open to public
22. GRAND COUNTY
    Trail Ridge Road, highest continuous highway (12,183 feet)
23. GRAND JUNCTION - Colorado National Monument
24. GREELEY
    Fort Vasquez State Museum, restored fur trading fort;
    Meeker Memorial Museum;
    Monfort Feedlot, one of largest in U.S.
25. GUNNISON NATIONAL PARK
    Black Canyon;
    Blue Mesa Lake, Colorado's largest lake
26. JEFFERSON COUNTY
    Buffalo Bill's Grave;
    Pahaska Tepee Museum;
    Mother Cabrine Shrine, to St. Frances Xavier Cabrini
27. KIOWA COUNTY - Sand Creek Massacre, Indian battle
28. LAKE CITY - Slumgullion Earthflow
29. LA PLATA COUNTY - El Pueblo State Museum, replica of Fort Pueblo
30. LAS ANIMAS
    Ben's Old Fort, restored fort;
    Baca House Pioneer Museum, Santa Fe Trail and Kit Carson Exhibits
31. LEADVILLE - Dexter Cabin State Museum, mid-Victorian exhibits
32. MEEKER - Meeker Massacre, site of Indian battle
33. MOFFAT COUNTY - Dinosaur National Monument, prehistoric dinosaurs
34. MONTEZUMA COUNTY - Durango-Silverton, historic narrow gauge railroad
35. MONTROSE - Ute Indian Museum
36. MORRISON - Red Rocks Park and Amphitheater, capacity: 8,040, open air in red sandstone
37. NAVAJO TRAIL - Scenic trail
38. PARK COUNTY - Christ of the Rockies, 52 foot porcelain statue of Christ
39. PITKIN COUNTY - Osgoo Castle, 42 room restored mansion
40. PLATTEVILLE - Nuclear Plant
41. PUEBLO - Thatcher Mansion, historical museum
42. RIO BLANCO COUNTY - Rangley Oil Field, largest in Colorado
43. STERLING - Summit Springs Massacre, Indian battlegrounds
44. TELLURIDE - Historic early-day district
45. TRINIDAD - Bloom House State Museum, Victorian furnishings
46. WELD COUNTY - Pawnee Buttes
47. YUMA COUNTY - Beecher Island, site of Indian battle

treasure trails / page 23

Narrow Gage Railroad at restored South Park City—Fairplay

Visitor Center Dinosaur Park—Northwest Colorado

Longs Peak—Rocky Mountain National Park

Ranger Headquarters—Dinosaur National Park

page 24 / treasure trails

STATE MOTTO: He Who Transplanted Still Sustains

STATE BIRD: American Robin

STATE FLOWER: Mountain Laurel

CONNECTICUT
Admitted to the Union in 1788

FOR FURTHER INFORMATION WRITE:

- Commissioner
  Connecticut Department of Commerce
  Tourism Division
  210 Washington Street
  Hartford, Connecticut 06106

- Director of Parks and Recreation
  Department of Environmental Protection
  State Office Building
  Hartford, Connecticut 06115

- Deputy Commissioner of Preservation and Conservation
  Department of Environmental Protection
  State Office Building
  Hartford, Connecticut 06115

From rolling hills to winding shoreline, colonial villages to towering skyscrapers, Connecticut is New England in capsule. Its farms and quiet colonial villages live door-to-door with bustling urban centers. Along the southern tier, the rambling shoreline of Long Island Sound is dotted with sandy beaches, pleasure boat marinas, great ports of call and quaint fishing villages. It's a state where history and geography place widely differing life styles within a few minutes of each other— where majestic 18th century church steeples in the heart of rural Connecticut cast their shadows to the edge of modern industrial centers.

Connecticut lies between New York City and Boston; contact with both cities is extremely easy. Motorists who follow Connecticut's winding byways discover that much of colonial Connecticut remains in its cities and villages, homes, museums and landmarks.

Almost a thousand homes dating back to colonial days are still standing. Some of them are filled with beautiful period furnishings and are open to the public. Historical museums also display priceless collections that tell us about an earlier age.

Connecticut, one of the most highly industrialized of the states, ranks sixth in the nation in the ratio of manufacturing employees to total nonagricultural employment and sixth in per capita value added by manufacturing. Connecticut's manufacturing firms turn out products such as aircraft engines and motor vehicle components. Other important industries include fabricated metals, machinery and electrical equipment. Connecticut's major agricultural industries are dairying and milk production, egg production, tobacco, and commercial horticultural products.

Above is the Joseph Conrad docked at the 19th century coastal village of Mystic Seaport in Connecticut.

treasure trails / page 25

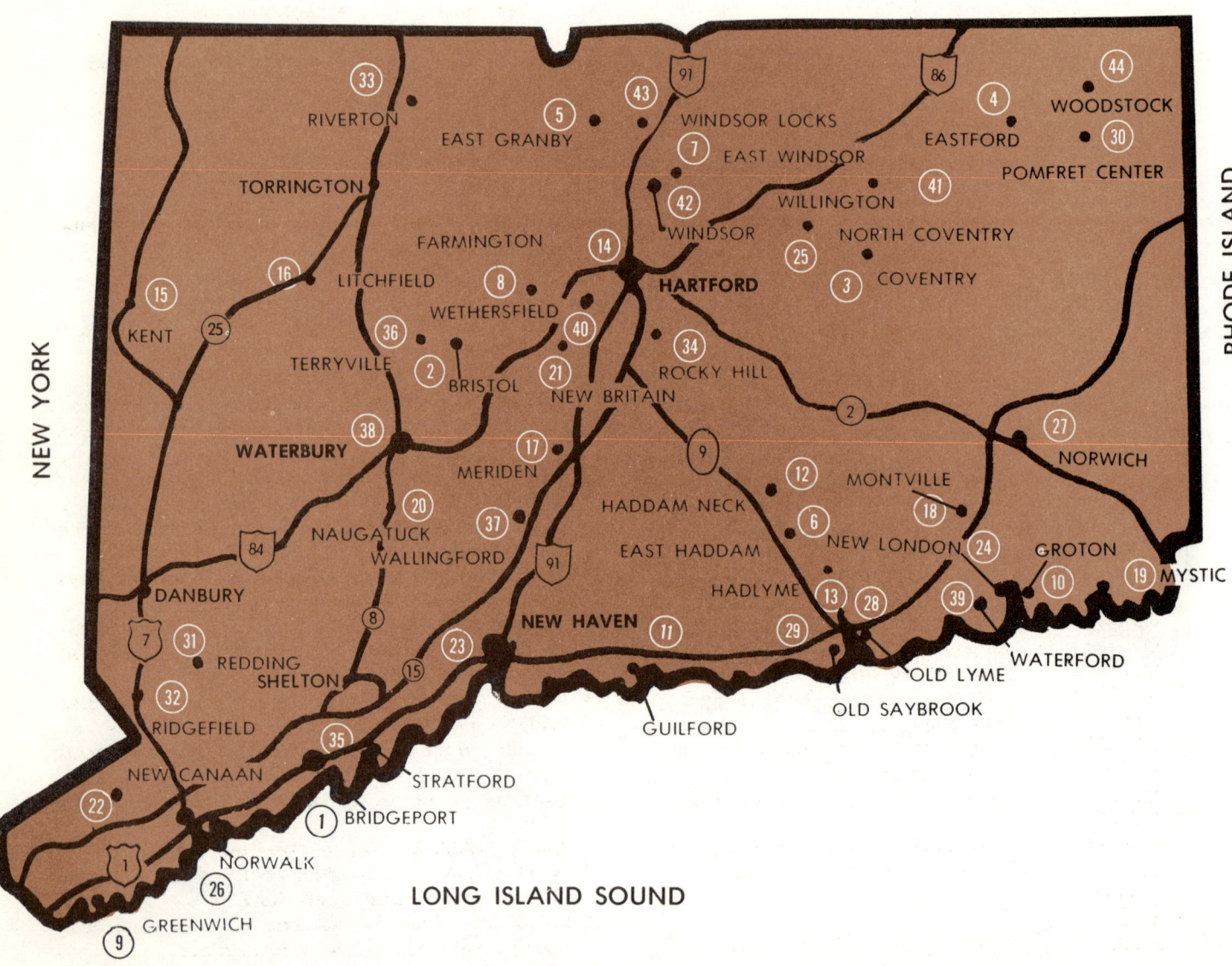

Key:

① relates to number 1 on the following page.

page 26 / treasure trails

CONNECTICUT POINTS OF INTEREST

1. BRIDGEPORT - P.T. Barnum Museum, circus mementoes
2. BRISTOL
   Chrysanthemum Gardens;
   American Watch and Clock Museum
3. COVENTRY - Nathan Hale Homestead
4. EASTFORD - Buell's Greenhouse, violets
5. EAST GRANBY - Old New-Gate Prison and Copper Mine - Historical exhibits from 1707
6. EAST HADDAM - Riverboat "Yankee Clipper" Cruises
7. EAST WINDSOR - Connecticut Electric Railway Trolley - trolleys from 1892; rides through museum
8. FARMINGTON
   Stanley-Whitman House, restored and furnished;
   Hill-Stead Museum, mansion with Impressionist Art
9. GREENWICH - Museum of Cartoon Art and Hall of Fame; cartoons and comic strips
10. GROTON
    Submarines By Boat, tours of New London Submarine Harbor;
11. GUILFORD - Whitfield House, oldest stone house in New England, 17th century exhibits
12. HADDAM NECK - Connecticut Yankee Atomic Power Company, exhibit of peacetime uses
13. HADLYME - Gillette Castle State Park, fieldstone mansion resembling medieval castle, 1919
14. HARTFORD
    Nook Farm, restored homes of Mark Twain and Harriet Beecher Stowe;
    Wadsworth Atheneum, art museum;
    Elizabeth Park Rose Gardens;
    Connecticut Historical Society;
    Old State House, Bulfinch architecture;
    State Library, contains the original Royal Charter
15. KENT - Sloane-Stanley Museum, early American craft and domestic tools
16. LITCHFIELD - White Memorial Foundation and Nature Museum, recreational center
17. MERIDEN - Castle Craig, crenelated stone tower
18. MONTVILLE
    Fort Shantok State Park, Indian burial grounds;
    Tantaquidgeon Indian Museum, museum and grounds
19. MYSTIC
    Mystic Seaport and Museum, living museum of homes, shops and ships, 19th century;
    Mystic Marinelife Aquarium, Marine life
20. NAUGATUCK - Peter Paul, Incorporated, candy manufacturer
21. NEW BRITAIN - Museum of American Art, 18th and 19th century American art
22. NEW CANAAN - Silvermine Guild of Artists
23. NEW HAVEN
    Yale Art Gallery, all periods of art;
    Peabody Museum of Natural History;
    New Haven Colony Historical Society
24. NEW LONDON
    Ocean Beach Park, recreation area;
    U.S. Coast Guard Academy, open to visitors;
    Connecticut College, American Dance Festival
25. NORTH COVENTRY - Capriland Herb Farm
26. NORWALK - Lockwood-Mathews Mansion, 60 rooms
27. NORWICH
    Leffingwell Inn, restored home, 1675
28. OLD LYME - Nut Museum, nutwood products
29. OLD SAYBROOK - Riverboat "River Queen", paddle-wheeler offering cruises
30. POMFRET CENTER - Hillandale Handweavers, Inc. hand loomed woolens mill and salesroom
31. REDDING - Putnam Memorial State Park, museum
32. RIDGEFIELD
    Keeler Tavern, colonial travelers stop-over;
    Aldrich Museum, Art gallery, sculpture gardens
33. RIVERTON - Hitchcock Chair Factory and Museum, tours available
34. ROCKY HILL - Dinosaur State Park, dinosaur tracks
35. STRATFORD - American Shakespeare Theatre, replica of Globe Theatre, Shakespearean drama and comedy
36. TERRYVILLE - historic collection of locks and keys
37. WALLINGFORD - Wallace Silversmiths, Inc., manufacturers of sterling flatware, cutlery, etc.
38. WATERBURY - Minature Holy Land, 200 figures on several acres, facsimiles of Bethlehem
39. WATERFORD - Eugene O'Neill Memorial Theatre
40. WETHERSFIELD
    Joseph Webb House, 1752, Colonial architecture;
    Silas Deane House, 1776, Isaac Stevens House, 1789;
    Buttolph-Williams House, Garrison design
41. WILLINGTON - Willington Wild Animal Farm, Connecticut's largest game farm
42. WINDSOR - Fyler House, one of state's earliest frame dwellings, authentic furnishings
43. WINDSOR LOCKS - Bradley Air Museum, vintage planes from W.W. II to jets
44. WOODSTOCK - Roseland (the Pink House) Classic Gothic Revival home, 1845

treasure trails / page 27

This lovely floriculture and display garden is found at the University of Connecticut, Storrs campus.

Gillette Castle, in Hadlyme, is found high atop the "Seven Sisters" mountains and overlooks the Connecticut River. The stately fortress, made of local fieldstone and wood, was built by actor William Gillette.

The Buttolph - Williams House, in Wethersfield, boasts the most authentically restored kitchen.

See submarines by boat on a tour of the New London Harbor. Above is a view of a submarine launch in Groton, Connecticut.

Photographs furnished by Connecticut Department of Commerce.

page 28 / treasure trails

STATE MOTTO: Liberty and Independence
STATE FLOWER: Peach blossom
STATE BIRD: Blue Hen's Chicken

DELAWARE
Admitted to the Union in 1787

FOR FURTHER INFORMATION WRITE:

- Mr. Melvin C. Luff
  Division of Economic Development
  45 The Green
  Dover, Delaware 19901

- Delaware Recreational Park Owners Association
  R.D. #1, Box 306D
  Millsboro, Delaware 19966

- Delaware State Development Department
  45 The Green
  Dover, Delaware 19901

Delaware was one of the 13 original colonies and became "the first state" because it was the first state to ratify the constitution on December 7, 1787. It is known as the "diamond state", possibly from Thomas Jefferson's reference to it as "a jewel among the states", or because Delaware poet John Lofland wrote, "Delaware is like a diamond, diminutive but having within it inherent value."

The State derived its name from "Lord De La War" an early Governor of Virginia and patron of Samuel Argall who explored the river and bay area.

The first settlement was made by the Dutch at Lewes in 1631; but was destroyed by the Indians the following year. The first permanent settlement was by the Swedes under Peter Minuit in 1638 on a site now part of Wilmington. A second Dutch settlement was made at what is now New Castle in 1651. In 1655 the Dutch extended their holdings to include the Swedish colony. What is now Delaware, as part of the province of Pennsylvania, later became a British colonial possession, and remained so until 1776 when the three lower countries became "The Delaware State".

On July 2, 1776 Caesar Rodney made his famous ride from Dover to Philadelphia to break the tie vote and insure Delaware's vote in favor of the Declaration of Independence. During the Revolution, Delaware men distinguished themselves by gallant fighting and sacrifice, although only one battle, at Cooch's Bridge, was fought, on Delaware soil. Captain Jonathan Caldwell's Co. of Kent County militia became known as "The Blue Hen's Chickens", a reference to the fighting cocks which were their mascots. As a result all Delawareans have become known as the Blue Hen's Chickens.

The Old State House, in Dover, Delaware, has been the center of state government since 1777.

treasure trails / page 29

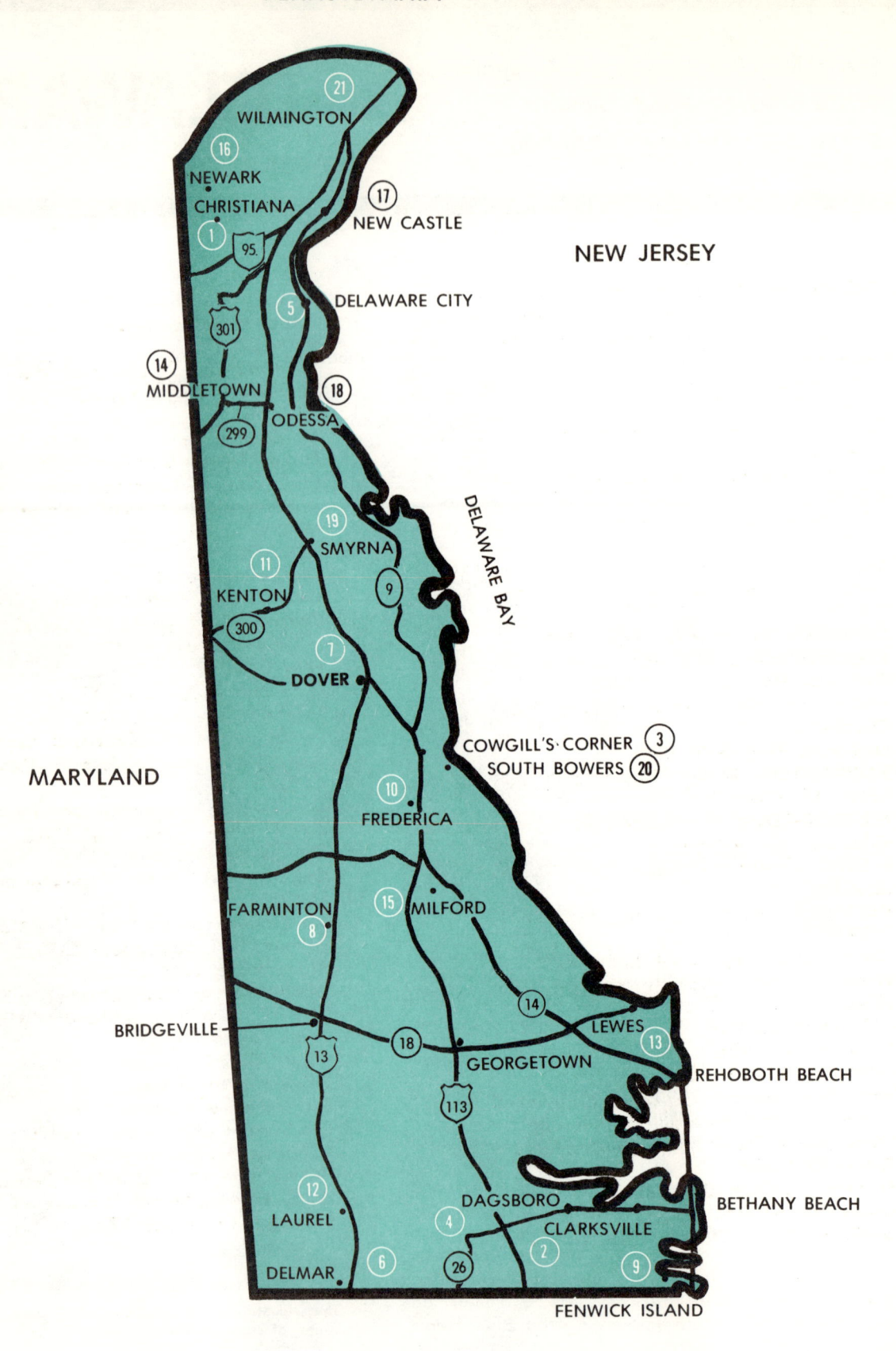

Key:

① relates to number 1 on the following page.

page 30 / treasure trails

DELAWARE POINTS OF INTEREST

1. CHRISTIANA - Christiana Hotel, built 1700
2. CLARKSVILLE - Blackwater Church, built about 1736
3. COWGILL'S CORNER - Octagonal Schoolhouse, built 1836, on route 9
4. DAGSBORO - Prince George's Church, Episcopal Church, built 1757
5. DELAWARE CITY - Fort Delaware, on Pea Patch Island
6. DELMAR - Mason-Dixon Monument, erected 1768
7. DOVER
   Old State House - center of state government since 1777;
   Christ Church - Episcopal Church, built in 1734;
   Delaware State Museum - once Presbyterian Church;
   Governor's House, built about 1790;
   Ridgely House, built 1728, private residence;
   Dickinson Mansion, built 1740;
   Hall of Records - contains original charter from Charles II;
   Legislative Hall, built 1933
8. FARMINGTON - William Tharp House, built before 1838, U.S. Hiway 13
9. FENWICK ISLAND - Fenwick Light, used to guide ships for over 100 years
10. FREDERICA - Barratt's Chapel, built 1780, Methodist Church
11. KENTON - Aspendale House, built 1773
12. LAUREL
    Christ Church - Episcopal, built 1771;
    Woodland Ferry - cable ferry, since 1793
13. LEWES
    1812 Memorial Park;
    De Vries Monument, marks the site of ill-fated Dutch colony of 1631;
    Many 18th century buildings, Cannonball house (Lewes Marine Museum), Thompson's Country Store, Rabitts Ferry house, Burton-Ingram house, The Plank house;
    St. Peter's Church, Episcopal, built 1858;
    Lewes Presbyterian Church, 17th century;
    Bethel Methodist Church, 17th century;
    St. George's Chapel, 1794, route 285;
    Zwaanendael Museum
14. MIDDLETOWN
    St. Ann's Church, Episcopal, built 1869;
    Middletown Academy, built 1826
15. MILFORD
    Mordington, built 1777, route 12;
    Parson Thorne Mansion, built 1740, route 14;
    Christ Church, Episcopal, built 1791;
    Abbott's Mill, built 1808, right off route 36 west of Milford
16. NEWARK
    Old College, built 1833;
    Welsh Tract Church - Baptist, built 1746;
    Cooch's Bridge, scene of only revolutionary battle in Delaware, 1777
17. NEW CASTLE
    Old Court House, built 1731;
    Amstel House, built 1707;
    Immanuel Church - Episcopal, built 1703;
    Buena Vista, home of John M. Clayton, built 1847
18. ODESSA
    Corbit-Sharp House, museum, built 1772;
    David Wilson House, built 1740;
    Friends Meeting, built 1780;
    Old Drawyers Church, Presbyterian, built 1773
19. SMYRNA
    The Lindens, colonial home built about 1765;
    Belmont Hall, built about 1753;
    Allee House, built 1753;
    Wildlife Refuge, Federal game refuge
20. SOUTH BOWERS - Island Field Site, Indian archeological site
21. WILMINGTON
    Delaware Art Center;
    Fort Christina Monument;
    Old Swedes Church, built 1698;
    Old Town Hall, built 1798;
    Hagley Museum, Old duPont Powder Mill;
    Henry Francis duPont Museum (5 miles west of Wilmington on route 52)

treasure trails / page 31

Here is a side view of the beautiful Winterthur Museum located five miles west of Wilmington, Delaware.

Barrett's Chapel, near Frederica, was built around 1778 and is called the "Cradle of Methodism in America."

The largest resort area in the state of Delaware, Rehoboth Beach, is a portion of the mainland that extends right to the surf of the South Atlantic coastline.

Hagley Museum, site of the first du Pont powder mills along the Brandywine River, is found three miles north of Wilmington.

Zwaanendael Museum, erected in Lewes, Delaware in 1931, commemorates the settling of the Dutch in 1631.

page 32 / treasure trails

WASHINGTON, D.C.

Became a District in 1790

FOR FURTHER INFORMATION WRITE:

- Chamber of Commerce of Washington, D.C.
  Visitors Information
  Washington, D.C. 20013

Washington, D.C., in reality, is the District of Columbia and vice versa. Unlike the 50 states it does not have a motto, bird or flower, but it has an interesting history. The United States is the first country to plan a special city to be the seat of its government. Others have taken up the idea in the 20th century. Eight cities had served for times as the seat of Congress before 1800 when Washington, D.C. became the capital of the United States. George Washington, Thomas Jefferson and Major Pierre Charles L'Enfant, a young French engineer, are among those who had a part in developing the area.

Washington, D.C. was planned to be the most beautiful and eminent capital in the world. Thomas Jefferson was instrumental in the planning of the city. Jefferson proposed astronomer and mathematician, Benjamin Baneker, as one of the three men to lay out the new Capitol. Pierre L'Enfant, an engineer from France, was the head of the three-man committee. The third member was George Ellicott, a Quaker scientist and businessman. This team created a plan carefully devised for the new Capital city. Washington was to have north-south and east-west streets with diagonal avenues extending from the Capitol and the White House. At the suggestion of Thomas Jefferson, these buildings were planned two miles apart to signify the separation of the legislative and executive branches of government.

The wide diagonal avenues were named after the states. The avenues extend like the spokes of a wheel. This was their plan for the "magnificent city."

The land of the District of Columbia lying alongside the Potomac River is mainly coastal plain land with Mt. St. Albans as the highest point.

Government is the business of first importance, real estate ranking second followed by tourism vieing with convention planning for third place. Manufacturing is a very small part of the economy.

Daniel Chester French created the stately 19-foot marble statue of Abraham Lincoln at the Lincoln Memorial in Washington, D.C.

treasure trails / page 33

MARYLAND

Map of Washington, D.C. locations:

- ⑥ CHESAPEAKE AND OHIO CANAL
- ㉑ JOHN F. KENNEDY CENTER
- ⑩ DEPARTMENT OF INTERIOR MUSEUM
- ㊳ WATERGATE HOTEL
- ⑦ CORCORAN ART GALLERY
- ㉓ LINCOLN MEMORIAL
- ⑤ CHERRY TREES
- ㊲ WASHINGTON MONUMENT
- ⑨ DEPARTMENT OF COMMERCE
- ㉕ NATIONAL ARCHIVES
- ⑲ JEFFERSON MEMORIAL
- ③ BUREAU OF ENGRAVING AND PRINTING
- ⑧ DEPARTMENT OF AGRICULTURE
- SMITHSONIAN INSTITUTE ㉜
- ② BOTANIC GARDENS
- NATIONAL GALLERY OF ART ㉗
- POTOMAC
- WASHINGTON CATHEDRAL ㊱
- NATIONAL ZOOLOGICAL PARK ㉚
- NATIONAL GEOGRAPHIC SOCIETY ㉘
- DUMBARTON OAKS ⑫
- GEORGETOWN ⑰
- WHITE HOUSE ㊵
- FORD'S THEATRE ⑮
- FEDERAL BUREAU INVESTIGATION ⑬
- U.S. TREASURY BUILDING ㉟
- INTERNAL REVENUE SERVICE ⑱
- NATIONAL AQUARIUM ㉖
- DEPARTMENT OF JUSTICE ⑪
- HOUSE WHERE PRESIDENT LINCOLN DIED ㉔
- NATIONAL SHRINE OF THE IMMACULATE CONCEPTION ㉙
- UNION STATION ㉞
- FRANCISCAN MONASTERY ⑯
- ① MUSEUM OF AFRICAN ART
- THE CAPITOL ④
- SUPREME COURT ㉝
- KENILWORTH AQUATIC GARDENS ⑳
- NAVY MEMORIAL MUSEUM ㉒
- FOLGER SHAKESPEARE LIBRARY ⑭
- WAX MUSEUM ㊴
- LIBRARY OF CONGRESS
- WOODROW WILSON HOUSE ㊶

VIRGINIA · MARYLAND

Key:
① relates to number 1 on the following page.

page 34 / treasure trails

WASHINGTON, D.C. POINTS OF INTEREST

1. MUSEUM OF AFRICAN ART
2. BOTANIC GARDENS - tropical and domestic plant life
3. BUREAU OF ENGRAVING AND PRINTING - paper money and stamps made here
4. THE CAPITOL - our symbol of government
5. CHERRY TREES - given by Japan, site of Cherry Blossom Festival
6. CHESAPEAKE AND OHIO CANAL - restored part runs from Georgetown to Lock 23
7. CORCORAN ART GALLERY
8. DEPARTMENT OF AGRICULTURE - second largest building in Washington, D.C.
9. DEPARTMENT OF COMMERCE - has electronic devises that record vital statistics
10. DEPARTMENT OF INTERIOR MUSEUM - paintings, movies, dioramas
11. DEPARTMENT OF JUSTICE - houses over 130,000,000 fingerprints, tours
12. DUMBARTON OAKS - formal gardens, historic markers
13. FEDERAL BUREAU INVESTIGATION - Government men explain the workings of the Department of Justice
14. FOLGER SHAKESPEARE LIBRARY - collection of English Renaissance books
15. FORD'S THEATRE - Theatre where President Lincoln was shot
16. FRANCISCAN MONASTERY - replicas of Holy Lands and catacombs
17. GEORGETOWN - elegant restored residential section
18. INTERNAL REVENUE SERVICE - shows roles of taxes in American History
19. JEFFERSON MEMORIAL - impressive marble memorial
20. KENILWORTH AQUATIC GARDENS - lilies, lotus, and other aquatic plants
21. JOHN F. KENNEDY CENTER - houses four theatres
22. LIBRARY OF CONGRESS - Gutenberg Bible and other great books
23. LINCOLN MEMORIAL - immense sculptured figure by Daniel Chester French
24. HOUSE WHERE PRESIDENT LINCOLN DIED - remains unchanged
25. NATIONAL ARCHIVES - original documents, including the Declaration of Independence
26. NATIONAL AQUARIUM - marine life from around the world
27. NATIONAL GALLERY OF ART - Mellon and Kress collections, etc.
28. NATIONAL GEOGRAPHIC SOCIETY - exhibits from around the world
29. NATIONAL SHRINE OF THE IMMACULATE CONCEPTION - largest Roman Catholic Church in the United States
30. NATIONAL ZOOLOGICAL PARK
31. NAVY MEMORIAL MUSEUM - relics from 1775
32. SMITHSONIAN INSTITUTE
    Air and Space Building, historic planes and space missiles;
    Arts and Industries Building, "Kitty Hawk" and "Spirit of St. Louis";
    Freer Gallery of Art, collection of Oriental art;
    National Collection of Fine Arts, shows development of American art;
    National Museum of Natural History, natural and man-made wonders;
    National Museum of Technology, many historic items;
    National Portrait Gallery, contains portraits of those who aided progress;
    Renwick Gallery
33. SUPREME COURT - our Nation's highest tribunal
34. UNION STATION - Roman Classic architecture
35. U.S. TREASURY BUILDING - supervises the printing and coining of money
36. WASHINGTON CATHEDRAL - one of the world's largest church buildings
37. WASHINGTON MONUMENT - towers 555 feet high
38. WATERGATE HOTEL
39. WAX MUSEUM
40. WHITE HOUSE - residence of every President except Washington
41. WOODROW WILSON HOUSE - 28th President's home

treasure trails / page 35

Overlooking the Potomac River is the beautifully restored plantation of George Washington. The lush floral gardens and landscaping enhance the scene.

Another attraction to view is the majestic Capitol building. The structure was partially completed in 1800 and the dome finished in 1863.

The Washington Monument, at 555 feet, is the tallest building in Washington, D.C. and the world's tallest masonry structure.

Photographs furnished by Washington Area Convention and Visitors Bureau.

page 36 / treasure trails

STATE MOTTO: In God We Trust
STATE BIRD: Mocking Bird
STATE FLOWER: Orange Blossom

FLORIDA
Admitted to the Union in 1845

FOR FURTHER INFORMATION WRITE:

- Mr. J. M. Bethea
  Director, Forestry Division
  Mayo Building
  Tallahassee, Florida 32304

- Major Jim Floyd
  Game & Fresh Water Fish Commission
  Farris Bryant Building
  Tallahassee, Florida 32304

Europeans, most likely the Spaniards, saw Florida for the first time. A Spanish map of 1502 depicts a peninsula like Florida. Peter Martyr writes in 1511 of land near the Bahama Islands with water of eternal youth.

Juan Ponce de Leon, who first had come to the New World on the second voyage of Columbus, sighted Florida on March 27, 1513. Going ashore between April 2 and 8 in the vicinity of St. Augustine, he named the land "Pascua Florida" because of its discovery "in the time of the Feast of Flowers." They had heard from the Puerto Rican Indians of a lush land in the northwest, with gold and a glorious fountain that would restore youth. The West Indians searched for the fountain of youth and named sections of the mainland. Some reached southeastern Florida and settled there. Andreas the Bearded, a West Indian told a Spanish historian, Peter Martyr, that his father found the fountain of youth and was restored to a youthful, vigorous man.

The unified government of Florida was established on March 30, 1822, when President Monroe signed into law the Congressional Act providing for a Governor and a Legislative Council of 13 citizens, appointed by the President. William P. DuVal, a Virginian who grew to manhood in Kentucky, became the first Territorial Governor.

Governor DuVal, on March 4, 1824 proclaimed the site of the present city of Tallahassee as the seat of the new Territory, with the Legislative Council meeting there in November at a log house erected in the vicinity of today's capitol.

Florida produces vegetables, mainly in the southern area, citrus crops in the central area, and cane in the Everglades. Sweet and Irish potatoes, corn, sugar cane, peanuts, and field peas are produced in central Florida. Tobacco and cotton are harvested in the north.

Major industries in Florida include tourism, fishing, lumber products, and the production of cigars.

This impressive headdress can still be seen at forts such as the Castillo de San Marcos in St. Augustine, Florida.

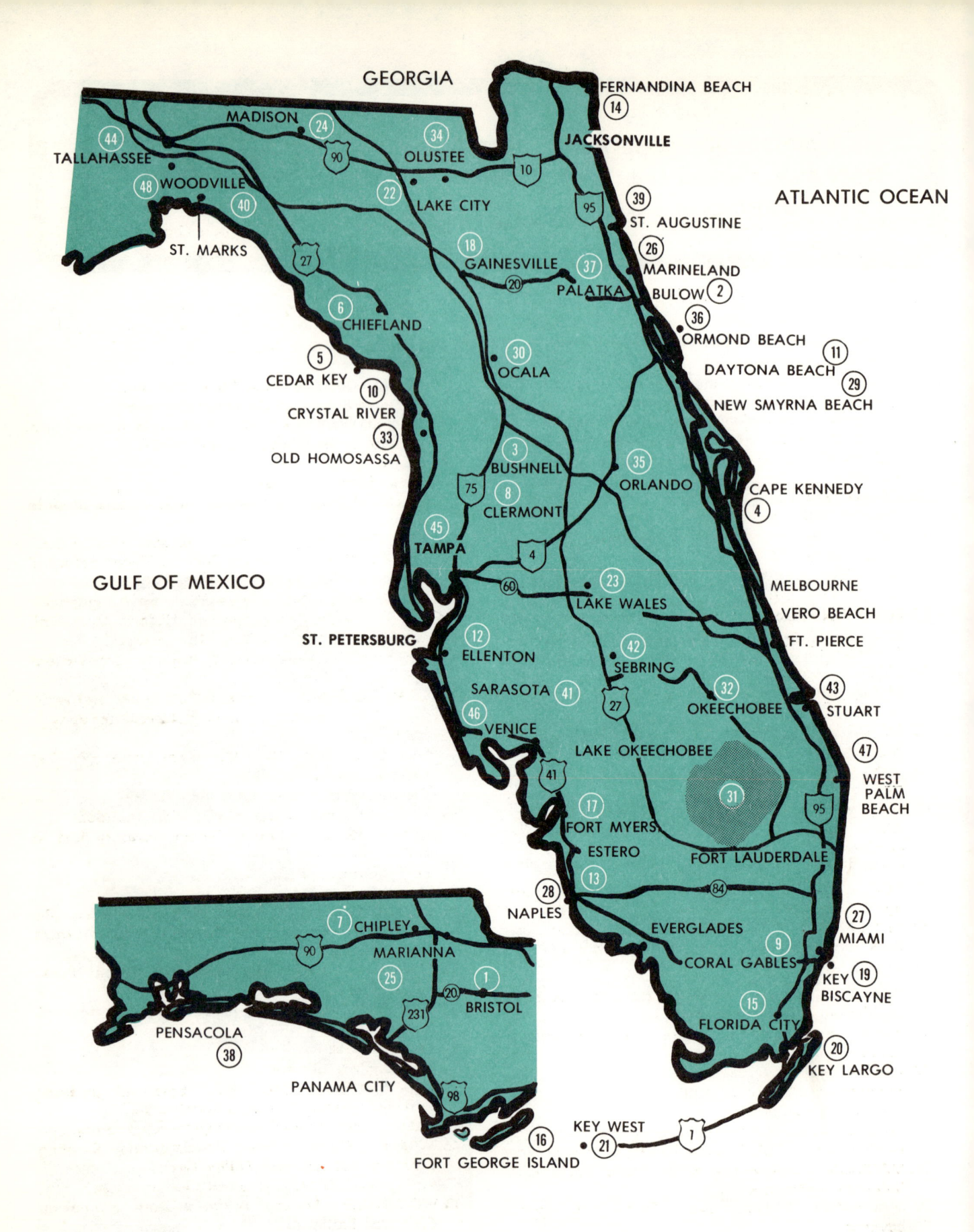

Key:
① relates to number 1 on the following page.

page 38 / treasure trails

FLORIDA POINTS OF INTEREST

1. BRISTOL - Torreya State Park, antebellum mansion and plantation
2. BULOW - Bulow Plantation Ruins and Historic Memorial
3. BUSHNELL - Dade, battlefield and historic memorial, site of Seminole massacre of 1835
4. CAPE KENNEDY - Space Center, site of man's exploration of space
5. CEDAR KEY - Cedar Key Memorial, museum
6. CHIEFLAND - Manatee Springs State Park: boardwalk, boat pier, major natural springs
7. CHIPLEY - Falling Waters State Park, waterfall
8. CLERMONT - Citrus Tower, overlooks acres of citrus groves
9. CORAL GABLES - Fairchild Tropical Gardens: classical villa, museum, Florentine gardens
10. CRYSTAL RIVER - Crystal River Indian Mounds, 1,000 years old
11. DAYTONA BEACH - Daytona Speedway, home of the Daytona 500
12. ELLENTON - Gamble Mansion, antebellum home and plantation, memorial to Judah Benjamin, Confederate Secretary of State
13. ESTERO - Koreshan State Park, art hall
14. FERNANDINA BEACH - Fort Clinch State Park, built in 1850
15. FLORIDA CITY - Everglades National Park, natural history museum, wildlife preserve
16. FORT GEORGE ISLAND - Fort George, site where Huguenots first landed, Indian mounds
17. FORT MYERS - Thomas Edison Home and Gardens, winter residence of inventor, museum, botanical gardens
18. GAINESVILLE - Home of University of Florida
19. KEY BISCAYNE - Cape Florida State Park, lighthouse, built in 1825
20. KEY LARGO - John Pennekamp Coral Reef State Park: undersea park, glass bottom boat tours
21. KEY WEST
    Audubon House, dedicated to famous ornithologist, John Audubon
    Ernest Hemingway's Home, author's Florida home
22. LAKE CITY
    Stephen Foster Memorial, bell tower plays melodies, museum;
    Osceola National Forest: ocean pond, hunting
23. LAKE WALES - Bok Singing Tower, bird sanctuary
24. MADISON - Suwannee River State Park, Confederate earthworks
25. MARIANNA - Florida Caverns State Park, lighted caverns
26. MARINELAND - Washington Oaks Gardens State Park: gardens, ocean fishing
27. MIAMI
    Crandon Park Zoo;
    Vizcaya, formal gardens, art museum;
    Museum of Science and Natural History, aquarium, planetarium with lectures
28. NAPLES
    Collier Seminole State Park, camping;
    Corkscrew Swamp Audubon Sanctuary
29. NEW SMYRNA BEACH - Turtle Mound, Indian burial mound, archaeological explorations
30. OCALA
    Silver Springs, museum;
    Prince of Peace Memorial, Ross Allen's Reptile Institute
31. LAKE OKEECHOBEE - second largest lake in U.S.
32. OKEECHOBEE - site where Zachary Taylor defeated the Seminoles, 1837
33. OLD HOMOSASSA - Yulee Mile, early sugar mill
34. OLUSTEE - Olustee Battlefield Historic Memorial, site of major Civil War Battle, museum
35. ORLANDO - Disney World, gigantic amusement center
36. ORMOND BEACH - Tomoka State park, statue
37. PALATKA - Ravine Gardens, botanical gardens
38. PENSACOLA
    Fort San Carlos De Barrancas, site of first settlement in U.S. 1559;
    Christ Church, oldest church in Florida
39. ST. AUGUSTINE - Oldest city in U.S., founded
    Castillo De San Marcos, oldest masonry fort in United States, 1672;
    Fort Matanzas, built 1737;
    Marineland, plant and fish life
40. ST. MARKS - Fort St. Marks, National Historic site
41. SARASOTA - Ringling Art Museum, circus artifacts from 16th century
42. SEBRING - Highlands Hammock State Park, subtropical
43. STUART - House of Refugee Museum, nautical history
44. TALLAHASSEE
    Florida State Capitol;
    Killearn Gardens State Park, botanical gardens;
    Wakulla Springs Audubon Sanctuary
45. TAMPA - Busch Gardens: tropical flora, birds, zoo
46. VENICE - Circus Winter Headquarters, Ringling Brothers, Barnum and Bailey Circus
47. WEST PALM BEACH - Norton Gallery of Art
48. WOODVILLE - Natural Bridge Historic Memorial, Civil War Battlefield

treasure trails / page 39

Here is a "friendly pet" for your home! This reptile can be found at the Alligator Farm in St. Augustine, Florida.

Photographs furnished by Florida Department of Commerce.

Cape Kennedy, site of Apollo moon shots.

Visitors to the Ringling Museum complex in Sarasota are transported to another time and era as they stroll the beautifully landscaped grounds. The art museum surrounds a garden courtyard.

The campanile at the Stephen Foster Memorial, near White Springs, houses a carillon on which American composers songs are played.

page 40 / treasure trails

STATE MOTTO: Wisdom, Justice and Moderation
STATE BIRD: Brown Thrasher
STATE FLOWER: Cherokee Rose

GEORGIA
Admitted to the Union in 1788

FOR FURTHER INFORMATION WRITE:

- Chattahoochee and National Forest Supervisors Office
  P.O. Box 1437
  Gainesville, Georgia 30501

- Tourist Division
  Georgia Department of Community Development
  P.O. Box 38097
  Atlanta, Georgia 30334

- Travel Council
  Georgia Chamber of Commerce
  1200 Commerce Building
  Atlanta, Georgia 30303

In a day's time, one can travel from the blue Appalachian range of mountains in the north of Georgia, through the rolling central plains, on to the great Okefenokee Swamp, then to the tide water marshes, the white beach sands, and to the famous Golden Islands.

Georgia is the youngest of the thirteen Colonies. In 1733, under the leadership of James Oglethorpe, the first colonists came. They arrived from Britain to settle along the Savannah River.

Seven years of conflict, during the fight for independence, stopped all growth and development in the colony. When statehood was attained on January 2, 1788, settlement began to increase. The American soldiers came home to take up land.

Through treaties with the Creek and the Cherokee Indians, new land was opened. The call of gold and land created swift expansion beyond the old frontier.

In 1860 the Georgia Legislature voted to secede from the Union. January 19, 1861, the delegates at the Secession Convention in Milledgeville adopted the Ordinance of Secession.

The real devestation of the War Between the States did not come to Georgia until 1863, when General Sherman pushed through the state on his "March to the Sea" destroying Atlanta.

During the Civil War years Georgia sent almost 125,000 men into battle and lost much of her material wealth. After the war, bankrupt and without machinery and seeds, Georgia began to rebuild. Slowly cities began to grow, and the impetus of those years of building has never stopped.

A unique collection of nautical memorabilia, The Ships of the Sea Museum is found in Savannah, Georgia.

treasure trails / page 41

TENNESSEE

COHUTTA MOUNTAIN (15)   BLUE RIDGE (8)
(13)   (12)   (19)
CHICKAMAUGA   (52)   AMICALOLA FALLS   (14) CLARKESVILLE
   75   ELLIJAY   (3)   (34) TOCCOA
(10)   (21)   (16)
CALHOUN   DAWSONVILLE (17)   DAHLONEGA
       23   SOUTH CAROLINA
ROME (30)   CARTERSVILLE   (20)
   (27)   11   85   ELBERTON
MARIETTA   29
   ATHENS
   78   ATLANTA (2)   (6)   (5)
       20   APPLING   AUGUSTA
       (19) EATONTON (16)   (7)
       JACKSON   (24)
   (29)   (22)   (28)   LOUISVILLE
       MILLEDGEVILLE
   (35)   MACON   DUBLIN
   (29) WARM SPRINGS   (26)   (18)
PINE MOUNTAIN   PERRY   80   80
   COLUMBUS
   (26)   ELLAVILLE   CORDELLE   1   (32)
ALABAMA   ANDERSONVILLE   SAVANNAH
   LUMPKIN   (4)
   (25)   JESUP
   82   95
   ALBANY (1)   TIFTON   (31)
           ST. SIMONS
       WAYCROSS   (9)   ISLAND
       (36)   BRUNSWICK
   84   VALDOSTA

FLORIDA

Key:
(1) relates to number 1 on the following page.

page 42 / treasure trails

GEORGIA POINTS OF INTEREST

1. ALBANY
   Banks Haley Art Gallery;
   Museum
2. ATLANTA
   Stone Mountain, 563 acres, 200 million years old;
   Cyclorama, circular painting of Civil War Battle of Atlanta;
   Wren's Nest, home of Joel Chandler Harris, contains his possessions and original editions;
   Six Flags Over Georgia, amusement park;
   Lion Country Safari, amusement park and zoo;
   Atlanta Art Association, galleries;
   Margaret Mitchell Memorial Room, in Carnegie Library, author of "Gone With The Wind"
3. AMICALOLA FALLS - Springer Mountain, beginning of Appalachian Trail
4. ANDERSONVILLE - Andersonville Prison Site, used during Civil War
5. APPLING - Kiokee Baptist Church, established in 1773, first in the state, second in the nation
6. ATHENS - Founders Memorial Garden and House, Ladies Garden Club was first started here, 1857;
   University of Georgia
7. AUGUSTA - Confederate Monument, 76 foot marble statue of a Confederate private and life-size figures of four generals, Lee, Jackson, Walker and Cobb
8. BLUE RIDGE - Blue Ridge Lake, mountain lake, camping, boating, swimming
9. BRUNSWICK
   Jekyll Island;
   St. Simon's Island, Fort Fredricka National Monument
10. CALHOUN - New Echota, site of capitol of last Cherokee nation in Georgia
11. CARTERSVILLE
    Etowah Mounds, built by prehistoric Indians;
    Museum
12. CHATSWORTH - Vann House, a real showplace, bricks, nails, hinges produced in blacksmith shop, 1804
13. CHICKAMAUGA - Chickamauga and Chattanooga National Military Park, nation's oldest and largest
14. CLARKESVILLE - Tallulah Gorge
15. COHUTTA MOUNTAIN - Marble and Talc Quarries
16. DAHLONEGA - Dahlonega Gold Museum, pan for gold
17. DAWSONVILLE - Amicalola Falls, 729 foot fall
18. DILLARD - Baburn Gap Nacoochee School, High school students compiled "Foxfire I" and "Foxfire II"
19. EATONTON - Uncle Remus Museum, two slave cabins used to build this museum, scenes from Joel Chandler Harris tales, Harris born here 1848
20. ELBERTON - Granite Quarries, number one in the nation
21. ELLIJAY - Fort Mountain
22. JACKSON - Indian Springs
23. JEFFERSON - Crawford W. Long Medical Museum, on site of Dr. Long's office, who performed first surgical operation using ether
24. LOUISVILLE - Old Slave Market, one of the nation's few slave markets still standing, its bell was cast in 1772 and warned settlers of Indian attacks
25. LUMPKIN
    Providence Canyon, "Little Grand Canyon";
    Westville, restored 18th century town
26. MACON
    Ocmulgee National Monument, remains of ancient Indian mounds;
    Museum, Indian history
27. MARIETTA - Kennesaw Mountain National Battlefield Park
28. MILLEDGEVILLE - Old State Capitol
29. PINE MOUNTAIN - Callaway Gardens, boating, dining, fishing, golfing, and swimming
30. ROME - The Berry Schools, largest campus in world, original building still stands, largest overshot water-wheel in U.S. on this campus
31. ST. SIMONS ISLAND
    Christ Church, built 1736;
    Beach resorts;
    Historic sights
32. SAVANNAH
    Betheseda, oldest orphanage in America;
    Ships of the Sea Museum, collection of ship models, many in bottles, in cotton warehouse, 1853;
    Midway Church, built 1792;
    Yamacrow Bluff, site of landing of James Oglethorpe in 1733;
    Fort Pulaski National Monument, early 19th century with moat and drawbridge;
    Telfair Academy of Arts and Sciences, art gallery;
    Tybee Lighthouse, partially destroyed by Confederates in 1862
33. THOMASVILLE - home of the Rose Show, April
34. TOCCOA - Toccoa Falls, 186 foot drop
35. WARM SPRINGS
    40 miles north of Columbus;
    Little White House, home of Franklin Roosevelt;
    Warm Springs Fountain, handicap center, started by Franklin Roosevelt
36. WAYCROSS
    Okefenokee Swamp, 700 square miles;
    State park and national wildlife refuge

Providence Canyons State Park near Lumpkin, Georgia, boasts chasms that drop 300 feet.

The smooth forms of modern sculpture against the skyscrapers of Atlanta, Georgia, create this scene on Peachtree Street.

Georgia's rolling miles of secluded beaches on the Golden Isles draw visitors to relaxation.

Brasstown Bald Mountain, near Blairsville, is the highest peak (4,768 feet above sea level) in Georgia.

page 44 / treasure trails

STATE MOTTO: The Life Of the Land Is Perpetuated In Righteousness
STATE FLOWER: Hibiscus
STATE BIRD: Hawaiian Goose (Nene)

HAWAII
Admitted to the Union in 1959

FOR FURTHER INFORMATION WRITE:

- Chamber of Commerce
  Honolulu, Hawaii 96813

- Hawaii Visitors Bureau
  2270 Kalakaua Avenue (Suite 801)
  Honolulu, Hawaii 96815

- State of Hawaii
  Department of Transportation
  896 Punchbowl Street
  Honolulu, Hawaii 96813

The Hawaiian Islands were visited by white men after being discovered by Captain James Cook in 1778. There are twenty-three islands in the chain, but fifteen of them are small coral reefs. Eight large islands are known as the High Islands and are inhabited. Each of the six main islands are unique and offer their own advantages.

HAWAII: The big island is large both in size and variety. Here are smoldering volcanoes, wild orchids, black sand beaches, Kona coffee plantations and quarter-ton trophy marlin. Along with acres of dense forest, and centuries of history to be explored.

MAUI: This valley island is a sweep of land between two volcanoes. Mile after mile of white sand beaches parallel scenic drives past mountain cascades and pools.

OAHU: From downtown Honolulu, bustling commercial capital of the Pacific, to the tranquillity of Makaha Valley, from the miles of sugar cane and pineapple fields to the beaches and night life of glittering Waikiki, Oahu is where Hawaii's action is happening.

KAUAI: Kauai is the oldest and some claim, loveliest, island in the Hawaiian chain. It's lush, green and tropical. The Polynesian Paradise of song and legend, Kauai was the setting for the movie "South Pacific".

LANAI: This island is primarily a pineapple plantation. However, its 90,000 acres include a wealth of scenery and landmarks, as well as new, but somewhat limited, visitor accomodations.

MOLOKAI: Molokai offers visitors a sweep of Hawaiian history. Accommodations, while Polynesian in character, provide many luxuries.

NIIHAU: The island of Niihua is seventh in size of the Hawaiian Islands. Niihua lies across the Kaulakahi Channel, 17 miles southwest of Kauai. Niihau has been called The Forbidden Island, Isle of Yesteryear, and the Aloof Island. Hawaiian legends and culture are well preserved on this little island.

KAHOOLAWE: Southeast of the island of Lanai is the small, rugged island of Kahoolawe, used as a target area for Navy and Marines.

This strange formation of lava, Nature's Needle is found in the beautiful Iao Valley on Maui Island.

treasure trails / page 45

page 46 / treasure trails

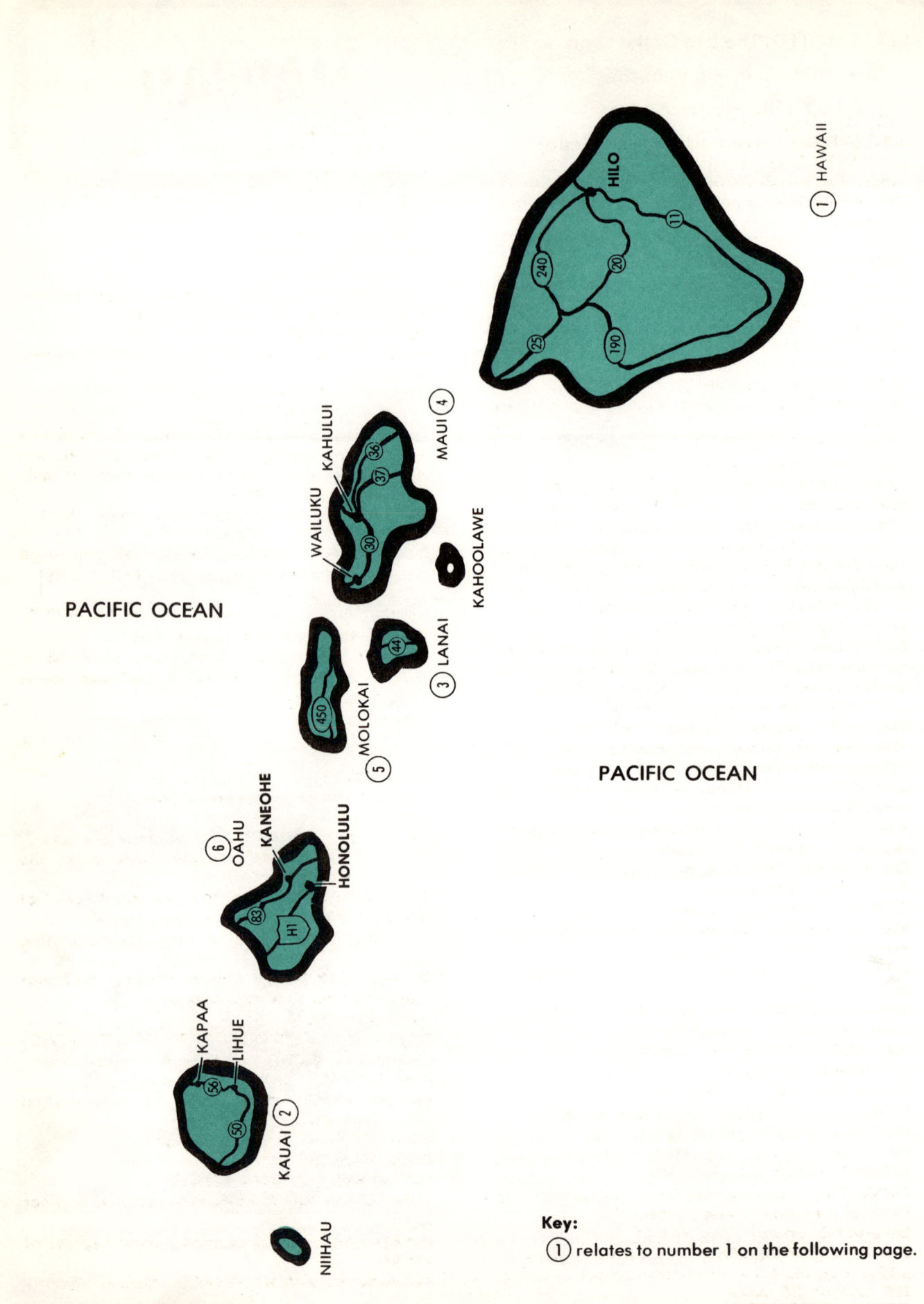

HAWAII POINTS OF INTEREST

1. **THE ISLAND OF HAWAII**
   AKAKA FALLS - 420 foot fall over volcanic cliff
   CAPTAIN COOK MONUMENT - Marks the spot where Captain Cook met his death
   CITY OF REFUGE - national park built 12th century to provide asylum
   HAWAII VOLCANOES NATIONAL PARK - Streaming craters and volcanological museum
   HULIHEE PALACE - summer palace of Hawaiian royalty, museum
   KAIMU BLACK SAND BEACH - pulverized lava rock
   KAMEHAMEHA STATUE - lost at sea, later recovered and erected
   LAVA FLOWS - marked by Warrior Signs which designate flows which surged down in prehistoric times
   LYMAN MEMORIAL MUSEUM - collection of ancient Hawaiian historic relics
   PARKER RANCH - second largest cattle ranch in the United States
   POLOLU VALLEY - site of ancient Hawaiian temples
   PUNA LAVA FLOW - recent lava flows
   PUUKOHOLA HEIAU - National Historical Park
   RAINBOW FALLS - water falls
   WAIPID VALLEY - Hawaii of yesteryear

2. **THE ISLAND OF KAUAI**
   BOTANICAL GARDENS - 4 gardens: Plantation Gardens, Olu Pua Gardens, Menehune Gardens and Paradise Pacifica
   CAPTAIN COOK'S WAIMEA BAY - landing place of the British explorer, January, 1778
   FERN GROTTO - cave with growing ferns
   KOKEE PARK - trail riding, trout fishing and hiking
   LUMAHAI BEACH - chosen for nurses' beach in the movie "South Pacific"
   MENHUNE DITCH - aqueduct, built before Hawaiians came to the island
   OLD RUSSIAN FORT - Russian fur trader built this in 1817 for his Czar
   OPAEKAA FALLS - waterfalls
   SLEEPING GIANT - outline of mountain ridge shows resemblance to reclining giant
   WAILUA - Royal Birthstones
   WAIMEA CANYON
   WAIOLI MISSION HOME - built 1834
   WAIPAHEE FALLS - waterfalls
   WET AND DRY CAVES OF HAENA

3. **THE ISLAND OF LANAI**
   CAVENDISH GOLF COURSE - 9 hole course
   GARDEN OF THE GODS - rock formations
   HULOPOE BAY AND MANELE BAY
   KAUNOLU BAY - ruins of ancient village
   KEOMUKU VILLAGE - ghost town
   LANAI CITY - picturesque town, surrounded by fields of pineapple. Dole's office
   LANAIHALE - view of six islands
   LUAHIWA PETROGLYPHS - old Mormon colony
   SHIPWRECK BEACH - fisherman's paradise

4. **THE ISLAND OF MAUI**
   BALDWIN HOME - early island missionary home
   HALEAKALA NATIONAL PARK - scenic crater
   HALE HOIKEIKE - museum
   HALEKII HEIAU - ancient temples of worship
   HAL PA'I - Hawaii's first newspaper
   IAO VALLEY - park, site of battle of 1790
   KAANAPALI - resort area
   KANAHA BIRD SANCTUARY
   KAPALUA BEACH - one of Hawaii's finest beaches
   KAUMAHINA PARK - picnic grounds
   PUAA KAA PARK
   SAVEN POOLS - crystal pools, photographers' paradise
   WHALER'S VILLAGE MUSEUM

5. **THE ISLAND OF MOLOKAI**
   FATHER DAMIEN'S STATUE - statue of missionary who worked among victims of Hansen's disease
   HALAWA VALLEY - site of two waterfalls: Moaula Falls and Hipuapua Falls
   KAPUIWA GROVE - 1,000 coconut trees
   MOAULA FALLS - waterfalls
   MOKUHOONIKI - offshore, used a bombing range
   PALAAU PARK - state park with phallic rocks

6. **THE ISLAND OF OAHU**
   ALOHA TOWER - landmark, in Honolulu, offering view of downtown and harbor area
   AQUARIUM - tropical fish aquarium at Waikiki
   BISHOP MUSEUM - Hawaiian and Polynesian antiquities
   CHINATOWN
   CORAL GARDENS - glass-bottom boat tours of coral growths
   DIAMOND HEAD - extinct volcano
   FOSTER GARDENS - botanical displays
   HANAUMA BAY - sea cove
   HAWAIIAN WAX MUSEUM - historical scenes
   IOLANI PALACE - only throne room under the American flag
   KAWAIAHAO CHURCH - "Westminster Abbey" of Hawaii, services in Hawaiian and English
   MAKAHA BEACH - site of International surfing meets
   MISSION HOUSES - oldest existing buildings erected by the first missionaries
   MORMON TEMPLE
   NATIONAL MEMORIAL CEMETERY OF THE PACIFIC - cemetery of W.W. II and Korean War veterans
   NUUANU PALI - Oahu's scenic masterpiece
   OLD SUGAR MILL - ruins of the first sugar mill on Oahu, built 1864
   PARADISE PARK - tropical exhibits
   PEARL HARBOR
   POLYNESIAN CULTURAL CENTER
   QUEEN EMMA SUMMER PALACE - restored summer palace
   SEA LIFE PARK - one of America's finest displays of sea life
   ULU MAU HAWAIIAN VILLAGE - historic village

treasure trails / page 47

Iolani Palace, located in Honolulu, was once the home of Hawaiian Royalty. The downstairs galleries, until recently, were used by the Hawaii State Legislature.

On the Kalaupapa Peninsula of Molokai Island, Father Damien cared for victums of leprosy.

On Maui Island, stands the largest dormant volcano in the world, Haleakala. 19 square miles in area, and 10,000 feet above sea level.

page 48 / treasure trails

Photographs furnished by Hawaii Visitors Bureau.

STATE MOTTO: Esto Perpetua, "Let It Be Perpetual"
STATE FLOWER: Syringa
STATE BIRD: Mountain Bluebird

IDAHO
Admitted to the Union in 1890

FOR FURTHER INFORMATION WRITE:

- Idaho Parks Department
  Boise, Idaho 83707

- Idaho Fish and Game Department
  600 South Walnut or P.O. Box 25
  Boise, Idaho 83707

- Division of Tourism and Industrial Development
  State Capitol
  Boise, Idaho 83720

In 1848, the U.S. Congress established the Oregon Territory, Oregon soon decided it did not want any of the land that is now Idaho. It became a part of the Washington Territory. Following the discovery of gold, on March 4, 1860, the Idaho Territory was formed in 1863, which included all of what is now Montana and nearly all of Wyoming. It was in 1864 that the Idaho Territory assumed the shape and size of its present state. On July 3, 1890, Idaho was added as the 43rd state in our country's flag.

The rolling hills in southeastern Idaho as well as in the Palouse-Lewiston-Moscow area, are the chief dry farming (not irrigated) croplands in the state, with wheat, other grain, hay and potatoes as the principal agriculture products.

Idaho mountains are blanketed with great evergreen forests. In fact, with more than 1/3 of its surface area in woods, Idaho is more widely forested than any other state in the Rocky Mountain group.

Idaho ranks among the 10 leading cattle and sheep raising states in the U.S. today. Manufacturing in Idaho, based on this industry, includes meat packing, cheese factories, and milk processing plants.

One of the fastest growing Idaho industries is food processing. Idaho processes nearly 60 percent of the nation's potatoes including: freezing, canning, dehydration, chips and flour, as well as potato starch.

Idaho's wildlife is unequaled by any other state. Valleys and mountains of the Lemhi Range have one of the few large antelope herds in the United States. There are bighorn sheep along the Salmon River as well as in the Owyhee Mountains. In the Panhandle are moose. Huge herds of elk and deer roam across Idaho. High mountain peaks are home to Rocky Mountain goats. Black bear, cougars, bobcats, and coyotes are found in Idaho. Fur-bearing animals—beaver, marten, otter, mink, fox and muskrat are still trapped here.

Chain upon chain of majestic mountains rise across the length and breadth of Idaho . . . plowed by glaciers . . . moistened by the snows of a million winters . . . split and twisted by earthquakes . . . built by the forces of nature.

Said to be the most perfect spatter and cone chain at Craters of the Moon National Monument, near Arco, Idaho, is centered along the Great Rift.

treasure trails / page 49

CANADA
95
39
SANDPOINT
COEUR D'ALENE
11
10
CATALDO
21
10
KELLOGG
35
POTLATCH
24
LEWIS AND CLARK ROUTE
MOSCOW
29
25
31
OROFINO
LEWISTON
33
PIERCE
12
SPAULDING
42
MONTANA
95
RIGGINS
36
46
8
CARMEN
SALMON
28
McCALL
38
TENDOY
43
MACKS INN
26
191
46
WEISER
GILMORE
15
12
55
DUBOIS
3
93
93
ASHTON
19
IDAHO CITY
27
SAINT ANTHONY
44
37
TETON
80-N
BOISE
4
22
MACKAY
2
KETCHUM
ARCO
20
OREGON
13
ELMORE COUNTY
IDAHO FALLS
80-N
MURPHY
30
1
15
GRAND VIEW
17
16
GLENN'S FERRY
AMERICAN FALLS
34
POCATELLO
5
40
41
BRUNEAU
HAGERMAN
SHOSHONE
SODA SPRINGS
18
30
7
23
6
BUHL
BURLEY
LAVA HOT SPRINGS
TWIN FALLS
CASTLEFORD
45
80-N
PARIS
32
9
14
FRANKLIN
NEVADA
UTAH

Key:

(1) relates to number 1 on the following page.

IDAHO POINTS OF INTEREST

1. **AMERICAN FALLS**
   American Falls Reservoir and Dam;
   Crystal Ice Caves;
   Massacre Rocks, site of Indian ambush
2. **ARCO**
   Craters of the Moon Monument, extinct volcanic craters, lava beds;
   Natural Bridge, 150 feet across, 100 feet high;
   Nuclear Reactor Testing Station;
   Big and Little Lost Rivers and Birch Creek Sink, rivers disappear into lava beds;
   Twin Buttes and Cinder Cone, extinct craters, landmarks for early settlers traveling west
3. **ASHTON** - Upper and Lower Mesa Falls of Henry's Fork of Snake River, scenic area
4. **BOISE**
   State Capitol Building;
   Pioneer Village, site of first buildings erected;
   Boise State University;
   Boise Art Gallery;
   Julia Davis Park and Zoo;
   Bogus Basin, ski area;
   Boise Valley, famous pioneer stop;
   Treasure Valley, irrigation area, rich farmland where once was a desert
5. **BRUNEAU**
   Indian Bath Tubs, hot springs;
   Bruneau Dunes State Park, sand dunes and recreational area
6. **BUHL** - Snake River Trout Farm, world's largest trout farm
7. **BURLEY** - Silent City of Rocks, 25 square miles of bizarre rock forms
8. **CARMEN** - Tower of Rocks, display of natural erosion
9. **CASTLEFORD** - Balanced Rock, rock shaped by wind (In Ripley's "Believe It or Not")
10. **CATALDO** - Cataldo Mission, oldest building still standing in Idaho, 1853
11. **COEUR D'ALENE**
    Mullan Tree;
    Fourth of July Canyon;
    Lookout Pass;
    Heyburn State Park;
    Lake Chalcolet, scenic area
12. **DUBOIS** - USDA Sheep Experiment Station
13. **ELMORE COUNTY** - Trinity Lakes, three lakes in primitive area
14. **FRANKLIN** - Idaho's oldest town, 1860
15. **GILMORE** - Charcoal kilns, used by early miners
16. **GLENN'S FERRY** - Three Islands State Park
17. **GRAND VIEW** - Strike Dam, on Snake River
18. **HAGERMAN** - Thousand Springs, outlet for underground rivers
19. **IDAHO CITY** - Frontier town
20. **IDAHO FALLS** - Idaho Falls, on Snake River
21. **KELLOGG** - Mining District, largest silver and lead-producers in U.S., home of Sunshine Silver Mine
22. **KETCHUM**
    Sun Valley - Famous resort, skiing;
    Sawtooth Mountains, known as "America's Alps"
23. **LAVA HOT SPRINGS**
    Indian Rocks, Indian writings (petroglyphs);
    Mineral Springs, springs known for therapeutic and recreational value
24. **LEWIS AND CLARK ROUTE**, entrance at Lolo Pass and along Lolo Trail
25. **LEWISTON**
    Potlatch Lumber Mill, one of the largest in the world
26. **MACKS INN** - Big Springs, head-waters of Henry's Fork of Snake River
27. **MACKAY** - Borah Peak, highest point in Idaho, 12,662 feet
28. **McCALL** - Brundage Mountain, winter and summer resort
29. **MOSCOW** - University of Idaho
30. **MURPHY** - Silver City, ghost town, rich mining town in 1860's
31. **OROFINO** - Dworshak Dam and Steel-head Hatchery, highest gravity dam in the U.S.
32. **PARIS**
    Minnetonka Caves;
    Bear Lake, recreational area
33. **PIERCE** - Site of first gold discovery in Idaho
34. **POCATELLO**
    Fort Hall Indian Reservation;
    Idaho State University
35. **POTLATCH** - White Pine Drive, largest stand of white pine timber in U.S.
36. **RIGGINS** - Seven Devils Scenic Area, high rugged mountains
37. **ST. ANTHONY**
    St. Anthony Sand Dunes, Idaho's "Miniature Sahara Desert";
    Fort Henry, trading post established 1810
38. **SALMON**
    Salmon River, known as "River of No Return", famous for raft trips;
    Sacajawea Monument, birthplace of Indian guide for Lewis and Clark
39. **SANDPOINT**
    Lake Pend Oreille, largest lake in Idaho;
    Kullyspell House, site of old trading post;
    Upper Priest Lake, scenic area;
    Schweitzer Basin, ski area
40. **SHOSHONE** - Shoshone Ice Caves, underground lava tubes hold ice year-round
41. **SODA SPRINGS**
    Phosphate mining and mills;
    Soda Springs, largest carbon dioxide geyser in world, contains 22 minerals
42. **SPAULDING** - Spaulding Log Cabin Mission and Museum, site of first missionary settlement in Idaho, 1836
43. **TENDOY** - Fort Lemhi, frontier site
44. **TETON** - Teton River and Basin, meeting place for early day mountain men and fur traders
45. **TWIN FALLS**
    Shoshone Falls, higher than Niagara Falls (212 feet)
    Twin Falls, on Snake River
46. **WEISER** - Hell's Canyon, deepest canyon in North America

treasure trails / page 51

The height of 10,229 feet of Mt. Heyburn in Idaho's Sawtooth Mountain Range of the Challis National Forest rises high above Redfish Lake in Custer County. Here one can seek peace and quiet in the Idaho wilderness.

Cataldo's Sacred Heart Mission, built in 1853 by the Jesuit missionaries and the Indians, is Idaho's oldest standing building.

Here is a beautiful view up Trail Creek and across the Sun Valley Trap Shoot grounds.

page 52 / treasure trails

Photographs furnished by Idaho Department of Commerce and Devel

STATE MOTTO: State Sovereignty, National Union
STATE FLOWER: Native Violet
STATE BIRD: Cardinal

ILLINOIS
Admitted to the Union in 1818

FOR FURTHER INFORMATION WRITE:

- Forest Supervisor: Shawnee National Forest
  317 East Poplar Street
  Harrisburg, Illinois 62946

- Department of Conservation
  Division of Fisheries
  605 State Office Building
  Springfield, Illinois 62706

- Illinois Adventure Center
  State of Illinois Building
  160 North LaSalle Street
  Chicago, Illinois 60601

The "Prairie State", situated near the midpoint in the continent binds north to south and east to west. The gently rolling countryside with the deep soil makes Illinois part of the great agricultural area of our country. The city of Chicago, second in size in the United States, situated on Lake Michigan, with a great deal of industry contributes toward making Illinois known as the Inland Empire. The state has had a longer and more varied history than any other state west of the Alleghenies. Illinois came from the Indian word, Illiniwek, meaning "the men." The French dropped the last two syllables and substituted their own ending.

Geologically, Illinois was invaded by four massive ice sheets. Many streams are found in Illinois. The very southern tip of the state has some rock outcropping from the Ozark Highlands. Here one finds the soil and climate suitable for growing fruit. Some of the highland is part of the Shawnee National Forest. The dairyland is toward the northern part of the state, the vegetable growing area is in the northeast, leaving the great grain and livestock raising area throughout most of the state.

Early settlers developed agriculture, lumbering and mining. They came from Kentucky and Tennessee and remained largely in the southern third of the state. The invention of the steel plow and other agricultural implements made agriculture the greatest industry until the industrialization of the late nineteenth century.

There are a total of sixty-five state parks, twenty-three historical memorials and twenty-four conservation areas in Illinois.

Visitors can feel a part of Illinois' past as they tour the grounds of old Ft. Chartres located in southern Illinois.

treasure trails / page 53

page 54 / treasure trails

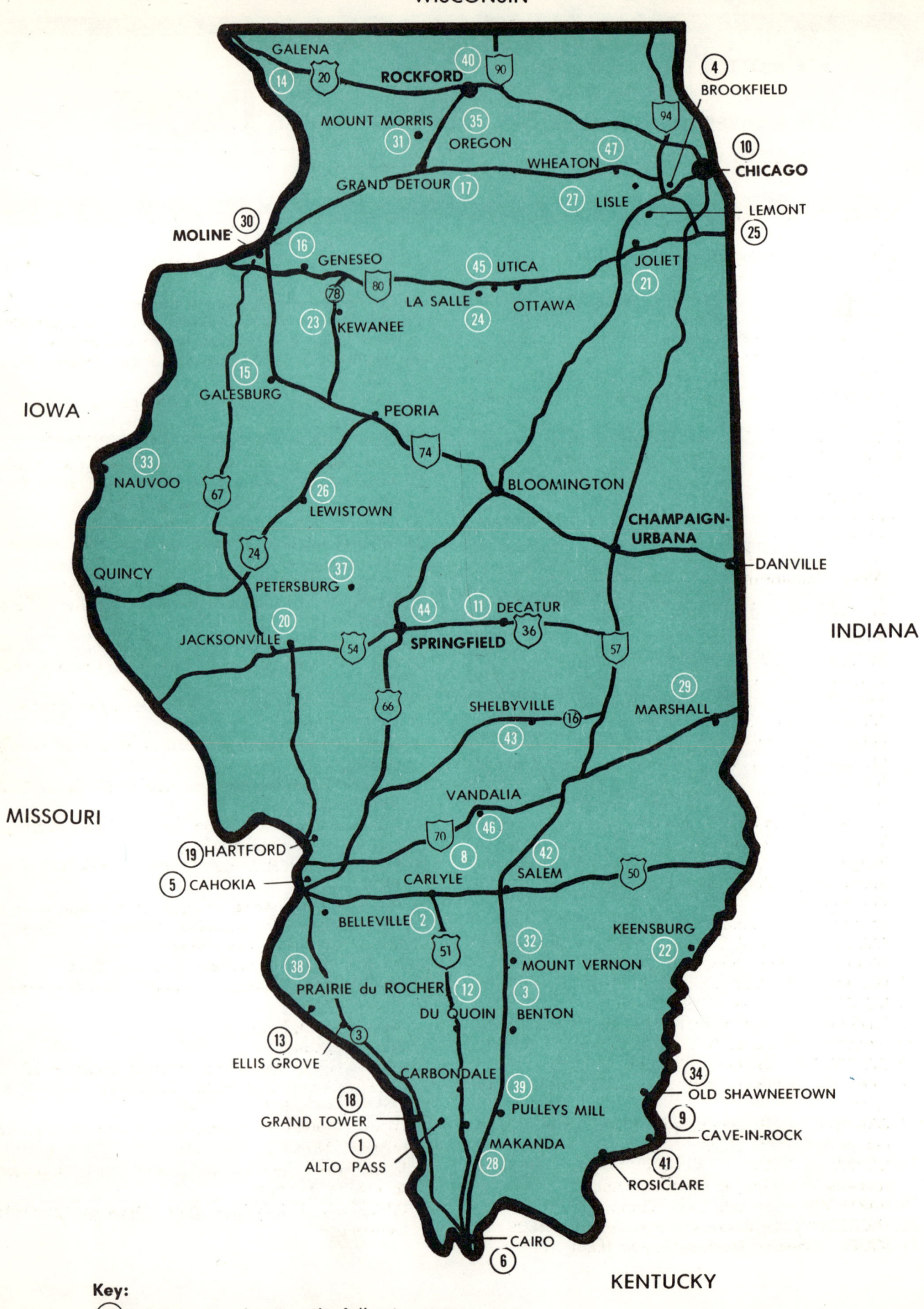

ILLINOIS POINTS OF INTEREST

1. ALTO PASS - Bald Knob Cross of Peace, Easter sunrise service
2. BELLEVILLE - Shrine of Our Lady of the Snows
3. BENTON - Rend Lake, recreation area
4. BROOKFIELD - Brookfield Zoo, year around attraction
5. CAHOKIA - Monk's Mound, prehistoric mound
6. CAIRO - Junction of Ohio and Mississippi rivers, cotton growing
7. CARBONDALE - Crab Orchard Lake, National Wildlife Refuge
8. CARLYLE - Carlyle Lake, recreation area
9. CAVE-IN-ROCK - Cave-in-Rock State Park, recreation area
10. CHICAGO
    Museum of Science and Industry, world famous;
    Field Museum of Natural History;
    John G. Shedd Aquarium, largest in world;
    Alder Planetarium;
    Art Institute, French impressionist collection;
    The "Chicago Picasso," five story sculpture by Picasso;
    McCormick Place, convention center;
    Chicago Public Library, glass mosaics;
    Sears Tower, world's tallest building;
    O'Hare Airport, world's largest;
    Robie House, by Frank Lloyd Wright;
    Chicago Water Tower, relic of the great Chicago fire, 1871;
    Buckingham Fountain, world's largest fountain;
    Chicago Mercantile Exchange, commodity trade;
    White Sox Park, American Baseball League;
    Wrigley Field, Cubs National Baseball League;
    Merchandise Mart, wholesale display;
    Chinatown;
    Soldier Field, mamouth sports center;
    Chicago Historical Society, Lincoln memorabilia;
    Wrigley Building, beautiful landmark
11. DECATUR - Soybean capital
12. DU QUOIN - scene of Hambletonian
13. ELLIS GROVE - site of first state capitol 1818-1820
14. GALENA - Home of Ulysses S. Grant
15. GALESBURG - Birthplace of Carl Sandburg
16. GENESEO - Johnson 1910 Farm, operating old-time farm
17. GRAND DETOUR - John Deere Historic Site, site of use of first steel plow
18. GRAND TOWER - world's longest pipeline suspension bridge across Mississippi
19. HARTFORD - Lewis & Clark Camp, 1803-1804
20. JACKSONVILLE - Illinois College, founded 1829
21. JOLIET - Dresden Nuclear Power Plant
22. KEENSBURG - Beall Woods Nature Preserve, primeval woodland
23. KEWANEE - Bishop Hill, Swedish village commune, restored
24. LA SALLE - Home of "Big Ben Clocks"
25. LEMONT - Argonne National Laboratory, research installation of Atomic Energy Commission
26. LEWISTOWN - Dickson Mounds, Indian burial mounds
    Spoon River, scene of writings by Edgar Lee Masters
27. LISLE - Morton Arboretum, nature preserve
28. MAKANDA - Giant City State Park, great bluffs
29. MARSHALL - Lincoln Trail Homestead State Park, site of Lincoln's first home in Illinois
30. MOLINE - John Deere Implement Works
31. MOUNT MORRIS - White Pines State Park, preserve of white pines
32. MOUNT VERNON - Mitchell Art Museum
33. NAUVOO - Joseph Smith Home, Mormon area restored
34. OLD SHAWNEETOWN - historic town
35. OREGON - Black Hawk Statue, in Lowden State Park
36. OTTAWA - site of first Lincoln-Douglas debate
37. PETERSBURG
    Lincoln's New Salem, replica of village at time of Lincoln;
    Home of Edgar Lee Masters, author of "Spoon River Anthology";
    Oakland Cemetery, burial place of Ann Rutledge and Edgar Lee Masters
38. PRAIRIE du ROCHER - Fort Chartres State Park, built 1720
39. PULLEYS MILL - Lake of Egypt, recreation area
40. ROCKFORD - Time Museum, ancient timepieces
41. ROSICLARE - Flourspar mines
42. SALEM - home of William Jennings Bryan
43. SHELBYVILLE - Shelbyville Lake, recreation area
44. SPRINGFIELD
    State Capitol;
    State Museum;
    Lincoln Home, residence until his presidency;
    Lincoln's Tomb, Oak Ridge Cemetery
    Old State Capitol, restored
45. UTICA - Starved Rock State Park, Father Marquette Mission, 1675
46. VANDALIA - The Madonna of the Trail, monument to pioneer woman
47. WHEATON - Cantigny War Museum, realistic trenches

This statue of Abraham Lincoln as a young man stands proudly at Illinois' port of entry.

This stately colonial home, in Nauvoo, Illinois, was the residence of the first Mormon prophet, Joseph Smith.

The home state memorial of General U.S. Grant overlooks his restored home of Galena, Illinois.

Photographs furnished by Illinois Division of Tourism.

page 56 / treasure trails

STATE MOTTO: The Crossroads of America
STATE BIRD: The Cardinal
STATE FLOWER: The Peony

INDIANA
Admitted to the Union in 1816

FOR FURTHER INFORMATION WRITE:

- The Hoosier National Forest
  Mr. Donald Girton
  Forest Supervisor
  Wayne-Hoosier National Forests
  1615 J. Street
  Bedford, Indiana 47421

- Mr. Frank Lockard
  Chief of Fisheries
  Division of Fish and Wildlife
  607 State Office Building
  Indianapolis, Indiana 46204

- Division of Tourism
  Department of Commerce
  366 State House
  Indianapolis, Indiana 46204

The Indianapolis 500 . . . the annual Memorial Day race . . . tells much about Indiana, past and present. The name of the capitol "City of the land of the Indians" . . . recalls the frontier past, and the 500 mile race, one of the most celebrated national sports events, reflects the State's position as a leader in the automobile world.

During its early history, Indiana was indeed the "land of the Indians." The Indian wars made General William H. Harrison famous, and his victory at Tippecanoe gave him his campaign slogan (Tippecanoe and Tyler, Too) when he ran for President in 1840. The first white men to enter Indiana were French Jesuits. The first white man to explore Indiana was Robert Cavelier, Sieur de la Salle, a French fur trader.

Since the beginning of this century, automobiles have been built in the South Bend area. Other important products are iron and steel, machinery, mobile homes, refrigerators, books and chemicals. The Bedford quarries are a major source of building stone, the mines in the southwest are a rich producer of bituminous coal. Gas and oil, clay and gysum are other valuable resources.

Most of the state is prairie with rich farmlands that produce rye, wheat, soybeans, spearmint and Peppermint, and on which are raised hogs and cattle. Fruit and tobacco are grown in the hilly area near the Ohio River.

Small lakes formed by glaciers abound in the north, man-made lakes in the south, which also boasts such natural features as huge caves and mineral springs.

Indianapolis, the capitol and largest city, lies near the center of the state. In 1820, commissioners selected this location, even though the site was then a dense forest. Today over half a million people live there in the nation's second largest city not on a navigable waters.

Notre Dame Library, South Bend, displays an impressive 132-foot-high mosaic mural of Christ with a host of saints and scholars.

treasure trails / page 57

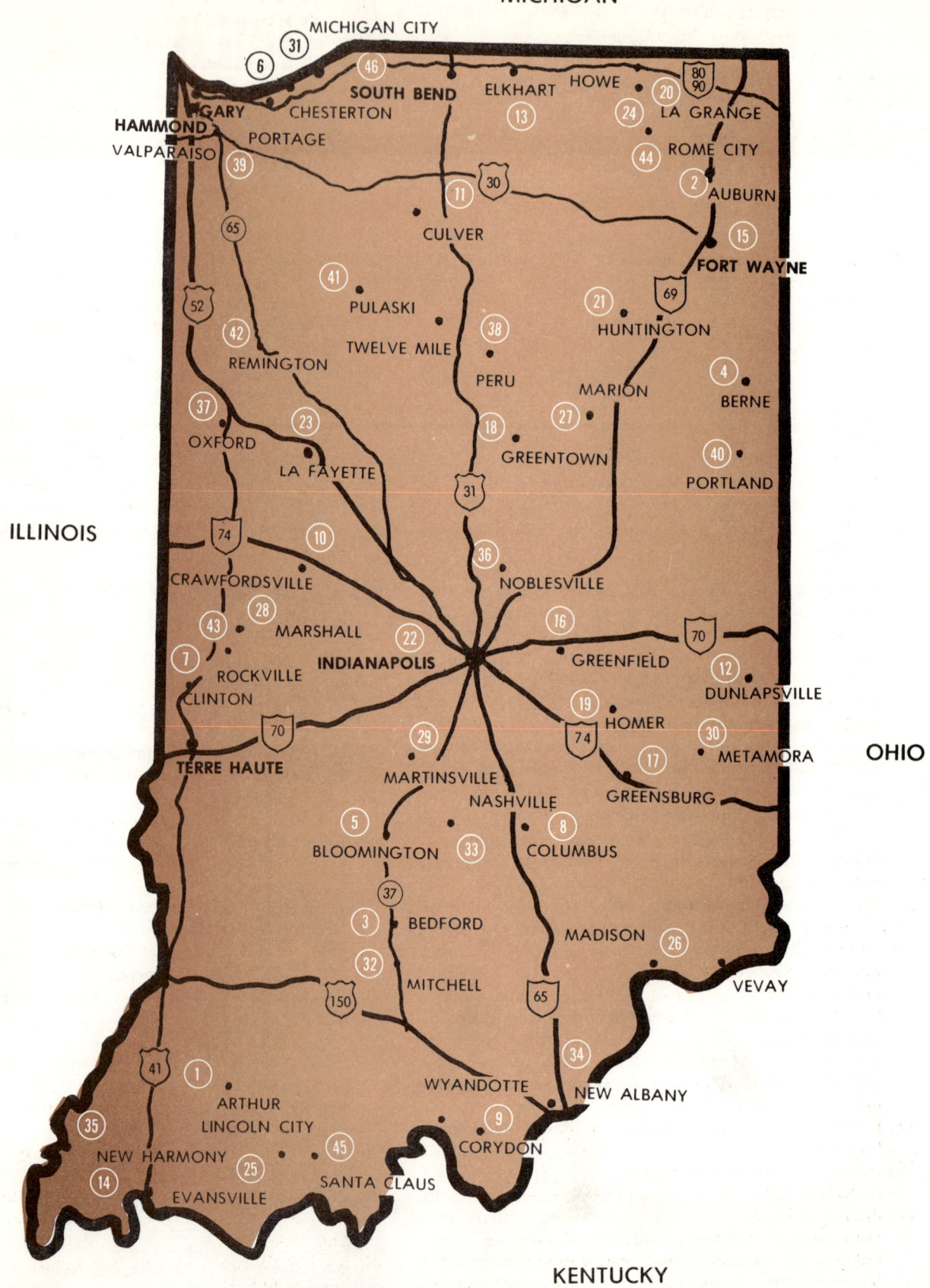

Key:
① relates to number 1 on the following page.

page 58 / treasure trails

INDIANA POINTS OF INTEREST

1. ARTHUR - Strip Mining, roads are made of waste coal, mining community
2. AUBURN - Auburn-Cord-Duesenberg Parade and Auction, antique automobile show
3. BEDFORD - Limestone Quarries
4. BERNE - Dunbar Furniture Company, manufacturers
5. BLOOMINGTON - Monroe Reservoir, largest body of water in Indiana
6. CHESTERTON - Indiana Dunes, 3 miles of lakeshore on Lake Michigan
7. CLINTON - Little Italy Festival, annual Italian heritage celebration
8. COLUMBUS - examples of 19th century and modern architecture
9. CORDYDON
   First State Capitol Building, built 1811;
   Squire Boone Caverns, underground caverns, orginally discovered by Daniel Boone's brother in 1790
10. CRAWFORDSVILLE
    Ben-Hur Museum;
    author Lee Wallace's Estate
11. CULVER - Culver Military Academy, boys 13 to 18 years, dress parades open to public
12. DUNLAPSVILLE - Treaty Line Museum, pioneer exhibits
13. ELKHART
    Ruthmere, 1910 House Museum;
    World center for manufacturing of mobile homes
14. EVANSVILLE
    Mesker Park, largest zoo in Indiana, sunken garden and amusement park;
    Temple of Fine Arts and History, museum;
    Angel Mounds Museum, site of ancient city of mound builders
15. FORT WAYNE
    Lincoln Museum and Library, collection of information of Abraham Lincoln;
    Franke Park, children's zoo;
    Johnny Appleseed Park & Gravesite, site of orchards planted by John Chapman, 1801;
    Fort Wayne Art Museum;
    The Old Fort, site of four forts dating to 1719
16. GREENFIELD - James Whitcomb Riley's birthplace and boyhood home
17. GREENSBURG
    Courthouse Tower Tree, tree growing out of concrete roof;
    Indiana Railway Museum, train rides offered
18. GREENTOWN - Greentown Glass Museum, 700 pieces of glassware
19. HOMER - Sampler, makers of Early American Furniture
20. HOWE - Howe Military School
21. HUNTINGTON - lake, recreational area
22. INDIANAPOLIS
    State Capitol Building, noted for dome;
    Indiana 500, world famous automobile race;
    Museum of Art, houses collection over 4,000 years old;
    Eli Lilly & Company, visitor center displays history of drugs;
    Union Station, built in 1888 of Romanesque style;
    State Library & Museum, made of Indiana limestone
23. LA FAYETTE - Fort Quiatenon, site of largest Indian settlement in middle west, museum
24. LA GRANGE - Amish settlement
25. LINCOLN CITY - Lincoln Boyhood National Memorial and Lincoln State Park, Lincoln's mother's grave here, reconstructed family cabin and farm
26. MADISON
    Hydroplane Regatta, world's largest and fastest hydroplane race;
    Clifty Fall State Park, scenic attractions;
    Tour historic homes
27. MARION - Marion Easter Pagent, 2,000 cast members, presented Holy Week
28. MARSHALL - Turkey Run State Park, canyons and gorges
29. MARTINSVILLE
    Bean Blossom Blue Grass Music Festival;
    Grassy Fork Fish Hatchery, world's largest producer of goldfish
30. METAMORA - Whitewater Canal, historic mill
31. MICHIGAN CITY - Friendship Gardens
32. MITCHELL - Gus Grissom Memorial, memorial to astronaut killed in test project for Apollo Space Program
33. NASHVILLE
    Brown County State Park, scenic woodland;
    Artist Colony
34. NEW ALBANY
    Shipyards and Steamboat builders;
    Scribner House, built 1814;
    Culbertson Mansion, state's finest Victorian River Mansion
35. NEW HARMONY - site of two communal living centers, groves of "golden rain trees"
36. NOBLESVILLE
    Museum of Transportation and Communication, railroad equipment, train rides;
    Conner Prairie Pioneer Settlement and Museum, 1830 pioneer museum
37. OXFORD - Home of Dan Patch, colt that broke existing pace record
38. PERU - winter quarters for five circuses
39. PORTAGE - Burnes Harbor
40. PORTLAND - Tri-State Engine & Tractor Show, display of restored antique gasoline engines, tractors
41. PULASKI - Wild Game Hatchery, one of world's largest wild game hatcheries, 5,200 acres
42. REMINGTON - Fountain Park Chautauqua, religious summer camp
43. ROCKVILLE - Covered Bridge Festival, 37 wooden bridges
44. ROME CITY - Gene Stratton Porter Home & Park, dedicated to author of "The Girl of the Limberlost" and "Freckles"
45. SANTA CLAUS - Santa Claus Land
46. SOUTH BEND
    The Mishawaka 100 Center, shops in former brewery;
    Studebaker Museum;

treasure trails / page 59

The stair-step Cataract Falls are found in Lieber State Park near Cuno, Indiana.

The Howard Mansion and Museum is a 26 room Victori[an] mansion containing the world's largest collection [of] steamboat models, photographs and river relics from 183[0].

Photographs furnished by the Indiana Department of Commerce.

The oldest covered bridge in the state, once at Raccoon, now crosses the scenic Clinton Falls creek in Turkey Run State Park.

The parish records of The Old Cathedral begin in 1749 when Vincennes was a French outpost.

George Rogers Clark Memorial, Vincennes, represents the capture of the Old Northwest from the British.

page 60 / treasure truils

STATE MOTTO: Our Liberties We Prize and Our Rights we will Maintain

STATE BIRD: Eastern Goldfinch

STATE FLOWER: Wild Rose

IOWA
Admitted to the Union in 1846

FOR FURTHER INFORMATION WRITE:

- Iowa State Conservation Commission
  Valley Bank Building
  4th and Walnut
  Des Moines, Iowa 50309

- Director of Tourism
  Iowa Development Commission
  250 Jewett Building
  Des Moines, Iowa 50309

In 1675, Louis Joliet and Father Jacques Marquette became the first white men to set foot on Iowa soil and in 1788 Julien Dubuque, a fur trader became the first permanent settler in the land that was to become Iowa.

The rich soil of Iowa has made it one of the outstanding agricultural producing areas of the world, producing 10 percent of the nation's food supply, Iowa ranks first in the number of hogs raised and in the number of cattle and calves marketed.

But Iowa is more than pork and beef, corn and soybeans.

Iowa is Indian for "the beautiful land," and it is truly that. Iowa has 91 state parks. Their unusual geological formations, hills and bluffs, streams and wildlife provide many opportunities for recreational enjoyment. The natural lakes in the northern part of the state and the newer man-made lakes in the south provide boating, swimming and fishing for those who love water sports. Skiing, snowmobiling and ice skating are available to the winter sports enthusiast.

Industry also finds its place in Iowa. Over one-fifth of the nation's 500 largest manufacturers operate more than 450 plants in Iowa. Iowa has the largest cereal plant, single brand home laundry equipment industry, popcorn processing plant, honey producer, aluminum plate rolling mill . . . and many others. Iowa ranks 17th in value of its manufactured exports.

The great state universities and the many small colleges and universities give educational leadership to the state whose people have the highest functional literacy rate in the nation. The new Hancher Auditorium at State University of Iowa in Iowa City and C.Y. Stephens Auditorium at Iowa State University in Ames present cultural performances of international renown, attracting state-wide audiences.

A favorite of hundreds of engaged couples and the theme of the hymn "Church in the Wildwood," the Little Brown Church in Nashua is open daily.

treasure trails / page 61

Key:

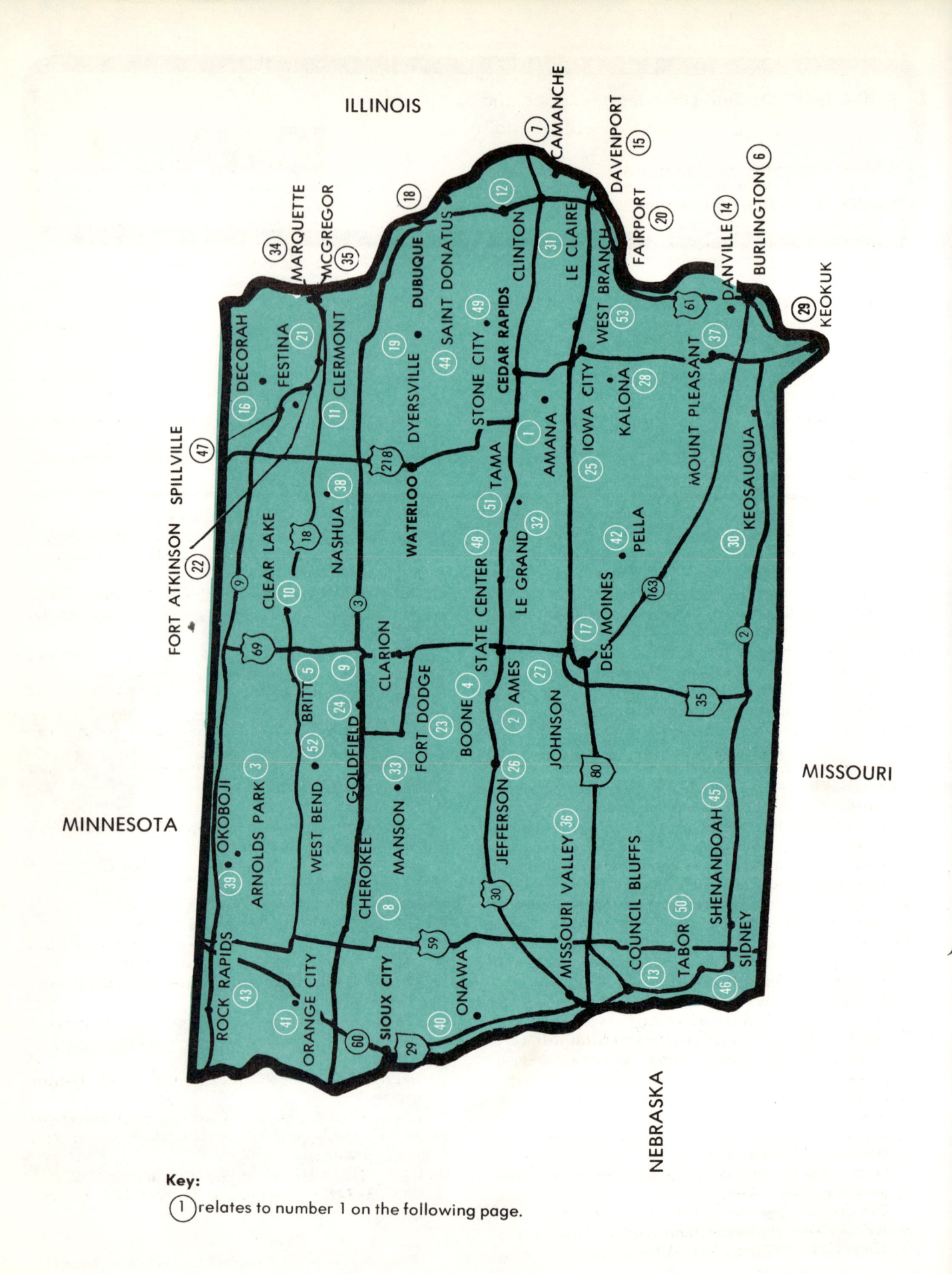

① relates to number 1 on the following page.

page 62 / treasure trails

IOWA POINTS OF INTEREST

1. AMANA - Amana Colonies, furniture factory, woolen mills, winery, Amana refrigeration
2. AMES - Iowa State University, U.S. Atomic Energy Laboratory, C.Y. Stephens Auditorium
3. ARNOLDS PARK - Gardner Cabin, site of Indian massacre in 1857
4. BOONE
   Kate Shelley High Bridge, highest and longest double track railroad bridge in U.S.;
   Ledges State Park, geologic formations
5. BRITT - National Hobo Day, mid-August
6. BURLINGTON - Steamboat Days and Dixie Land Jazz Festival, mid-June
7. CAMANCHE - E. I. DuPont de Nemours
8. CHEROKEE - Sanford Museum
9. CLARION - 4-H Country School House, where 4-H emblem originated
10. CLEAR LAKE - Clear Lake, resort area
11. CLERMONT - Historic Home of William Larabee, Iowa's twelfth governor
12. CLINTON - Riverboat Days, first week in July
13. COUNCIL BLUFFS - Dodge House, home of railway magnate, General Grenville Dodge
14. DANVILLE - Geode State Park, crystal-filled hollow rocks
15. DAVENPORT - Bix Lives Traditional Jazz Festival, Bix Beiderbecke Memorial Society
16. DECORAH - Decorah Annual Norwegian Festival, in July; Norwegian Museum
17. DES MOINES
    State Capitol Building;
    Historic Building;
    Art Center;
    Meredith Publishing Company, Home of "Better Homes and Gardens";
    Living History Farms.
18. DUBUQUE - New Mellary Abbey, Trappist Monastery, founded 1849
19. DYERSVILLE - St. Francis Basilica, reminiscent of cathedrals of Europe
20. FAIRPORT
    Old Grist Mill;
    Wildcat Den State Park
21. FESTINA - St. Anthony of Padua Chapel, world's smallest cathedral, seats eight
22. FORT ATKINSON - Fort Atkinson, restored fort
23. FORT DODGE - Old Fort Dodge, replica of original, museum
24. GOLDFIELD - Cheese Factory, buy cheese where it is made
25. IOWA CITY
    University of Iowa;
    Plum Grove, home of Iowa Territory's first governor, built 1844;
    Old Capitol, first seat of state government
26. JEFFERSON - Mahanay Memorial Carillon Tower
27. JOHNSON - Pioneer, hybrid seed farm
28. KALONA - Amish Settlement, founded by religious sect, uses only horse and buggy for transportation
29. KEOKUK - Riverboat Museum
30. KEOSAUQUA - Hotel Manning, "steamboat gothic" architecture
31. LE CLAIRE - Birthplace of Buffalo Bill Cody
32. LE GRAND - Doll Museum, 45 settings, dolls, Indian craft
33. MANSON - Kalsow Prairie, land untouched by the plow
34. MARQUETTE
    Effigy Mounds National Monument, pre-historic Indian burial grounds;
    "Little Switzerland", rugged hills overlooking Mississippi River
35. McGREGOR - Spook Cave, longest underground water tour in America
36. MISSOURI VALLEY
    DeSoto Bend National Wildlife Refuge;
    Museum, raised Missouri Riverboat on display;
    Corn Museum, display of pioneer farm implements
37. MOUNT PLEASANT
    Harlan House, home of Iowa Senator whose daughter married Robert Todd Lincoln, son of the President;
    Midwest Old Settlers and Threshers Reunion, second week in September
38. NASHUA - Home of The Little Brown Church in the Vale
39. OKOBOJI - Iowa Great Lakes Region, resort area
40. ONAWA - Lewis and Clark State Park
41. ORANGE CITY - Dutch Settlement, Tulip Time Celebration (May)
42. PELLA
    Dutch Settlement, annual Tulip Festival (May);
    Boyhood home of Wyatt Earp;
    Red Rock Dam, colorful rock formations;
    Covered Bridge Area
43. ROCK RAPIDS - farm tours
44. SAINT DONATUS - Old World Village
45. SHENANDOAH - Seed and nursery capital of Iowa
46. SIDNEY - Sidney Rodeo, August
47. SPILLVILLE - Bily Clock Museum and Antonin Dvorak Memorial
48. STATE CENTER - Rose capital of Iowa, displays
49. STONE CITY - Grant Wood art colony
50. TABOR
    John Brown's one-time headquarters, historic house;
    Forney's Lake, state game preserve for waterfowl
51. TAMA - Mesquakie Indian settlement, annual Pow Wow in August
52. WEST BEND - Grotto of the Redemption
53. WEST BRANCH - Birthplace of President Hoover, library

treasure trails / page 63

The State Capitol Building in Des Moines projects a gilded dome designed from the Hotel des Invalides in Paris.

At Spirit Lake Fish Hatchery, fish native to Iowa lakes are bred in large aquariums to provide sport for the outdoorsman.

The Herbert Hoover birthplace (above) and presidential library are found in West Branch, Iowa.

Iowa leads the nation in the production of corn, oats, eggs, poultry and the fattening of cattle. The state is known as the symbol of the Corn Belt.

Here is a sky view of the large J. I. Case Building located in Bettendorf, Iowa.

page 64 / treasure trails

STATE MOTTO: To The Stars Through Difficulties
STATE FLOWER: Wild Native Sunflower
STATE BIRD: Western Meadowlark

KANSAS
Admitted to the Union in 1861

FOR FURTHER INFORMATION WRITE:

- Kansas Fish and Game Department
  Pratt, Kansas 67124

- George Mathews
  State Department of Economic Development
  State Office Building
  Topeka, Kansas 66612

The area that is now Kansas was a land of Indians and buffalo when the Spanish "conquistodor" Coronado reached it in 1541 on his fruitless search for the fabled riches of Quivera.

In 1803, with the purchase of the Louisiana territory, the interest of the United States in the Western territory heightened. The following year Lewis and Clark touched the northeastern corner of present day Kansas as they made their way up the Missouri River. The first Kansas white settlements were Indian missions and military posts like Fort Leavenworth. Eastern Kansas became dotted with mission stations which served as both churches and schools and as stopping places for early western travelers. Several of these buildings survive today. Inextricably woven into its background are the early trails—Santa Fe, Oregon, Chisholm, and the Pony Express Route. Wagon trains of emigrants to the Far West, "Forty-Niners" hurrying to the gold fields of California, traders traveling to do business in Santa Fe plus the hundreds of thousands of cattle which came up from Texas, were some of the travelers on these famous trails. Out of this mostly raw wilderness was created Kansas territory, with the signing of the Kansas-Nebraska bill in 1854.

After the Civil War the railroads began building in earnest. With the railroads came the disappearance of the Indians and buffalo. This was also the time that the Mennonite emigrants from Russia arrived in central Kansas with their famous Red Turkey hard winter wheat and other agricultural innovations which combined to help make Kansas the "bread basket" of the nation.

Kansas produces wheat, grain sorghum, corn, soybeans, alfalfa, airplanes, oil, gas, salt, and farm machinery. There is abundant wildlife, game and fish. There is also swimming, fishing, boating and water skiing in any of the 20 federal reservoirs located throughout Kansas.

Visitors pay tribute to former President Dwight D. Eisenhower at his final resting place.

treasure trails / page 65

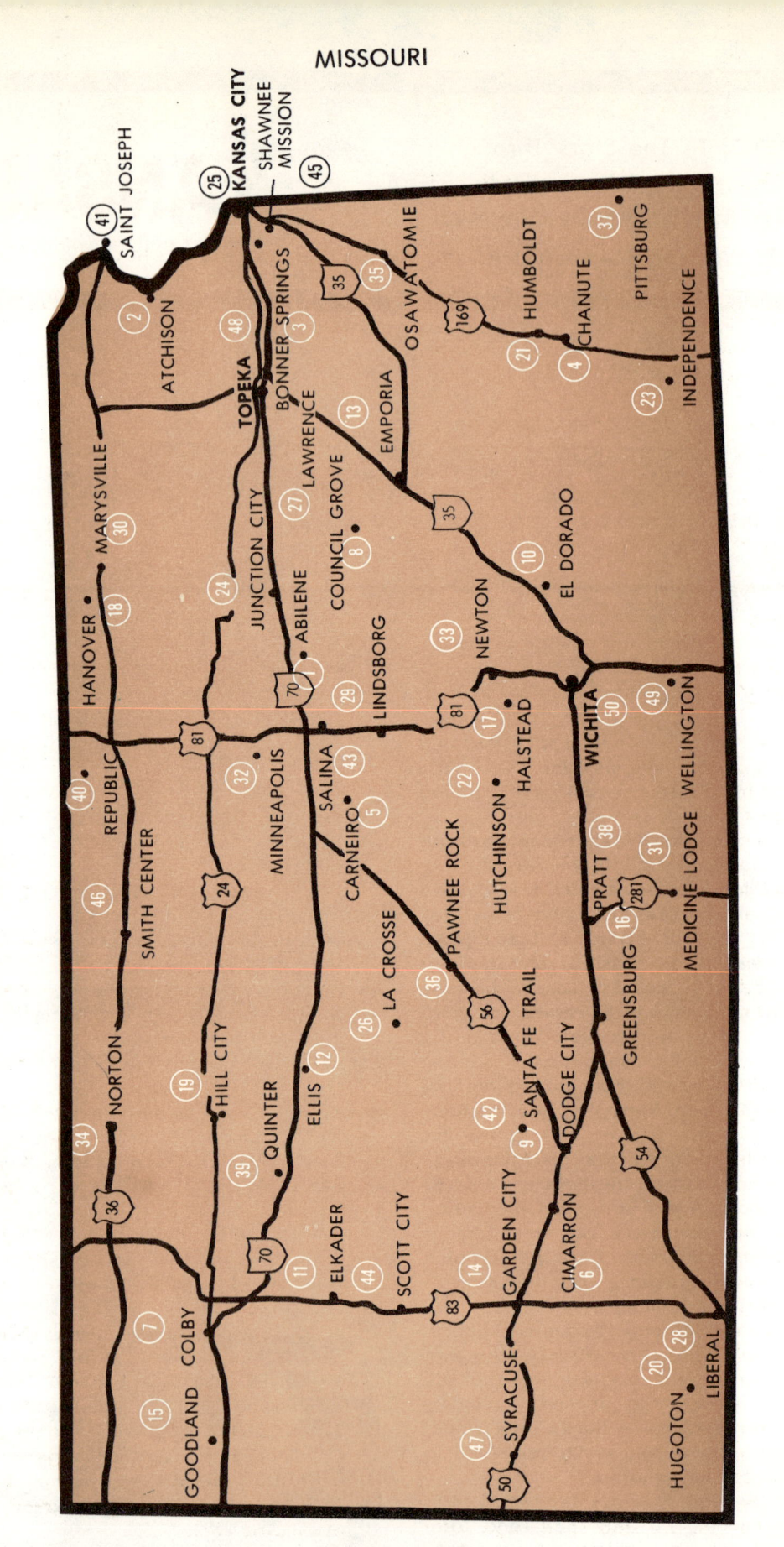

Key:
① relates to number 1 on the following page.

page 66 / treasure trails

KANSAS POINTS OF INTEREST

1. ABILENE
   Eisenhower Center, museum, library, chapel, and boyhood home;
2. ATCHISON
   Santa Fe Railway Monument, commemorates organization of Santa Fe Railway, 1860;
   Birthplace of Amelia Earhart, aviatrix
3. BONNER SPRINGS - Agricultural Hall of Fame, history of agriculture
4. CHANUTE - Osa and Martin Johnson's Safari Museum, hometown of African explorers
5. CARNEIRO - Mushroom Rock Park, sandstone formations
6. CIMARRON - Cimarron Crossing, dividing point for north and south routes of Santa Fe Trail
7. COLBY - Sod House Town, headquarters for "Sons and Daughters of the Soddies"
8. COUNCIL GROVE
   Kaw Methodist Mission;
   Last Chance Store;
   Council Grove, town named for agreement with Osage nation for travel on Santa Fe Trail, mission now museum, historic landmark
9. DODGE CITY
   Front Street, replica of 1872 "Queen of the Cow Towns";
   Home of Stone;
   Cultural Heritage and Arts Center
10. EL DORADO - Oil Refineries, oil discovered here in 1915
11. ELKADER - Chalk Pyramids, scenic fossil area, Point of Rocks
12. ELLIS - Walter P. Chrysler Home, birthplace of automobile industrialist
13. EMPORIA - William Allen White Memorial, birthplace and home of famed journalist
14. GARDEN CITY
    Cattle feed lots
    Windsor Hotel, unique architecture
15. GOODLAND - Sugar beet industry, beet fields, processing plant
16. GREENSBURG - United State's largest hand dug well
17. HALSTEAD - Kansas Health Museum, models of human body, hospital built by Arthur Hertzler, author of "Horse and Buggy Doctor"
18. HANOVER - Hollenberg Pony Express Station, original station used in 1860-61
19. HILL CITY - Oil Museum, history of oil
20. HUGOTON - Gas field, large natural gas area
21. HUMBOLDT - Biblesta, panorama of Bible, parade, floats, etc., first Saturday in October
22. HUTCHINSON
    Largest single grain elevator;
    Major salt producing area, since 1901;
    State Fair, 3rd week in September
23. INDEPENDENCE - Beginning of the Oregon Trail
24. JUNCTION CITY - Fort Riley, established 1853, 7th cavalry organized here, today is army training post
25. KANSAS CITY - Huron cemetery, tribal burial ground for Wyandotte Indians;
26. LA CROSSE - Post Rock Museum, limestone fence posts
27. LAWRENCE - Dyche Museum, campus of Kansas University
28. LIBERAL - Pancake Derby, annual competition
29. LINDSBORG
    Birger Sandzen Memorial Art Gallery, Swedish artist's home;
    Bethany College, Messiah Festival during Holy Week since 1882;
    McPherson County Museum complex;
    Coronado Heights, scenic point
30. MARYSVILLE - Flint Hills country, scenic bluestem grass cattle pastures
31. MEDICINE LODGE
    Medicine Lodge Peace Treaty Park, commemorates 1867 treaty, pageant October;
    Carry A. Nation Museum, home of anti-liquor crusader;
    Red Hills Country, scenic drive
32. MINNEAPOLIS - Rock City, spherical sandstone concretions, state park
33. NEWTON
    Memorial to Mennonite settlers;
    Warkentin Home
34. NORTON - Stagecoach station 15, where Horace Greeley once stopped on way west
35. OSAWATOMIE - John Brown Museum, cabin of famed abolitionist, state museum
36. PAWNEE ROCK - Pawnee Rock, natural sandstone landmark on Santa Fe Trail
37. PITTSBURG
    Mining operations, strip mining coal production begun in 1860's;
    W.S. Dickey Clay Manufacturing Company, 1885, large clay pipe producers
38. PRATT - Kansas Forestry, Fish and Game Commission, fresh-water hatchery, museum, aquarium and zoo
39. QUINTER - Castle Rock, landmark on California Trail
40. REPUBLIC - Pawnee Indian Village Museum, archeological site, state museum
41. SAINT JOSEPH - Pony Express Route
42. SANTA FE TRAIL - 500 miles of trail
43. SALINA
    Milling center, major flour milling center;
    Cathedral of the Sacred Heart, architecture symbolic of agricultural enterprises
44. SCOTT CITY - Scott County State Park, archeological site of Pueblo Indian habitations, historic landmark
45. SHAWNEE MISSION - Shawnee Methodist Mission, established 1830 for Indian children
46. SMITH CENTER - Dr. Higley's cabin, pioneer, doctor, writer of "Home on the Range"
47. SYRACUSE - Sand dunes, scenic area
48. TOPEKA - Menninger Foundation, world famous psychiatric clinic
49. WELLINGTON - Chisholm Trail Museum
50. WHICHITA
    Largest City in Kansas;
    Air Capitol of the World, home of Boeing, Beech, Cessna, Lear Jet, etc.

treasure trails / page 67

A young visitor to Front Street, Dodge City, Kansas, enjoys riding "shotgun" on a Boot Hill Stage Line run.

Coronado Heights - Lindsborg

This wagon train is charted by nationally-recognized Wagons Ho, Inc., which offers tourists and vactioners in Kansas authentic one-to-four-day trips across the West-Central Kansas grasslands.

Fort Larned National Historical Site - Larned

page 68 / treasure trails

STATE MOTTO: United We Stand, Divided We Fall
STATE BIRD: Kentucky Cardinal
STATE FLOWER: Goldenrod

KENTUCKY
Admitted to the Union in 1792

FOR FURTHER INFORMATION:

- Department of Fish and Wildlife
  Capital Plaza 4th Floor
  Frankfort, Kentucky 40601

- W. L. Knight
  Travel Director
  Department of Public Information
  Capital Annex Building
  Frankfort, Kentucky 40601

- Director of Forestry
  Natural Resources
  Capital Plaza 5th Floor,
  Frankfort, Kentucky 40601

Kentucky boundaries traditionally divide the northern and southern states and form a link between two great land features of the United States. The long northern border is formed by the Ohio River, the eastern touches the Appalachian Mountains, the western the Mississippi River.

Prehistoric, Indians, who lived along the streams and in caves were the first Kentuckians. French and British trappers began crossing into Kentucky in 1740, and were followed by Dr. Thomas Walker and a small party of Virginia land scouts in 1750. They entered Cumberland Gap thus opening the curtain to modern Kentucky history. Kentucky became the fifteenth state of the union in 1792.

Issac Shelby, a revolutionary war hero, became the first governor. The government organization was first set up in Lexington with the state capital locating one year later in Frankfort.

Rich tobacco, bourbon and champion race horses have long been symbols of Kentucky and thoroughbred race horses still graze in the bluegrass region around Lexington. This grass with dusty blue blossoms gave Kentucky the nickname, "Bluegrass State." Each May, huge crowds thrill to the excitement of the Kentucky Derby, held at Churchill Downs in Louisville.

Stephen Foster wrote of the state's traditional life in his immortal song, "My Old Kentucky Home," the state song.

Kentucky leads the nation in the production of whiskey, ranks first in burley tobacco, and second in total tobacco production, third in total coal production and second in miles of streams.

Such natural phenomenas as rock bridges, one being the Natural Bridge in Powell County, deep caves including Mammoth Cave in Edmonson County, bring thousands of visitors each year inside Kentucky boundries.

An uncanny work of Mother Nature, the Natural Bridge in Slade, Kentucky is certainly an aesthetic pleasure.

treasure trails / page 69

Key:
① relates to number 1 on the following page.

page 70 / treasure trails

KENTUCKY POINTS OF INTEREST

1. ASHLAND - Armco Steel Corporation, one of the largest blast furnaces in the world
2. AUBURN - "Shakertown Revisited", outdoor drama of Shaker movement
3. BARBOURVILLE - Dr. Thomas Walker State Shrine, discovered Cumberland Gap, 1750
4. BARDSTOWN
    "Stephen Foster Story", outdoor musical drama;
    "My Old Kentucky Home", home of Judge Rowan;
    Old Talbot Tavern, oldest American hotel;
    Wickland, home of three governors;
    Barton Museum of Whiskey History, depicts 170 years of distilling;
    Annual Antique Flea Market, held in April;
    John Fitch Monument, inventor of the steamboat
5. BEREA - "Wilderness Road", musical drama of pioneer Kentuckians
6. BERNHEIM FOREST - 10,000 acre nature sanctuary
7. CALVERT CITY - Calvert Auto Museum
8. CAMPTON - Burial Mounds of Adena People, 2,700 years old
9. CAVE CITY - Mammoth Cave, one of the largest cave networks, 150 miles charted
10. COLUMBUS - Belmont Battlefield State Park, Civil War artillery
11. CORBIN - Cumberland Falls, "Niagara of the South", only moonbow in western hemisphere
12. COVINGTON
    Daniel Carter Beard Home, founder of Boy Scouts, 1910;
    Crawford Memorial Museum, archeological collections
13. DANIEL BOONE NATIONAL FOREST - Daniel Boone hunted here
14. DANVILLE
    Isaac Shelby State Shrine, burial site of Kentucky's first governor;
    Constitution Square State Shrine, reproduction of Kentucky's first courthouse square;
    Wilderness Road, Village of the Arts, depicts Kentucky in the 1890's
15. FAIRVIEW - Jefferson Davis Monument, birthplace of the Confederate President
16. FORT KNOX
    U.S. Gold Depository, holds U.S. gold reserve;
    General Patton Museum, personal effects of George Patton, Jr.;
    Fort Knox Military Reservations, United States Army Armor School
17. FRANKFORT
    State Capitol building, 1910;
    Old State House, museum;
    Floral Clock, lawn clock in 100 ton planter
18. HARRODSBURG
    Fort Harrodsburg, state's oldest town, 1774;
    Old Fort Harrod Amphitheatre, drama, "Legend of Daniel Boone";
    Pleasant Hill, community restored to tell Shaker history;
    Morgan Row Houses, only true row house in Kentucky, built 1807;
    Beaumont Inn, white columned brick structure, built 1845
19. HAWESVILLE - Sorghum Festival
20. HAZARD - Lilly Cornett Woods, 554 acres of virgin forest, wildlife
21. HENDERSON - John James Audubon State Park, from here he gathered material for the paintings of "The Birds of America"
22. HODGENVILLE - Abraham Lincoln's birthplace 100 acre farm of Thomas Lincoln
23. KENTUCKY PALISADES - rocky cliffs on the banks of the Kentucky River
24. LEXINGTON
    Largest tobacco warehouse in the world;
    Ashland, Henry Clay's Home;
    Headley Jewell Museum, only private collection of valuable bibelots open to the public
25. LICKING RIVER - Sherburnes Covered Bridge, only covered suspension bridge known
26. MAYFIELD
    Mayfield Ceramic Clay, world's largest ball clay depository;
    'Old Tip", cannon used in Battle of Tippecanoe, 1811
27. MIDDLESBORO - Cumberland Gap, break in Cumberland Mountains
28. MOREHEAD - Rowan County "Digs", ancient relics, 15,000 years old
29. OWENSBORO - Sassafras Tree, 300 years old
30. PADUCAH
    Kentucky Dam, TVA's largest dam;
    William Clark Market House Museum, riverboat memorabilia;
    Irvin S. Cobb Memorial, famous journalist's monument
31. PERRYVILLE - Perryville Battlefield State Shrine, site of Kentucky's greatest Civil War battle
32. PINEVILLE
    Pine Mountain State Park, Kentucky Mountain Laurel Festival
33. POWELL COUNTY - Sinking Creek, creek disappears underground, then reappears
34. RICHMOND
    White Hall, home of Cassius Clay, early abolitionist;
    Home of Bybee Pottery, established 1845
35. RUSSELLVILLE - Old Southern Bank of Kentucky, built 1810, site of James Brothers robbery
36. SLADE
    Natural Bridge, carved by wind and rain;
    Red River Gorge, forest with rare plant life
37. SPRINGFIELD - Lincoln Homestead State Shrine, restored settlement of Abraham Lincoln's grandparents, Nancy Hank's home
38. STANFORD - William Whitley House State Shrine built 1787, America's first oval horse racing track
39. TOMPKINSVILLE - Old Mulky Meeting House, oldest log church in the state
40. WICKLIFFE - The Ancient Buried City, remains of ancient city of mound builders

The cabin where Abraham Lincoln was born has been preserved within the walls of this beautiful memorial in Hodgenville, Kentucky.

Frozen Niagara is only a portion of one of the largest cave networks in the world, Mammoth Cave, with at least 150 miles charted on five levels.

Sunning is a popular pastime near Cumberland Falls, the "Niagara of the South," southwest of Corbin, Kentucky.

Kentucky ranks first in the nation in the production of burley tobacco and second in total tobacco production.

STATE MOTTO: Union, Justice, Confidence
STATE BIRD: The Brown Pelican
STATE FLOWER: Magnolia

LOUISIANA
Admitted to the Union in 1812

FOR FURTHER INFORMATION WRITE:

- U.S. Forest Service
  2500 Shreveport Highway
  Pineville, Louisiana 71360

- Louisiana Wild Life and Fisheries Commission
  400 Royal Street
  New Orleans, Louisiana 70130

- Louisiana Tourist Commission
  P.O. Box 44291
  Baton Rouge, Louisiana 70804

Louisiana, named by Robert de LaSalle, early French explorer, for Louis XIV, King of France was discovered by the Spanish 27 years after Columbus landed in the New World. After the Seven Years War, the French ceded all their lands to Spain and England. The territory west of the Mississippi was returned to France in 1801, and Napoleon sold it in 1803 to the United States. On April 30, 1812, Louisiana became the 18th state admitted to the Union.

Louisiana is a beautiful blend of old world charm and new world excitement. In New Orleans, the French Quarter still looks much the same as it did when Andrew Jackson and the pirate Jean Lafitte fought the British at Chalmette in the War of 1812.

Moss-draped and dreamlike, the bayou country of South Louisiana is a land of shrimp boats, fishing nets, and magnificent architecture.

Louisiana's climate is relatively moderate all year, with comfortable summers and mild winters. The average annual temperature for the state as a whole is 67 degrees.

With the discovery of oil in 1901, Louisiana began its industrial progress. Today it ranks second in the nation in oil and gas production, and more than a dozen refineries in the state process the output of the state's many wells.

Louisiana ranks near the top in many other fields such as production of furs, fish, paper, sugar cane, strawberries and cane syrup.

Louisiana State Capitol, Baton Rouge, built in 1932 during Huey Long administration. Tallest capitol building in U.S.

treasure trails / page 73

ARKANSAS

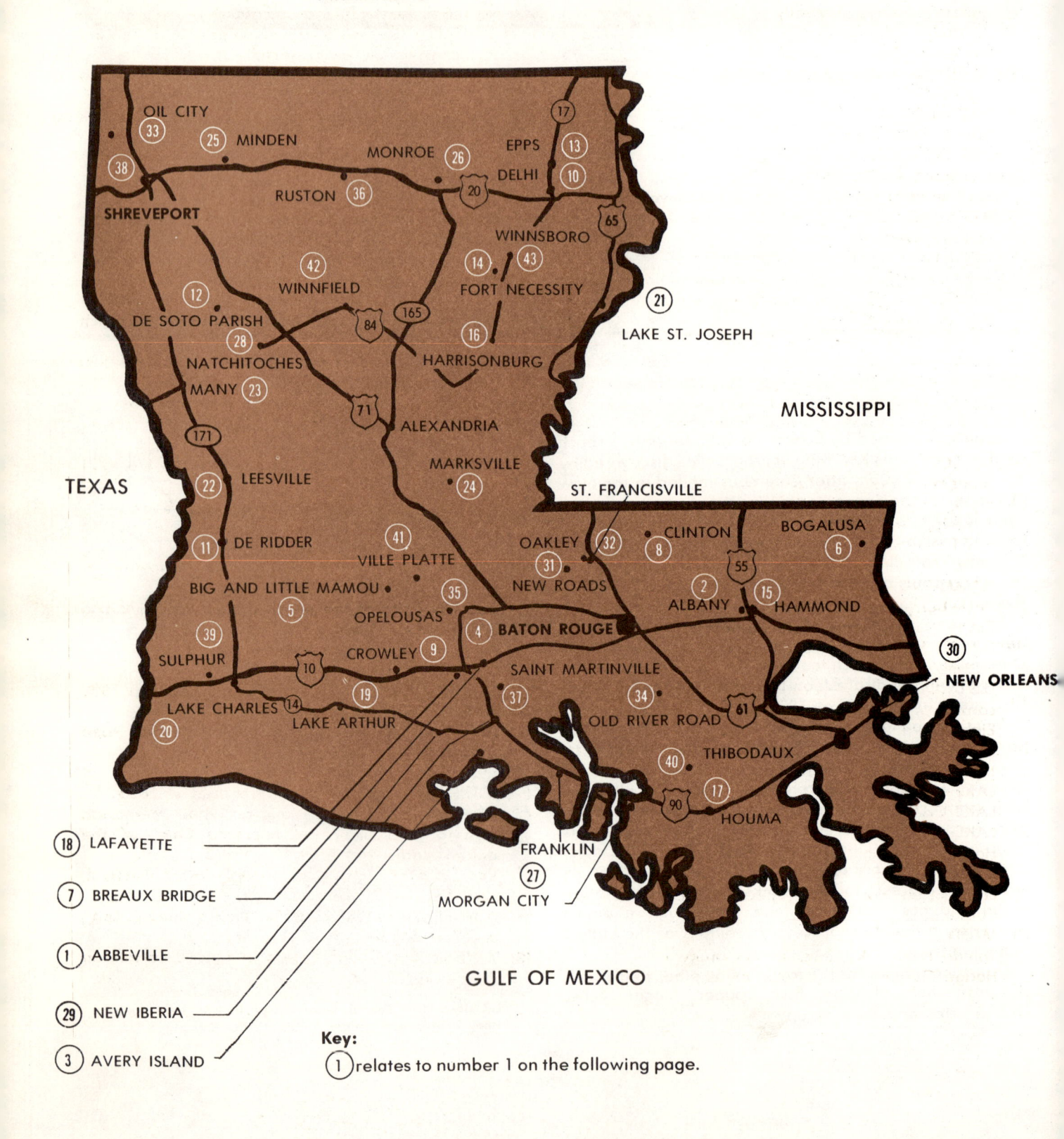

OIL CITY (33)
(38)
(25) MINDEN
MONROE (26) EPPS (17)
(13)
DELHI (10)
(20)
SHREVEPORT
RUSTON (36)
(65)
WINNSBORO
(42)
(14) (43)
WINNFIELD
FORT NECESSITY
(12)
(84)
DE SOTO PARISH
(165)
(21)
(28)
(16)
LAKE ST. JOSEPH
NATCHITOCHES
HARRISONBURG
MANY (23)
(71)
MISSISSIPPI
ALEXANDRIA
(171)
MARKSVILLE
TEXAS
(22) LEESVILLE
(24)
ST. FRANCISVILLE
BOGALUSA
(11)
OAKLEY (32) CLINTON
DE RIDDER
(41)
(8)
(6)
VILLE PLATTE
(31)
(55)
BIG AND LITTLE MAMOU
(35)
NEW ROADS
(2)
(15)
(5)
ALBANY HAMMOND
(39)
OPELOUSAS
(4) BATON ROUGE
SULPHUR
CROWLEY (9)
(30)
(10)
SAINT MARTINVILLE
NEW ORLEANS
LAKE CHARLES (14)
(19)
(37) (34)
(20)
LAKE ARTHUR
OLD RIVER ROAD (61)
(40) THIBODAUX
(90) (17)
HOUMA
(18) LAFAYETTE
(7) BREAUX BRIDGE
FRANKLIN
(1) ABBEVILLE
(27)
MORGAN CITY
(29) NEW IBERIA
(3) AVERY ISLAND
GULF OF MEXICO

Key:
(1) relates to number 1 on the following page.

page 74 / treasure trails / **Louisiana**

LOUISIANA POINTS OF INTEREST

1. ABBEVILLE - Steen Syrup Mill, produces 800,000 gallons of syrup annually
2. ALBANY - Hungarian Settlement, oldest in U.S., Hungarian Festival, October
3. AVERY ISLAND - Jungle Gardens, pepper fields, tabasco plants and birds
4. BATON ROUGE
   Site of State Capitol;
   Old State Capitol Building, built 1847, houses Louisiana Art Commission;
   Southern University, largest black university in U.S.
5. BIG AND LITTLE MAMOU - quaint Acadian communities
6. BOGALUSA - Lake Vista Nature Perserve
7. BREAUX BRIDGE - Crawfish Capital of the world
8. CLINTON - Old Town, courthouse square, Greek-Rivival Courthouse
9. CROWLEY - Crowley Rice Museum, history of rice production
10. DELHI - Dehli Manufacturing Corporation, world's largest manufacturers of fishing boats
11. DE RIDDER - Boise Southern Pulpwood and Paper Mill
12. DE SOTO PARISH - Lands End Plantation, 1830 mansion in the same family for seven generations
13. EPPS - Poverty Point, oldest civilization in North America, 3000 B.C.
14. FORT NECESSITY - Boeuf Prairie Methodist Church, built 1833
15. HAMMOND
    Strawberry Capital of the World;
    Camp Moore Confederate Cemetery
16. HARRISONBURG - Fort Beauregard
17. HOUMA
    U.S.D.A. Sugar Experiment Station, study for control of pests, etc.;
    Eight seafood factories
18. LAFAYETTE - Evangeling Downs, newest thoroughbred race track
19. LAKE ARTHUR - largest oak tree in the world
20. LAKE CHARLES - three wildlife refuges
21. LAKE ST. JOSEPH - Winter Quarters Plantation Home, used by General Grant at seige of Vicksburg, 1863
22. LEESVILLE - Fort Polk, Special Forces Training Center
23. MANY
    Toledo Bend Lake, largest man-made lake;
    Hodge Gardens, 4700 acres of scenic gardens
24. MARKSVILLE - prehistoric Indian Park and State Museum, ruins date to 300-600 A.D.
25. MINDEN - Germantown Settlement, 19th century socialist community, restored
26. MONROE - Louisiana Purchase Gardens and Zoo
27. MORGAN CITY - Shrimp Festival
28. NATCHITOCHES - oldest city in Louisiana Purchase Territory, 1714
29. NEW IBERIA - Shadow-on-the-Teche, plantation home, built 1830
30. NEW ORLEANS
    Lake Ponchartrain Causeway, longest bridge in the world;
    Avondale Marine Ways, largest shipyard in the South;
    Vieux Carre', historic French Quarter contains Jackson Square, St. Louis Cathedral, French Market, etc.;
    Chalmette National Historical Site, scene of last engagement of War of 1812
31. NEW ROADS - Parlange, antibellum mansion
32. OAKLEY - Grace Episcopal Church, original Henry Pilcher pipe organs
33. OIL CITY - first marine well in U.S., drilled in 1911
34. OLD RIVER ROAD
    Bonfires at Christmas, on Mississippi Leves;
    Oak Alley Plantation, built 1830;
    Four miles of antibellum homes
35. OPELOUSAS - Jim Bowie Museum, mementoes of designer of Bowie knife
36. RUSTON - site of the peach industry in Louisiana
37. SAINT MARTINVILLE
    Longfellow Evangeline State Park;
    Acadian House Museum;
    St. Martin de Tours Catholic Church, built in 1833
38. SHREVEPORT
    American Rose Society, experimental rose gardens;
    State Fair
39. SULPHUR - Sulphur mine, discovered in 1868
40. THIBODAUX - Edward Douglas White Memorial, Former Chief Justice of Supreme Court of the United States
41. VILLE PLATTE - Home of annual Cotton Festival, each fall
42. WINNFIELD - birthplace of Governors Huey P. Long and Earl K. Long
43. WINNSBORO - Union Cotton Compress, largest in the world

treasure trails / page 75

Oaklawn Manor, near Franklin, named for magnificent live oaks, said to have been growing when Columbus discovered America. Restored manor house is white-pillared prototype of Southern plantation. Open daily to public.

Grace Episcopal Church at St. Francisville, built 1858, shelled in Civil War by Union gunboats on Mississippi River.

Acadian House Museum, at St. Martinville, located on grounds of Longfellow-Evangeline State Park. Louisiana's Acadiana culture expressed.

page 76 / treasure trails

Photographs furnished by Louisiana Tourist Development Commission.

STATE MOTTO: I Direct or Guide
STATE BIRD: Chickadee
STATE FLOWER: White Pinecone And Tassel

MAINE
Admitted to the Union in 1820

- Maine Publicity Bureau
  Gateway Circle
  Portland, Maine 04102

When Maine, by separation from Massachusetts, became a state in 1820, a number od cities and towns were very desirous of the honor of being the capital and having the new State House. The legislative finally chose Augusta. The lot now occupied by the State House and State grounds was selected by the governor and the commissioners. After careful consideration 34 acres extending from the old Hallowell road to the Kennebec River was conveyed to the state.

The granite used to build the State House was from the quarry in Hallowell. The length of the building is three hundred feet. The dome rises to a height of 185 feet, surmounted by the figure of Wisdom made of copper covered with gold. The rotunda is a room of great dignity with eight Doric columns. Here are displayed battle flags in plate glass cases. On the walls throughout the corridors and halls hang portraits of Maine's distinguished sons. The State Museum is located in the south wing. The House of Representatives occupies the third and fourth stories of the north wing and the Senate and the Executive Chamber are in the south wing.

Maine is located in the extreme northeastern corner of the United States. Half of Maine is surrounded by two provinces of the Dominion of Canada which borders it on the west, north and east, while New Hampshire forms the remainder of its western boundry, and the Atlantic Ocean bounds it on the south.

Maine is famed for the fine taste, texture and fresh color of its lobsters, shrimp, salmon, and other fish.

Maine has vast timber and wood lots, they comprise almost 80% of the land. Forest resources have yielded lumber, wood, and pulp.

Aroostook County in northern Maine is the largest seed producing area of the 50 states. There are also acres of potatoes raised in this part of Maine.

Maine also raises 3/4 of the nation's blueberries. In the remote wilderness of the upper St. John River, the northwestern strip of Maine along the Quebec boundry is the largest sugar-bush in the world.

Angel Falls in the Rangeley Region is one of the more beautiful scenic spots in Maine.

treasure trails / page 77

page 78 / treasure trails / Maine

MAINE POINTS OF INTEREST

1. ASHLAND - Maine Forest and Logging Museum, open June to September
2. ATHENS - Harding's Maple Syrup Farm
3. AUGUSTA
   Blaine House, Governor's Residence, period funishings;
   State Capitol Building;
   Fort Western, original barracks, 1754
4. BANGOR
   Morse Bridge, longest covered bridge;
   Symphony House, built 1833
5. BATH - Marine Museum, open May 30 to October 15
6. BAXTER STATE PARK - Maine's highest peak, Mount Katahdin
7. BELFAST
   Broiler Festival, held each August;
   Historic Colonial Homes
8. BELGRADE LAKES - vacation resort
9. BOOTHBAY HARBOR
   Railway Museum, steam train rides, antique auto displays;
   Marine Aquarium, seals and fish;
   Playhouse, Broadway shows
10. BRIDGTON - summer and winter resort, skiing on Pleasant Mountain
11. CAMDEN
    Mary Meeker Cramer Museum in Conway House, restored 18th century farm house and barn;
    Still and Shevis Gallery, prints featuring Maine artists
12. CARIBOU - Nylander Museum, Indian artifacts of Professor Olaf Nylander, Swedish geologist
13. CUSHING - Christina Olson Home Museum, made famous by Andrew Wyeth
14. DAMARISCOTTA
    Chapman Hall House, built 1874, furnished;
    Pemaquid Diggings, ancient settlement;
    Fort William Henry
15. DORTHEA DIX PARK - on Penobscot River
16. DRESDEN - Pownalborough Courthouse, built 1761
17. EAST MACHIAS - Site of the first trading post
18. EASTPORT - Fort Sullivan, built 1810
19. ELLSWORTH - Black House Mansion
20. EMBDEM - Trout and Salmon Fish Hatchery
21. FARMINGTON - Home of Lillian Nordica, great American singer, built in 1850's
22. THE FORKS - Indian Pond and Dam, historic ovens
23. FORT KENT - State Memorial, built 1839
24. HALLOWELL - Worster House, built 1832
25. HARMONY - Harmony Castle
26. HOULTON
    Aroostock Historical and Art Museum, White Memorial;
    Pearce Homestead, built 1826;
    Black Hawk Putnam Tavern, built 1813
27. KINGFIELD - residence of Maine's first Govenor, historical house
28. LEE - Mount Jefferson Ski Run
29. LEEDS - Annual Folk Art Festival, annually in July
30. LEWISTON - Bates College: Treat Art Gallery, Slanton Biological Museum, bird collection
31. LIVERMORE FALLS - Washburn Memorial Library, 19th century architecture
32. LUBEC - Roosevelt - Campbello International Park, Canadian - American recreational area
33. MOOSE RIVER - Maine's oldest house, site of original settler
34. NEWFIELD - Willowbrook, completely restored village
35. NEW SWEDEN
    Capitol Hill;
    New Sweden Day, July;
    Historical museum
36. NEWRY - Artists' Bridge, built 1872
37. NORTH BERWICK - Quaker Cemetery
38. OGUNQUIT
    Art centers and galleries;
    Summer Ogunquit Playhouse
39. POLAND SPRINGS - Shaker Village
40. PORTLAND
    Portland Museum of Art, 19th century American painting and sculpture;
    Wadsworth-Longfellow House, built in 1785, National Historic Landmark;
    Victoria Mansion, built 1859;
    Tate House Museum, 1755, restored;
    Portland Head Light, 1791, oldest on the Atlantic Coast
41. RANGELEY - resort area
42. RICHMOND - Peacock Tavern, 18th century
43. ROCKLAND
    William A. Farnsworth Library and Art Museum;
    Annual Seafood Festival, August
44. ROCKPORT
    Town Hall, restored;
    Vesper Hill Chapel, for children
45. SAINT CROIX ISLAND
46. SOUTH BERWICK - Home of Sarah Orne Jewett, museum
47. SUGARLOAF MOUNTAIN - recreation area
48. THOMASTON - Montpelier State Memorial, mansion built by Henry Knox
49. UNION - Union Farm Maine Blueberry Festival
50. WALPOLE - Old Walpole Meeting House, 1772, has original pew box
51. WARREN - Georges River Canal System, on National Register of Historic Sites
52. WASHINGTON COUNTY - water level varies 28 feet every sixth house
53. WEST PEMBROKE - Reversing Salt Water Falls, beautiful natural wonder, park
54. WINSLOW - Fort Halifax, built in 1754, National Historic Landmark, America's oldest block-house
55. WINTHROP - Oldest Methodist Church, built 1795
56. WISCASSET
    Lincoln County Museum and Jail;
    Peabody Museum;
    Musical Wonder House Museum
57. YORK - Old Gaol Museum

treasure trails / page 79

Portland Headlight in Portland is at the tip of one of the many rocky peninsulas in Maine.

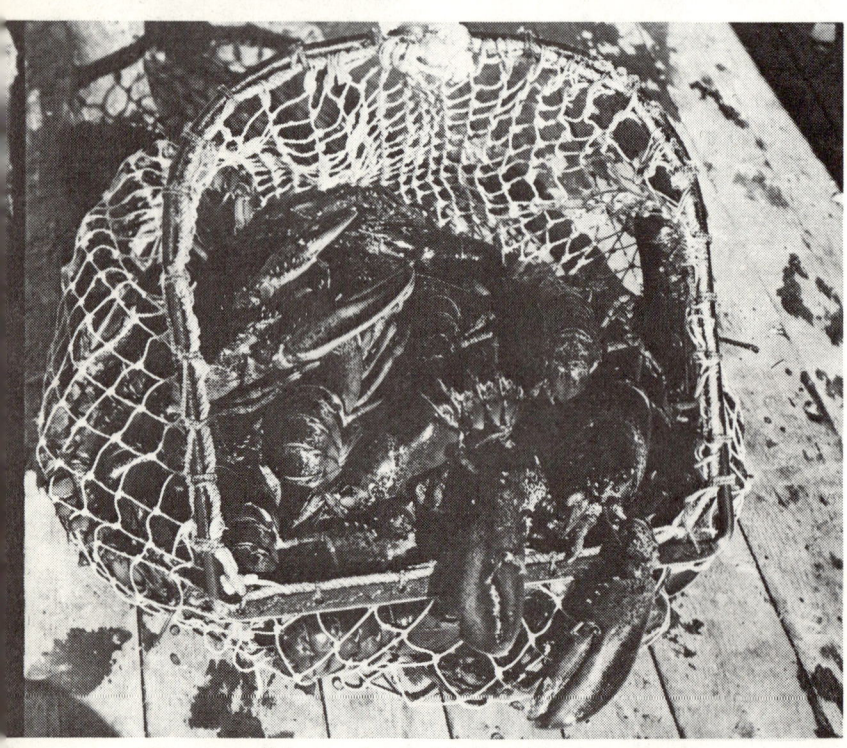

Maine is a land of variety with rolling hills and beautif[ul] mountains. This is Maine's highest, Mt. Katahdin.

Maine is well known for its lobster, which is a popular delicacy in the United States.

Much of Maine's rural winter countryside reflects the days o[f] the early settlers.

Photographs furnished by Maine Department of Commerce and Industry.

page 80 / treasure trails

STATE MOTTO: With The Shield Of Thy Goodwill
STATE BIRD: Baltimore Oriole
STATE FLOWER: Blackeyed Susan

MARYLAND
Admitted to the Union in 1788

FOR FURTHER INFORMATION WRITE:

- Assateague National Seashore Park
  Berlin, Maryland 21811

- Jacob M. Yingling
  Department of Tourism
  2525 Riva Road
  Annapolis, Maryland 21401

- Blackwater National Wildlife Preserve
  Cambridge, Maryland 21613

- Tawes State Office Building
  2525 Riva Road
  Annapolis, Maryland 21401

Maryland is named for Queen Henrietta Maria. She was the wife of Charles I, the English ruler who, in 1632, granted the territory now known as Maryland and Delaware to the first Lord Baltimore. Maryland is often called "The Old Line State" because its troops of the line won special praise from George Washington for gallantry during the Revolutionary War.

Maryland is like a northern state in some ways, and in others it is like a southern state. The state is both colonial and modern, conservative and progressive, agricultural and industrial.

Much of the life of Maryland is centered in Baltimore, where about one-half of the people of the state live. In this industrial center may be found one of the largest steel plants in the world, and great mills and plants which turn out a wide variety of products.

Maryland has a varied climate because of its nearness to the Atlantic Ocean, and the differences in elevation in the state.

More than 150 varieties of trees grow in Maryland's forests. Maryland also offers great hunting.

Chief products are dairy products, vegetables, especially sweet potatoes, spinach, and tomatoes. Maryland is rich in coal, sand and gravel and crushed stone. Manufactured products include chemicals, transportation equipment, textiles, lumber, furniture and tobacco.

Maryland is a great natural playground. The many sandy beaches of the Atlantic and Chesapeake shores provide swimming, fishing, and boating. In winter, skiing and tobogganing are popular sports in the western mountains. More than 140,000 acres of national and state forests, parks and historic battlefields add to the recreation that can be found in Maryland.

Swallow Falls is only one of the many breath-taking scenes of the Maryland countryside.

treasure trails / page 81

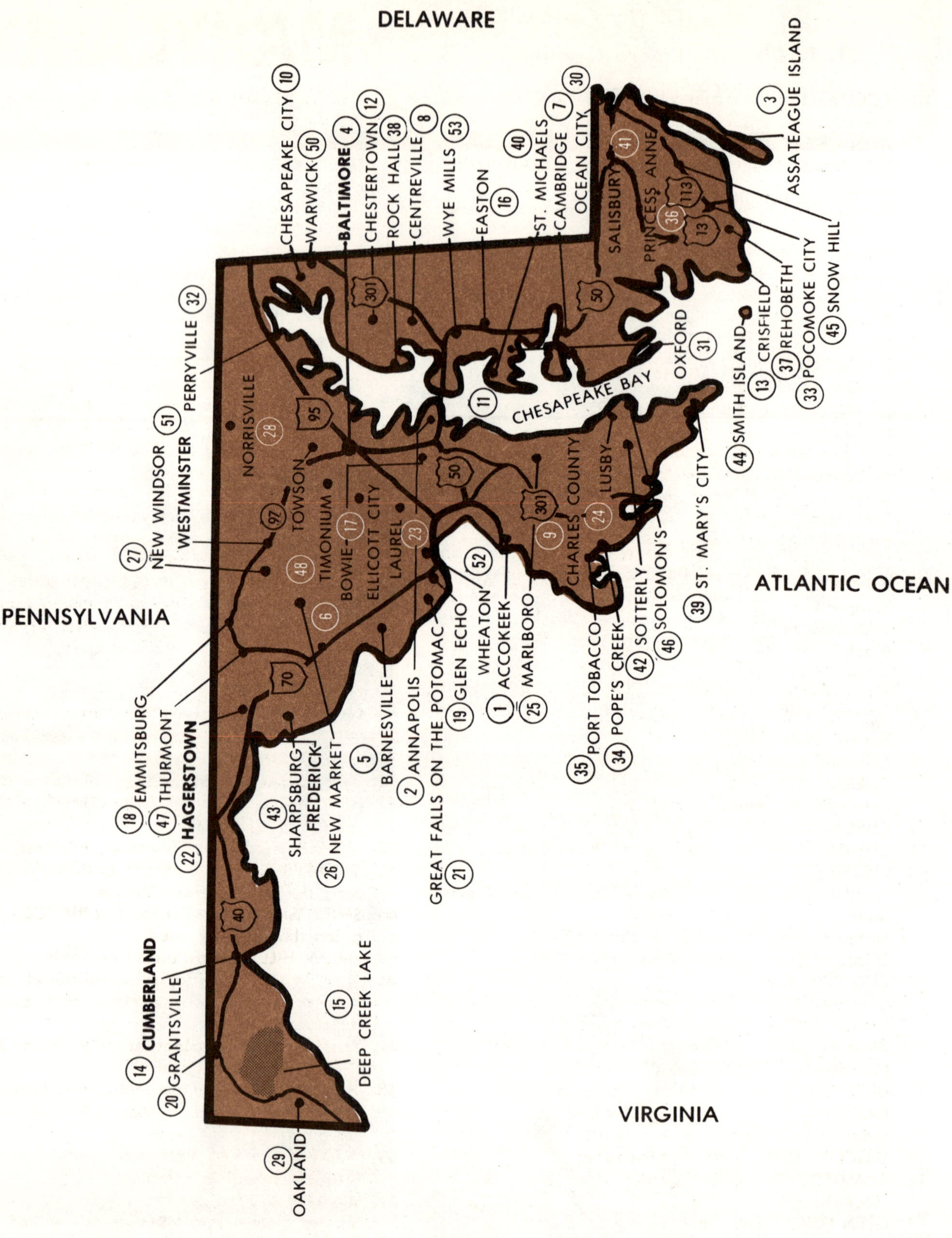
DELAWARE
PENNSYLVANIA
ATLANTIC OCEAN
VIRGINIA
CHESAPEAKE BAY
CHESAPEAKE CITY (10)
WARWICK (50)
BALTIMORE (4)
CHESTERTOWN (12)
ROCK HALL (38)
CENTREVILLE (8)
WYE MILLS (53)
EASTON (16)
ST. MICHAELS (40)
CAMBRIDGE (7)
OCEAN CITY (30)
SALISBURY (41)
PRINCESS ANNE (36)
ASSATEAGUE ISLAND (3)
SNOW HILL (45)
POCOMOKE CITY (33)
REHOBETH (37)
CRISFIELD (13)
SMITH ISLAND (44)
OXFORD (31)
(11)
PERRYVILLE (32)
NORRISVILLE (28)
WESTMINSTER (51)
NEW WINDSOR (27)
TOWSON (97)
TIMONIUM (48)
BOWIE (17)
ELLICOTT CITY
LAUREL (23)
(52)
(6)
LUSBY
CHARLES COUNTY (9)
(24)
ST. MARY'S CITY (39)
SOLOMON'S (46)
SOTTERLY (42)
POPE'S CREEK (34)
PORT TOBACCO (35)
MARLBORO (25)
ACCOKEEK (1)
WHEATON
GLEN ECHO (19)
GREAT FALLS ON THE POTOMAC (21)
ANNAPOLIS (2)
BARNESVILLE (5)
NEW MARKET (26)
FREDERICK
SHARPSBURG (43)
HAGERSTOWN (22)
THURMONT (47)
EMMITSBURG (18)
CUMBERLAND (14)
GRANTSVILLE (20)
DEEP CREEK LAKE (15)
OAKLAND (29)
95
50
301
70
40
113
13

Key:

(1) relates to number 1 on the following page.

MARYLAND POINTS OF INTEREST

1. ACCOKEEK - Colonial National Farm Museum, operating example, 18th century
2. ANNAPOLIS
   U.S. Naval Academy, chapel, crypt of John Paul Jones;
   Chesapeake Appreciation Day, nation's last oyster fleet sailing;
   Downtown listed as national historic landmark, walking tours
3. ASSATEAGUE ISLAND - barrier reef, home of Chicoteague ponies, national park
4. BALTIMORE
   B & O Transportation Museum, world's greatest collection of locomotive equipment;
   Ft. McHenry, birthplace of the National Anthem, museum;
   U.S. Frigate Constellation, first U.S. naval ship;
   McCormick & Company Spice Company, tours;
   Bethlehem Steel Plant, world's largest steel mill;
   Baltimore Museum of Art
5. BARNESVILLE - Al-Marah, 2,800 acre Arabian Horse Farm, open to public
6. BOWIE - Bowie Race Track, thoroughbred competition
7. CAMBRIDGE
   Blackwater Refugee, greatest concentration of water fowl, tours;
   Trinity Church, oldest Protestant church in America
8. CENTREVILLE - 18th century tidewater plantation house, museum
9. CHARLES COUNTY - Tobacco Auctions, April-June
10. CHESAPEAKE CITY - Chesapeake & Delaware Canal pump house, water wheel
11. CHESAPEAKE BAY - Parallel Bridge, 7.7 miles long
12. CHESTERTOWN - colonial waterfront village
13. CRISFIELD
    "Seafood Capital of the World", port for excursion boats;
    National Hard Crab Derby, September;
    Skipjack Races, Deal Island, Labor Day
14. CUMBERLAND
    Cumberland Narrows, gateway is a rocky gorge rising 1000 feet above Wills Creek;
    Washington's first headquarters, Toll House;
    Chesapeake & Ohio Canal
15. DEEP CREEK LAKE - Maryland's largest lake
16. EASTON - The Third Haven Meeting House, 1684, oldest frame church in America in use
17. ELLICOTT CITY - historic structures
18. EMMITSBURG - Lourdes Grotto, Anne Seton House, "Stonehouse"
19. GLEN ECHO - Clara Barton House, founder of Red Cross
20. GRANTSVILLE - Cassleman River Bridge, longest single span stone arch bridge
21. GREAT FALLS ON THE POTOMAC
22. HAGERSTOWN - Hager House, historical museum
23. LAUREL - Laurel Race Course, determines horse of the world
24. LUSBY
    Cliffs of Calvert, fossil treasures;
    Baltimore Gas and Electric Co. Nuclear Power Plant, museum
25. MARLBORO - Marlboro Park Speedway, sports car racing
26. NEW MARKET - major antique center
27. NEW WINDSOR - International Gift Shop
28. NORRISVILLE - Amos Mill, 18th century grist mill
29. OAKLAND
    Cranesville Swamp, sub-arctic swamp;
    Autumns Glory Festival, October
30. OCEAN CITY - largest resort area in Maryland
31. OXFORD - Robert Morris Inn, yachting center
32. PERRYVILLE - Roger's Tavern, 18th century stage coach station, museum
33. POCOMOKE CITY - Pocomoke River, tropical river, bald cypruss home of National Bass Round-Up, May-October
34. POPE'S CREEK - Waterman's Haven, crab houses
35. PORT TOBACCO - restored ghost town
36. PRINCESS ANNE - Teackle Mansion, museum
37. REHOBETH - Rehobeth Presbyterian Church, first in America, 1705
38. ROCK HALL
    Commercial and sport fishing area;
    Remington Farms, wildlife demonstrations
39. ST. MARY'S CITY - Maryland's mother country, founded 1634
40. ST. MICHAELS - Chesapeake Maritime Museum
41. SALISBURY - Atlantic Flyway Waterfowl carvings & art exhibit, October
42. SOTTERLY - Sotterly Mansion, museum
43. SHARPSBURG - Antietam Battlefield, Civil War National Shrine, stone bridges
44. SMITH ISLAND - Smith Island, settled 300 years ago, accessible only by boat
45. SNOW HILL - Julia Purnell Museum
46. SOLOMON'S - Chesapeake Biological Laboratory, research center for oysters and aquatic life, aquarium
47. THURMONT - Colorfest, Cacoctin Mountain Folkcraft Center, October
48. TIMONIUM - Maryland State Fair, August
49. TOWSON - Georgian Mansion, formal gardens, National Historic Shrine
50. WARWICK - Old Behemia Church, site of first Catholic school in colonies
51. WESTMINSTER
    Shriver Homestead Museum, 23 rooms;
    Carroll County Farm Museum, demonstrations
52. WHEATON - Trolly Car Museum, American and foreign streetcars
53. WYE MILLS - Colonial village, school, grist mill, 450 year old tree

treasure trails / page 83

At the Wye Oak and Colonial School House in Wye Mills stands the state tree, the White Oak, one of the largest in the world.

Fort McHenry, birthplace of the "Star Spangled Banner", is located in Baltimore City.

Maryland State House is the oldest state capitol in the U.S. still in legislative use. It was here that the United States Congress ratified the Treaty of Paris to end the Revolutionary War.

Photographs furnished by Maryland Division of Tourism.

STATE MOTTO: By The Sword We Seek Peace, But Peace Only Under Liberty
STATE BIRD: Chickadee
STATE FLOWER: Mayflower

MASSACHUSETTS
Admitted to the Union in 1788

FOR FURTHER INFORMATION WRITE:

- Department of Commerce & Development
  100 Cambridge Street
  Boston, Massachusetts 02202

In 1602, the English navigator Bartholomew Gosnold visited Massachusetts Bay and named it Cape Cod. In 1620 a permanent colony of 102 arrived on "The Mayflower" and settled at Plymouth. In 1630, a fleet of ships transported nearly 1,000 emigrants to Massachusetts Bay, where they settled. A search for religious freedoms brought the Pilgrims to Plymouth Rock and the Puritans to Salem and Boston.

Massachusetts is about 192 miles long. It extends 1,519 miles, when all bays and inlets have been measured. Much of Massachusetts is rough and hilly and covered with glacial deposits. Conditions of soil and climate in Massachusetts are favorable for raising vegetables and some kinds of tobacco. It ranks as one of the great industrial states and stands first in the production of leather, shoes, woolen and worsted goods. It, also, is first in the manufacturing of saws, textile machinery, jeweler's accessories, rubber footwear and fine paper for books. More than three-fifths of the nation's cranberries grow in the coastal bogs of Massachusetts. It leads the world in the value of its scollop catch.

Massachusetts was one of the original 13 states and the birthplace of many precious American freedoms. The influence of Massachusetts in life of the nation has been notable. The telephone was invented by Alexander Graham Bell in Boston in 1876. The sewing machine was invented by Elias Howe at Cambridge in 1845. The first college in the colonies, Harvard, was founded at Cambridge in 1636.

The coastal region of Massachusetts offers all types of water sports. Cultural activities draw many tourists as do the many historical sites.

Daniel Chester French's "Minuteman" guards the reproduction of the original Concord Bridge.

treasure trails / page 85

Massachusetts

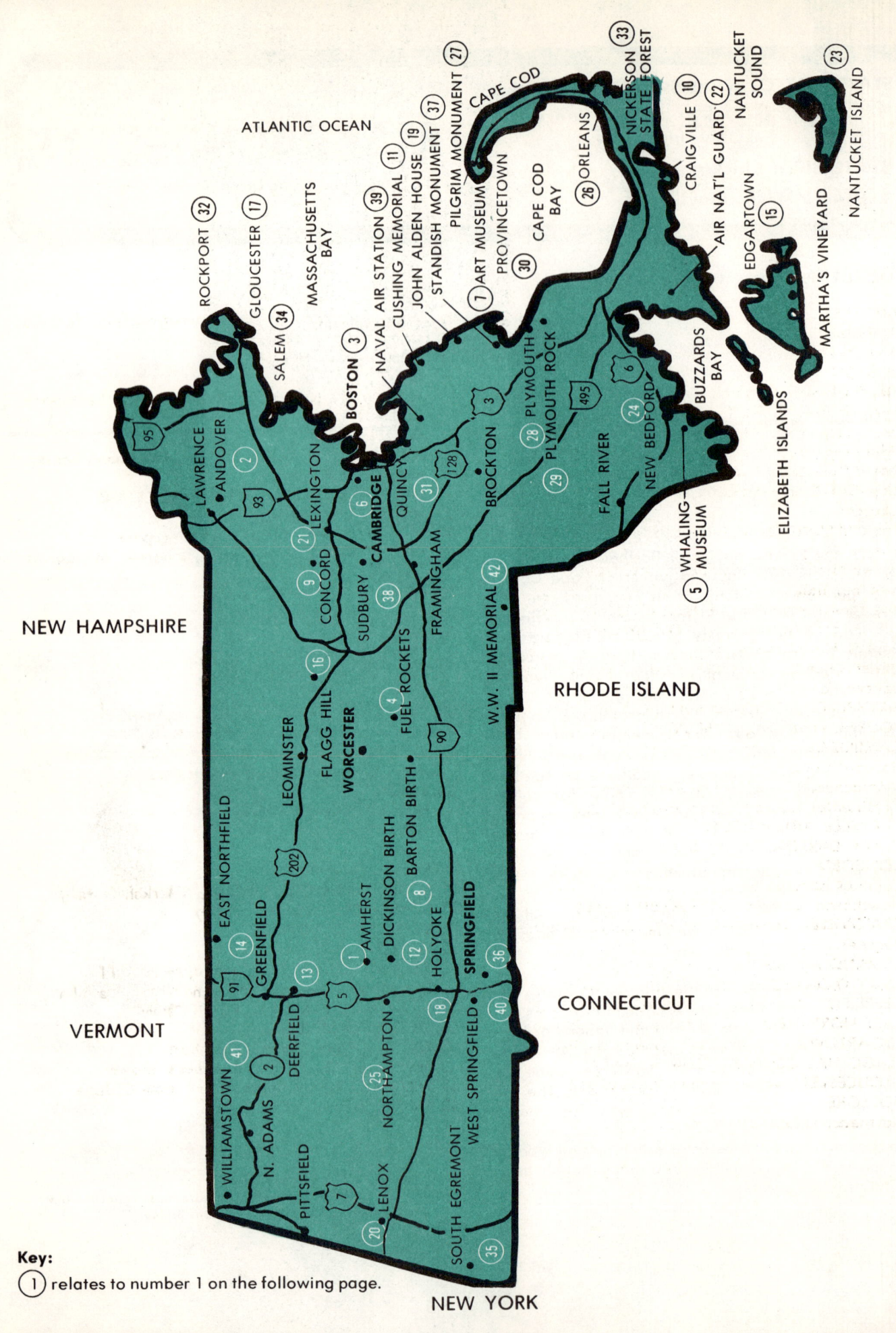

Key:
① relates to number 1 on the following page.

page 86 / treasure trails / Massachusetts

MASSACHUSETTS POINTS OF INTEREST

1. AMHERST - University of Massachusetts, and Amherst College
2. ANDOVER - Phillips Academy
3. BOSTON
   The Park Street Church, "America" was first sung here on July 4, 1831;
   Boston common, fifty acres of land that contain The Whipping Post, The Cage for Sabbath Breakers;
   The Pillory and Stocks for punishment;
   The Old South Meeting House, Congregational Church;
   The Old State House, first religious services of The Boston Massacre;
   Faneuil Hall, "The Cradle of Liberty", the first town meeting hall;
   The Paul Revere House, built in 1676;
   U.S. Frigate Constitution, "Old Ironsides";
   Bunker Hill Monument;
   Christ Church, "The Old North Church of Paul Revere Fame"
4. BIRTHPLACE OF LIQUID FUEL ROCKETS
5. BOURNE WHALING MUSEUM
6. CAMBRIDGE
   Harvard College;
   Massachusetts Institute of Technology;
   Continental Hotel, in historic Cambridge
7. CHRYSLER ART MUSEUM
8. CLARA BARTON BIRTHPLACE
9. CONCORD
   Colonial history;
   Hawthorne, Emerson, and Alcott Homes
10. CRAIGVILLE - famous Craigville Beach, water 72 degrees
11. CUSHING MEMORIAL
12. EMILY DICKINSON'S BIRTHPLACE
13. DEERFIELD - historical village restored
14. EAST NORTHFIELD - ski-lift areas, tobogganing
15. EDGARTOWN - on Martha's Vineyard, resort
16. FLAGG HILL COUNTRY CLUB SKI AREA
17. GLOUCESTER - world renown fishing port
18. HOLYOKE
    Northeast industrial center;
    Yankee Pedlar Inn, "Early American Inn" famous for Yankee cooking, skiing
19. JOHN ALDEN HOUSE
20. LENOX
    Avaloch Inn, summer home of Boston Symphony Orchestra;
    Ski area
21. LEXINGTON - Birthplace of American liberty, historical landmark
22. MASSACHUSETTS AIR NATIONAL GUARD
23. NANTUCKET ISLAND
24. NEW BEDFORD - historic whaling port
25. NORTHHAMPTON - former home of Calvin Coolidge
26. ORLEANS - on Cape Cod
27. PILGRIM MONUMENT
28. PLYMOUTH
    Plymouth Plantation;
    Fishing and boating
29. PLYMOUTH ROCK
30. PROVINCETOWN - historically famous
31. QUINCY - Adams National Historic Site.
32. ROCKPORT - seacoast town, artists' paradise
33. ROLAND NICKERSON STATE FOREST
34. SALEM
    House of Seven Gables;
    Witch House;
    Esses Institute;
    Peabody Museum
35. SOUTH EGREMONT - village in Berkshire Hills
36. SPRINGFIELD - Pioneer Valley
37. STANDISH MONUMENT
38. SUDBURY
    Restored colonial buildings, open to public;
    Longfellow's Wayside Inn, America's oldest Inn
39. S. WEYMOUTH NAVAL AIR STATION
40. WEST SPRINGFIELD
    Site of Eastern States Exposition;
    Storrowton Music Fair, Broadway shows
41. WILLIAMSTOWN - home of Williams College
42. WORLD WAR II MEMORIAL

Tanglewood, a 210 acre estate in Lenox, is world famous as the summer home of the Boston Symphony, and the Berkshire Music Festival.

This half-scale reproduction of the whaler Lagoda, in New Bedford, welcomes thousands of visitors annually.

Wychemere Harbor, Harwichport, provides a scenic port for pleasure boats.

The only 17th century structure now standing in Boston, Paul Revere's home has been fully restored for visitors.

Photographs furnished by Massachusetts Department of Commerce.

page 88 / treasure trails

STATE MOTTO: If You Seek A Pleasant Peninsula, Look Around You
STATE BIRD: Robin
STATE FLOWER: Apple Blossom

MICHIGAN
Admitted to the Union in 1837

FOR FURTHER INFORMATION WRITE:

- State of Michigan Tourist Council
  Charles Budd, Director
  300 South Capital Avenue
  Lansing, Michigan 48926

- Upper Peninsula Travel & Recreational Association
  Box 400
  Iron Mountain, Michigan 49801

- East Michigan Travel Commission
  1 Wenonah Park
  Bay City, Michigan 48706

Michigan is named for the lake which forms the western boundary of its lower peninsula. The name is Indian, and probably means great lake.

White men came to Michigan at an early date. More than three hundred years ago, Etienne Brule, a young French explorer discovered the falls of the St. Marys River. He was followed by missionaries, traders, and trappers. The first permanent settlement was founded at Sault Sainte Marie by Father Marquette in 1668. Britain gained possession of the area in 1763. Between 1820 and 1835 Michigan grew rapidly and was ready to become a state. On January 26, 1837 Michigan became the twenty-sixth state in the Union. Few states have as great of a variety of factory, farm, mine, and forest resources as Michigan. It is the automobile manufacturing center of the world, and the center for high-grade furniture making in the United States. It is first among the states in the production of cherries. It is also first in salt mining. One of the world's largest chemical industries is based on the state's salt industry. Michigan ranks high in dairy products, choice apples and peaches, cereal grains and breakfast foods.

Michigan is a picturesque state of hills and mountains, low-lying lands and swamps. Cut-over lands and virgin forests, rushing rivers and thousands of inland lakes cover Michigan.

The region has two great peninsulas separated by the Straits of Mackinac.

Michigan is nearly surrounded by four of the Great Lakes; therefore, it has a climate that is very different from that of neighboring states. On the whole, the state enjoys a more even climate than other states in the same latitude.

Mackinac Bridge, linking Michigan's two peninsulas, spans the Straits of Mackinac between Mackinaw City and St. Ignace.

treasure trails / page 89

Map of Michigan

FORT WILKINS STATE PARK (15)
(38) LAKE LINDEN
ISLE ROYLE NATIONAL PARK (32)
(57) ROCKLAND
(40) L'ANSE
(41) (37)
LAC VIEUX DESERT TRAIL (46) MARQUETTE
TAHQUAMENON STATE PARK
(60) SAULT STE MARIE
(49)
(66)
JOHNSTON (34)
(30) IRON COUNTY
MUNISING (53)
PALMS BROOK STATE PARK
(75)
WISCONSIN
(31) IRON MOUNTAIN
(2)
ST. IGNACE
(14) (63) (65) STRAITS OF MACKINAC
FAYETTE
(64)
MACKINAW CITY
ST. JAMES
(44)
(47)
(23) HARBOR SPRINGS
(58) ROGERS CITY
MENOMINEE
ELK RAPIDS
(12)
(75)
(1) ALPENA
TORCH LAKE
TRAVERSE CITY (69)
(68) (36)
(20)
(24) HARRISVILLE
FRANKFORT
(17) KALKASKA
GRAYLING
(13) ESSEXVILLE
(45)
(26)
HIGGONS LAKE
(62)
BAY CITY
(39)
MANISTEE (131)
(27) STERLING
(4)
LAKE MICHIGAN
(3) (56) REED CITY
(75) (48)
BALDWIN
(6)
MIDLAND
(21) GREENLEAF TOWNSHIP
BIG RAPIDS
SAGINAW
(71) WATROUSVILLE
(19) FREMONT
(16) FRANKENMUTH
(50) (43)
(22)
OVID
(52) (42) LAPEER (55)
MUSKEGON
GREENVILLE
IONIA
(51) OWOSSO
PORT HURON
GRAND RAPIDS
(28)
(54)
(10)
HOLLAND
LOWELL (29)
(96)
(59) ROMEO
(41) LANSING
HASTINGS (25) (9)
(18)
SOUTH HAVEN
(61) (35)
DETROIT
KALAMAZOO
CHARLOTTE
(94)
(11) DEARBORN
(33) JACKSON
BATTLE CREEK
(10) BLOOMFIELD
BERRIEN SPRINGS
(5) (70) (8)
HILLSDALE
(7) HILLS
VANDALIA
PARSHALLVILLE
FRANKLIN-SOUTHFIELD
CENTREVILLE
(67) TIPTON
TOWNSHIP
(2) ANN ARBOR

INDIANA

OHIO

Key:

(1) relates to number 1 on the following page.

page 90 / treasure trails

MICHIGAN POINTS OF INTEREST

1. ALPENA - Huron Portland Cement Company, 1908, world's largest cement plant
2. ANN ARBOR - Francis W. Kelsey Museum of Archaeology, antiquites from Near Eastern excavations
3. BALDWIN - Marlborough, ruins of a million-dollar cement plant
4. BAY CITY - Defoe Shipbuilding Company
5. BERRIEN SPRINGS - Berrien Springs Courthouse, 1830, Greek temple
6. BIG RAPIDS - Mescosta County Museum
7. BLOOMFIELD HILLS - Cranbrook Educational and Cultural Center
8. CENTREVILLE - Langley Covered Bridge, 1887
9. CHARLOTTE - Vermontville, colony from Vermont, 1836
10. DEARBORN - Greenfield Village
11. DETROIT
    Fort Wayne, historic landmarks, now museum; Indian and military exhibits
12. ELK RAPIDS - Elk Rapids Company Furnace, 1873
13. ESSEXVILLE - Essexville Sugar Plant, one of the largest refineries of sugar in the United States
14. FAYETTE - town built 1867, restored and is state park
15. FORT WILKINS STATE PARK - built, 1844
16. FRANKENMUTH - German community, Bavarian Festival
17. FRANKFORT - Point Betsie Lighthouse, built, 1858
18. FRANKLIN-SOUTHFIELD TOWNSHIP - village founded, 1835
19. FREMONT - Windmill Gardens, collection of windmills
20. GRAYLING - Fred Bear Museum, bow and arrow collection
21. GREENLEAF TOWNSHIP - Sanilac Petroglyphs
22. GREENVILLE - Annual Potato Festival
23. HARBOR SPRINGS - Chief Andrew Blackbird Ottawa Indian Museum
24. HARRISVILLE - Springport Inn, built in 1878
25. HASTINGS - Bristol Inn, historic village
26. HIGGONS LAKE - beautiful lake
27. HILLSDALE - Old Central Hall, magnificent clock tower
28. HOLLAND
    De Zwann and Dutch exhibits, 200 year old windmill; Tulip Festival, spring
29. IONIA - Hall-Flower Memorial Library, Italian villa style
30. IRON COUNTY - Chippewa burial ground, last major powwow in the upper Great Lakes area took place here in 1920's
31. IRON MOUNTAIN - Immaculate Conception Church,
32. ISLE ROYALE NATIONAL PARK - island in Lake Superior, majestic wilderness
33. JACKSON - Ella Sharp Museum, Victorian furnishings
34. JOHNSTON - John Johnston House, built 1815
35. KALAMAZOO - Ladies Library Association Building, 1852
36. KALKASKA
    Old Mill Museum;
37. LAC VIEUX DESERT TRAIL - ancient Indian village and burial ground
38. LAKE LINDEN - Houghton County Historical Museum, displays on transportation, communication, forestry
39. LAKE MICHIGAN - Sleeping Bear Dunes
40. L'ANSE - Zeba Methodist Church, continues to serve Indians, since 1882
41. LANSING
    State Capitol;
42. LAPEER - Lapeer County courthouse, oldest active courthouse in state, 1845
43. LOWELL - Fallasburg Covered Bridge, built 1860's
44. MACKINAW CITY - Fort Michilimackinaw, built by French in 1715, archeological excavation
45. MANISTEE - Our Savior's Evangelical Lutheran Church, built 1869, oldest Danish Lutheran church in America
46. MARQUETTE
    Father Marquette Statue;
    United States Ski Association Hall of Fame
47. MENOMINEE - The Alvin Clark (Mystery Ship) Great Lakes schooner, sunk in 1864
48. MIDLAND - Bradley House, restored, furnished, 1874
49. MUNISING - Pictured Rocks National Lakeshore
50. MUSKEGON
    Hackley House, built 1888, reflects the wealth of the lumber era;
51. OVID - Main Street Building, United Church, 1972
52. OWOSSO - Curwood Castle, architectural fantasy
53. PALMS-BROOK STATE PARK - associated with legends of Hiawatha
54. PARSHALLVILLE - Grist mill, in operation
55. PORT HURON - Huron Lighthouse, one of the first on the upper Great Lakes
56. REED CITY - The Old Rugged Cross, honors composer of that hymn
57. ROCKLAND - Victoria Road, log buildings, old foundations
58. ROGERS CITY - world's largest limestone quarries
59. ROMEO
    Victorian village;
    Romeo Peach Festival
60. SAULT STE. MARIE - Soo Locks, built 1855
61. SOUTH HAVEN - Liberty Hyde Baily birthplace, home of famed botanist
62. STERLING - Chick Museum, chick hatching
63. ST. IGNACE - St. Ignace Mission, grave of Father Marquette is here
64. ST. JAMES - Mormon Print Shop
65. STRAITS OF MACKINAC
    Mackinac Island;
    Mackinaw Bridge
66. TAHQUAMENON STATE PARK - Tahquamenon Falls, wilderness area
67. TIPTON - Hidden Lake Gardens
68. TORCH LAKE - fifth most beautiful lake in world
69. TRAVERSE CITY - Interlochen Center for the Arts
70. VANDALIA - Underground Railroad
71. WATROUSVILLE - Watrousville Museum,

treasure trails / page 91

Isle Royale National Park in Lake Superior attracts thousands each summer to its undeveloped wilderness.

Detroit, Michigan, the automotive capital of the world is the nation's fifth largest city.

More tonnage is passed through the Soo Locks at Sault Ste. Marie each year than combined total of the Panama and Suez canals.

page 92 / treasure trails

Photographs furnished by Michigan Tourist Council.

STATE MOTTO: The Star Of The North
STATE BIRD: Goldfinch
STATE FLOWER: Pink And White Lady's Slipper

MINNESOTA
Admitted to the Union in 1858

FOR FURTHER INFORMATION WRITE:

- Minnesota Department of Economic Development
  Tourism Divison
  480 Cedar Street Box B.C.
  St. Paul, Minnesota 55101

- Minnesota Historical Society
  Main Historical Building
  690 Cedar Street
  St. Paul, Minnesota 55101

- Greater Minneapolis Chamber of Commerce
  15 South 5th Street
  Minneapolis, Minnesota 55402

From the Indians to the French, and then to the British after the French and Indian War in 1763 we have a quick sketch of Minnesota's early history.

Fur trading and treaties lead from peaceful development to the area's becoming a state in 1858. The eastern part of the state was a part of the Northwest Territory, the rest a part of the Louisiana Purchase.

A land of lakes and rivers tells a story of glacial periods. The soil is generally rich and well-drained. All drainage goes into the Atlantic and Arctic Oceans, some by way of the Hudson Bay. The mighty Mississippi has its origin in Minnesota. The climate is subject to rapid changes, from 35 to 108 degrees F. Heavy snowfall is not unusual in Minnesota. The highest point, Eagle Mountain, is 2301 feet above sea level. The northernmost part of the 48 states is in Minnesota.

Agriculture, manufacturing, mining and lumbering make for a varied economy. In 1966 only 9.9% of the state's expenditures went for public welfare. Two-thirds of our nation's iron ore is produced in the mines of Minnesota. In the Mesabi Range, just 50 miles from Lake Superior, is the deepest open-pit mine in the world. Most of the original forests have already been cut by lumber companies. But the remaining forests provide raw materials for pulp, paper, and many other products.

About a million visitors from other states enjoy vacations in Minnesota every year. Tall, pine-covered cliffs face the blue waters of Lake Superior along the highway on the north shore. The deep forest of the Arrowhead Country attract campers and hunters. Sportsmen shoot more than 1,000,000 ducks and about 70,000 deer annually. Wooded wilderness trails and clear blue waterways lure hikers and canoeists. California is the only state in the union that issues more fishing licenses each year. A variety of sportsmen, including campers and hikers, wander through thousands of square miles of wilderness in the rugged northern and northeastern sections of Minnesota.

Split Rock Lighthouse on North Shore of Lake Superior. The lighthouse is now a State Park and open for tours.

treasure trails / page 93

Key:
① relates to number 1 on the following page.

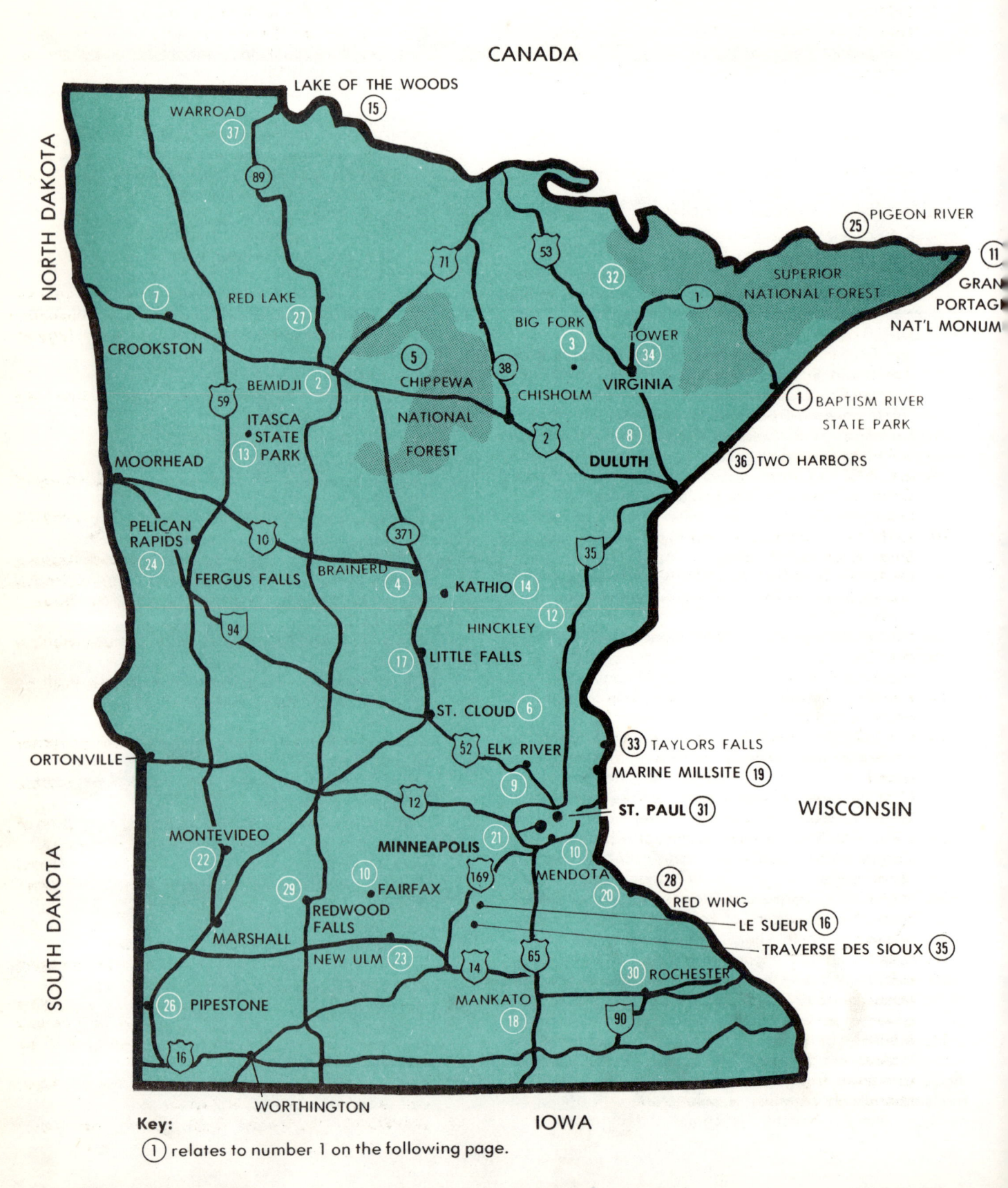

page 94 / treasure trails

MINNESOTA POINTS OF INTEREST

1. BAPTISM RIVER STATE PARK - 706 acres on the north shore of Lake Superior
2. BEMIDJI
   Lake Bemidji, features 286 acres of public camp and picnic grounds;
   Historical Wildlife Museum, lake and recreational area;
   Aquarium
3. BIG FORK - Scenic State Park, 2,121 acres of primitive surroundings
4. BRAINERD - Lumbertown, U.S.A., reconstruction of a typical early logging town
5. CHIPPEWA NATIONAL FOREST
6. CHISHOLM - "Iron Ore Country", Mesabi Range, open pit mines
7. CROOKSTON - Old Crossing Treaty Site, in 1863, Chippewa Indians gave up claim to nine million acres in Minnesota and North Dakota
8. DULUTH
   Jay Cooke State Park, falls of the St. Louis River;
   Aerial Lift Bridge;
   Skyline Drive, scenic beauty;
   North Shore Drive, view of the lake;
   Duluth Ship Canal, dug in 1870's, 300 feet wide and 1,734 feet long
9. ELK RIVER - Oliver H. Kelley Homestead, founded Order of the Patrons of Husbandry, (National Grange), 1867
10. FAIRFAX - Fort Ridgely, scene of turning point of Sioux Uprising of 1862
11. GRAND PORTAGE NATIONAL MONUMENT - site of one of North America's most important fur trade posts
12. HINCKLEY - St. Croix State Park
13. ITASCA STATE PARK - Lake Itasca, source of Mississippi River
14. KATHIO - (Izatys) major Sioux Indian village from prehistoric times to 1740's
15. LAKE OF THE WOODS - Fort St. Charles, French fur trade post established in 1732 by La Verendrye on island
16. LE SEUER - Mayo House, early home of Dr. William W. Mayo, built in 1859
17. LITTLE FALLS - Charles A. Lindbergh House, home of Congressman Lindbergh, father of Charles, Jr., "Lone Eagle"
18. MANKATO - Minneapa State Park, site of the last battle between the Sioux and Chippewa Indians, two waterfalls
19. MARINE MILLSITE - sawmill built in 1839
20. MENDOTA - Sibley House, oldest stone house in Minnesota built in 1836 by Henry H. Sibley, first governor
21. MINNEAPOLIS
    Walker Art Center;
    University of Minnesota;
    Minnehaha Parkway, scenic drive;
    Minnehaha Falls;
    Tyrone Guthrie Theatre;
    Falls of St. Anthony, first power for Minneapolis;
    Fort Snelling, "cradle of Minnesota", northwestern-most military post in nation for many years, established in 1819
22. MONTEVIDEO - Lac Qui Parle Mission, established in 1835
23. NEW ULM - Flandrau State Park, 837 acres
24. PELICAN RAPIDS - "Minnesota Man", skeleton of young girl supposed to have drowned in Glacial Lake Pelican 11,000 years ago
25. PIGEON RIVER
    High Falls, plunges over 1,200-foot cliff;
    Ft. Charlotte, trading post built in late 1700's
26. PIPESTONE
    Pipestone National Monument, Indians used red stone here for making ceremonial pipes, museum;
    Song of Hiawatha Pageant, Indian legend performed
27. RED LAKE
    Red Lake Indian Reservation, home of the Red Lake Chippewa Tribe;
    largest sawmill in Minnesota
28. RED WING
    Frontenac State Park, 945 acres on the shore of Lake Pepin;
    Fort Beauharnois, built by the French in 1727;
    Hiawatha Valley, rich in Indian legends
29. REDWOOD FALLS - Lower Sioux (Redwood) Agency, agency established in 1853 as administrative center for Indians, destroyed in 1862 by Sioux
30. ROCHESTER
    Mayo Clinic and Foundation, world famous medical center;
    Mayowood, four story, forty room house built by Dr. Charles H. Mayo, completed 1912
31. ST. PAUL
    Alexander Ramsey House, home of first governor of Minnesota Territory;
    State Capitol, completed 1904, elaborate marble and granite structure;
    Minnesota Historical Society, excellent collection of books, pictures, manuscripts, and newspapers;
    Mounds Park, preserves six large prehistoric burial sites, believed to have been built over 3,000 years ago
32. SUPERIOR NATIONAL FOREST
33. TAYLORS FALLS - Interstate State Park
34. TOWER - Tower State Park, state's first and deepest iron mine
35. TRAVERSE DES SIOUX - in 1851 thirty five Indian chiefs signed treaty with U.S. Government opening southern half of Minnesota for settlement by whites
36. TWO HARBORS - Gooseberry State Park, Gooseberry River and waterfalls
37. WARROAD - Northwest Angle, scenic boat trip

Fort Snelling, restored and operated by guides dressed in costumes of the period. Located between Twin Cities.

Even children can walk across the Mississippi River at its birthplace in Itasca State Park in Minnesota.

The Steamboat Museum in Winona is a steamboat converted into a display of riverboat history and artifacts.

The bluffs along the Mississippi River in southeastern Minnesota provide magnificent vistas for motorists. The Apple Blossom Scenic Drive from LaCrescent shows the huge apple orchards in the area.

STATE MOTTO: By Valor And Arms
STATE BIRD: Mockingbird
STATE FLOWER: Magnolia

MISSISSIPPI
Admitted to the Union in 1817

FOR FURTHER INFORMATION WRITE:

- Mississippi Game & Fish Commission
  Robert E. Lee Building
  Jackson, Mississippi 39203

- Mississippi Forestry Commission
  Robert E. Lee Building
  Jackson, Mississippi 39203

- Agricultural and Industrial Board
  Travel and Tourism Department
  Walter Sillers State Office Building
  Jackson, Mississippi 39203

Mississippi's past is a romantic one, dating back to 1540, when Hernando De Soto and his soldiers marched through what is now Mississippi in search for gold. Instead he discovered the mighty Mississippi River. Since that time, seven flags have flown over the state. The flags of Spain, France, England, the U.S., the Republic of West Florida, the Confederate States, and the Mississippi State flag have been unfurled overhead.

In 1669, d'Iberville, a Frenchman, founded the first permanent settlement in the lower Mississippi Valley at Old Biloxi. The purpose was to gain control of the Mississippi River which was felt to be the key to the control of the North American continent.

Prior to settlement by the white man, the principal Indian tribes inhabiting Mississippi were the Choctaw, Chickasaw and Natchez. After a series of wars and treaties, these tribes scattered with the exception of the Choctaws remaining at Philadelphia.

On January 9, 1861, Mississippi became the second state to secede from the Union. During the War Between the States, Mississippi played a pivotal role in the western campaigns. Then came Brice's Crossroads and Harrisburg, then surrender, and after the war, reconstruction.

Mississippi moved forward economically, and in the middle 1930's constructed a highway system second to none. During this surge of progress, vast timber and soil resources were recognized, oil was discovered, and industry was on the move.

Mississippi has a sub-tropical climate. The winters are brief and mild. The growing season is long.

Here, more than in any other state, the plantation system of the Old South still survives. Hundreds of mansions with white pillars were built in the days when cotton first became king and many still stand.

Mynelle's Gardens, in Jackson, the state capitol of Mississippi, is a year-round delight for garden lovers.

treasure trails / page 97

MISSISSIPPI

MISSOURI

ARKANSAS

- HOLLY SPRINGS ⑮
- ㉝ SARDIS
- ㉖ OXFORD
- ⑥
- CLARKSDALE
- 55
- ㉙ PONTOTOC
- 78
- TUPELO
- ㊳
- MERIGOLD
- ㉔
- 49
- ⑪ GRENADA
- Natchez Trace Parkway 39
- GREENVILLE
- LELAND
- ⑱
- WINONA
- 82
- ⑤
- COLUMBUS
- ㊶ WINSTON COUNTY
- SHARKEY COUNTY
- 61
- ㉟
- YAZOO CITY
- 45
- ㊷
- FLORA ⑨
- BARNETT RESERVOIR
- ①
- VICKSBURG
- ㊴
- EDWARDS
- ⑦
- ㉒ MADISON
- MERIDIAN
- 20
- ㉓
- RAYMOND
- STONEVILLE ㉛ JACKSON
- ㊱ ㉚
- ⑯ SCOTT COUNTY
- PORT GIBSON ㉞
- 59
- LORMAN
- ⑲
- FAYETTE
- ⑧
- 49
- ⑰ LAUREL
- 84
- NATCHEZ ㉕
- 55
- ⑪ HATTIESBURG
- WILKINSON COUNTY
- ㊵
- 98 COLUMBIA ④
- 98
- ⑳ LUCEDALE
- SANDY HOOK ㉜
- 49
- ㉑ LUMBERTON
- HARRISON COUNTY
- SEAWALL ⑭ GAUTIER
- ㉘ BILOXI ⑩ ㉗ PASCAGOULA
- PICAYUNE GULFPORT ⑬ ②
- 90
- ③ ㊱ ⑥ DEER ISLAND
- CAT ISLAND SHIP ISLAND
- ⑫ GULF COAST

LOUISIANA

ALABAMA

Key:

① relates to number 1 on the following page.

page 98 / treasure trails

MISSISSIPPI POINTS OF INTEREST

1. BARNETT RESERVOIR - recreational center
2. BILOXI
   Beauvoir, last home of Jefferson Davis;
   Shrimp and oyster canning plants;
   Biloxi Lighthouse, built in 1848;
   St. Michael's Church, unusual architecture and stained glass windows;
   Six Gun Junction Ghost Town and Deer Ranch, includes action shoot-outs;
   Shrimp Tour Train, 10 mile fun ride
3. CAT ISLAND - offshore of Mississippi
4. COLUMBIA - Red Bluff, scenic cliff
5. COLUMBUS - Friendship Cemetery, Confederate burial grounds
6. DEER ISLAND - offshore at Biloxi, beautiful coastal island
7. EDWARDS - Adams Egg Farm, largest in world
8. FAYETTE - Springfield, antebellum home which Andrew Jackson and Rachel Robards were married
9. FLORA - Petrified Forest, second largest such forest in the U.S.
10. GAUTIER - Old Place Plantation, antebellum home
11. GRENADA - Grenada Lake, recreational center
12. GULF COAST - world's longest and largest man-made beach, 26 miles
13. GULFPORT
    Banana terminal, deep sea port and terminal;
    Marine Life, porpoises, seals, skin divers, giant sea turtles, sharks
14. HARRISON COUNTY SEAWALL - largest step seawall and protection in the world
15. HOLLY SPRINGS
    Antebellum cotton, one of the oldest in Mississippi;
    Kate Freeman Clark Art Gallery
16. JACKSON
    Governor's Mansion;
    Jackson City Hall, built in 1854 by slave labor;
    State capital;
    Sub Rosa, antebellum home, authentically furnished;
    Jackson Municipal Art Gallery;
    Jackson Municipal Zoo;
    Manship House, one of only six homes which survived Sherman's destruction;
    Mynelle's Gardens, open March-November;
    Old Capitol, state's historical museum
17. LAUREL - Lauren Rogers Library & Museum of Art, Indian artifacts;
    Masonite Corporation, one of world's largest hardboard plants
18. LELAND - Walker Farms Dairy, largest privately owned dairy in Mississippi
19. LORMAN - Old Country Store, tourist delight
20. LUCEDALE - Model of Holy Land, 3 1/2 acres
21. LUMBERTON - Bass Pecan Company, world's largest pecan nursery
22. MADISON - Episcopal Chapel of the Cross, used as headquarters of General Sherman
23. MERIDIAN - Merrehope, antebellum home
24. MERIGOLD - McCarty's Barn, ceramic creations
25. NATCHEZ
    King's Tavery, antebellum home;
    Longwood, antebellum home;
    Natchez Museum, history of old Natchez;
    Buggy Museum, relics, buggies, clocks;
    Mt. Locust, restored frontier home
26. OXFORD
    Rowan Oak, home of William Faulkner;
    St. Peter's Episcopal Church, "Home from The Hill", filmed here;
    Stark Young Home, author of "So Red the Rose"
27. PASCAGOULA - Old Spanish Fort, oldest building in Mississippi Valley
28. PICAYUNE - Mississippi Test Facility, testing site for America's largest missiles
29. PONTOTOC - Lochinvar, antebellum home, Chickasaw Queen buried here
30. PORT GIBSON
    Grand Gulf State Park, museum and remains of many forts;
    Windsor, once the most pretentious mansion in the South
31. RAYMOND - Raymond Courthouse, served as confederate hospital
32. SANDY HOOK - John Ford House, oldest frontier-type house in Mississippi
33. SARDIS - Sardis Lake, recreational center
34. SCOTT COUNTY - Delta and Pine Land Company, world's largest cotton plantation, 38,000 acres at Scott, Mississippi, near point 24.
35. SHARKEY COUNTY - Panther Burn Plantation, larger plantations in Mississippi Delta
36. SHIP ISLAND - Fort Massachusetts, General Butler planned capture of New Orleans here
37. STONEVILLE - Delta Branch Experiment Station, cotton research center
38. TUPELO - Chickasaw Village
39. VICKSBURG
    Steamer Sprague, last of the sternwheelers;
    National Military Park, monuments of the Seige of Vicksburg;
    Cairo, relics of federal gunboat;
    Cedar Grove, antebellum home;
    Planters Hall, old Southern and English architecture;
    Warren County Courthouse, museum
40. WILKINSON COUNTY - Rosemont, Jefferson Davis' boyhood home
41. WINSTON COUNTY - Nanih Waiya Mound, birthplace of Choctaw race
42. YAZOO CITY - John Sharp Williams Home, has original floors, plaster, doors and locks

treasure trails / page 99

"Windsor" ruins, near Port Gibson, are all that remains of the once splendorous estate built in 1860 for $175,000.

Perhaps the most famous landmark along the Mississippi Gulf Coast is the 120-year-old lighthouse in Biloxi.

Originally a French Inn, this historic fort at Pascagoula, built in 1718, is the oldest structure in the lower Mississippi Valley.

Photographs furnished by Mississippi A & I Board, Travel Dept.

page 100 / treasure trails

STATE MOTTO: The Welfare Of The People Shall Be The Supreme Law
STATE BIRD: Bluebird
STATE FLOWER: White Hawthorne Blossom

MISSOURI
Admitted to the Union in 1821

FOR FURTHER INFORMATION WRITE:

- State Liaison Officer
  U.S. Travel Service
  Missouri Tourism Commission
  Jefferson City, Missouri 65101

- Forestry Division,
  State Department of Conservation
  Jefferson City, Missouri 65101

Missouri is located in the center of the North American Continent and is the setting of three great rivers, the Ohio, the Missouri, and the Mississippi, forming the entire eastern boundary of the state. In early history these streams provided roadways for exploring, settlement and commerce.

Other attractions in Missouri that help make it the vacation land it is, include 11 giant springs, 350 recorded caves, and 25 clear-water streams, some having health properties.

Missouri has a very favorable climate. Everything necessary to man is grown or produced there.

The earliest permanent settlers were of Spanish and Scotch-Irish descent. They found fertile farmland and many lead deposits. On August 10, 1921 Missouri officially attained statehood. The last vestige of Post Civil War bitterness vanished after the turn of the century, as the mining industry boomed and more smelters had to be built. Factories mushroomed in St. Louis and Kansas City. The wagon and carriage industry slowed and the automobile industry picked up the slack. The livestock business, flour milling, and meat processing soared to new records.

Today Missouri is fifth among the states in defense manufacturing. They also rank high in production of walnut lumber, corn, wheat, fruit, horses, and mules. Also in Missouri are fresh-water fish, plants, and granite quarries.

Missouri leads in poultry and egg production. Jasper County leads in zinc ore mining. Missouri produces more lead ore, cobalt, nickel, plus tobacco, and corncob pipes than any other state.

St. Joseph, Missouri, was the eastern starting point for the famous mail carriers of the Pony Express who blazed a trail through the wild west.

treasure trails / page 101

IOWA

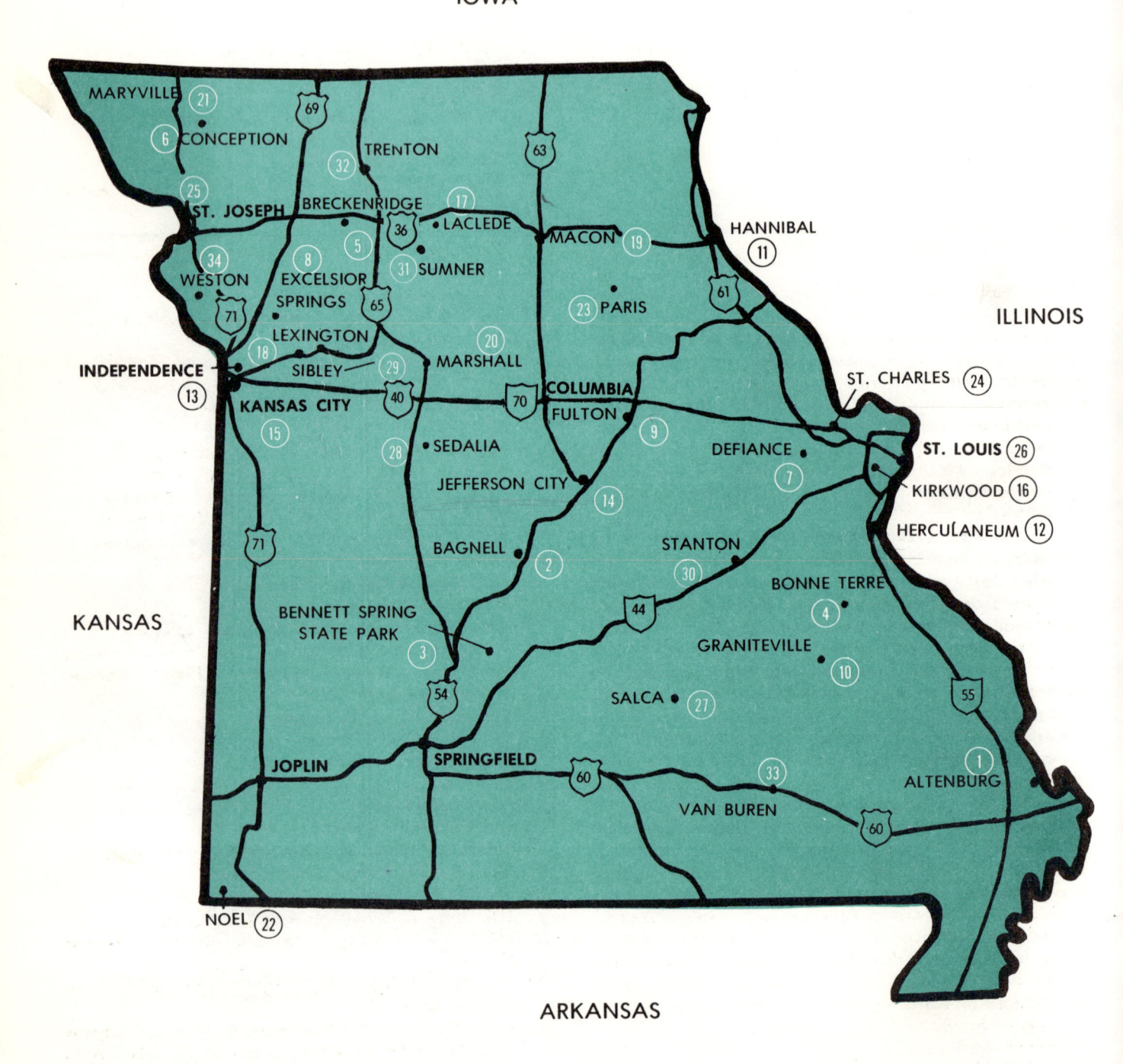

MARYVILLE (21)
(6) CONCEPTION
(69)
(25)
ST. JOSEPH BRECKENRIDGE (17)
(32) TRENTON
(63)
(34) (8) (36) LACLEDE
WESTON EXCELSIOR (5) (31) SUMNER MACON (19) HANNIBAL (11)
(71) SPRINGS (65)
LEXINGTON (20) (23) PARIS (61)
(18) MARSHALL
INDEPENDENCE SIBLEY (29) COLUMBIA ST. CHARLES (24)
(13) KANSAS CITY (40) (70) FULTON
(15) (28) SEDALIA (9) DEFIANCE ST. LOUIS (26)
JEFFERSON CITY (7) KIRKWOOD (16)
(14) HERCULANEUM (12)
BAGNELL (2) STANTON
(71) (30) BONNE TERRE
(44) (4)
BENNETT SPRING GRANITEVILLE
STATE PARK (10)
(3) SALCA (27) (55)
(54)
JOPLIN SPRINGFIELD (60) (33) ALTENBURG (1)
VAN BUREN (60)

NOEL (22)

KANSAS   ILLINOIS

ARKANSAS

Key:
(1) relates to number 1 on the following page.

page 102 / treasure trails

MISSOURI POINTS OF INTEREST

1. ALTENBURG - first home of Concordia Seminary, oldest log structure, restored
2. BAGNELL - Lake of the Ozarks and Bagnell Dam, houses Missouri's largest hydroelectric plant
3. BENNETT SPRING STATE PARK
4. BONNE TERRE - St. Joseph Lead Company, lead mining since 1864
5. BRECKENRIDGE
   J.C. Penney Farms, horse breeding farm;
   Old Hillstone, commemorating the Morman Massacre
6. CONCEPTION - Abbey Church of the Immaculate Conception
7. DEFIANCE - Daniel Boone Home, Judgement Tree
8. EXCELSIOR SPRINGS
   Mineral Water Springs, internationally known;
   Watkins Woolen Mill, built 1860, has original machinery and steam engines
9. FULTON - Winston Churchill Memorial, rebuilt church of St. Mary's Aldermanbury, dedicated to Winston Churchill
10. GRANITEVILLE
    Elephant Rocks State Park, rock formations;
    Graniteville Quarry
11. HANNIBAL
    Mark Twain Statue, tribute to Samuel Clemens;
    Tom Sawyer and Huck Finn Memorial and Mark Twain Cave, memorial to Samuel Clemens
12. HERCULANEUM - Governor Daniel Dunklin's Grave, 5th Governor, father of modern public school system
13. INDEPENDENCE - Truman Home and Library, manuscript collection
14. JEFFERSON CITY
    State Capitol Building;
    Executive Mansion
15. KANSAS CITY
    Sheffield Steel Plant;
    Nelson Art Gallery;
    J.C. Nichols Memorial Fountain and Giralda Tower, Spanish replica;
    American Royal, horse and livestock showing in August;
    Starlight Theatre, musical and stage productions;
    Nelson Art Gallery;
    Swope Park, zoo;
    William Rockhill Nelson Gallery
16. KIRKWOOD - Transport Museum, vehicles
17. LACLEDE - Pershing State Park, home of General John J. Pershing
18. LEXINGTON - Civil War Battleground, 1861
19. MACON - Strip Coal Mining
20. MARSHALL
    Arrow Rock State Park, historic arrow rock landmark of Santa Fe Trail;
    Van Meter State Park, archeological site
21. MARYVILLE - Homer Croy's Home, famous author
22. NOEL - Noel Bluffs, scenic drive
23. PARIS
    Mark Twain State Park, memorial shrine of Samuel Clemens;
    Union Covered Bridge
24. ST. CHARLES - First State Capitol, restored to its 1821 appearance
25. ST. JOSEPH
    Jesse James Home, famous Missouri outlaw;
    Pony Express Route, starting point
26. ST. LOUIS
    St. Louis Art Museum, 70,000 paintings;
    St. Louis Waterfront and Gateway Arch;
    Anheuser-Busch Brewing Company, brewery;
    Missouri Botanical Garden, orchid display;
    Jefferson Memorial Forest Park, trophies of Charles Lindberg's flight;
    Six Flags, recreational center;
    McDonnel Planetarium;
    Lucas Sunken Garden, botannical splendor;
    Polychrome Electric Fountain, limestone formation;
    American Wine Company Plant, makes champagne, built 1832;
    Forest Park, house of glass;
    Clinatron, Shaws Gardens;
    Old Cathedral built in 1834
27. SALCA
    Trout hatchery;
    Old Grist Mill, intact
28. SEDALIA - home of Missouri State Fair, August
29. SIBLEY - Fort Osage, 19th century
30. STANTON - Meramec State Park, springs
31. SUMNER - Fulbright Museum, antiques
32. TRENTON - Crowder State Park, historic Anderson House
33. VAN BUREN - Big Spring, largest single spring in the United States
34. WESTON - Tobacco Warehouse and Market, largest loose-leaf tabacco market west of the Mississippi

treasure trails / page 103

Big Spring, in Van Buren, is the largest single spring in the United States with a maximum flow of 846 million gallons per day.

Personal belongings of the famed American author Mark Twain are restored for the public at the Mark Twain Home and Museum in Hannibal.

The former home of the famous outlaw Jesse James, is a site to see in St. Joseph, Missouri.

St. Louis Riverfront and Gateway Arch, the tallest National Monument in America, signifies St. Louis' contribution to the development of the West.

Photographs furnished by Missouri Division of Tourism.

page 104 / treasure trails

STATE MOTTO: Gold And Silver
STATE BIRD: Western Meadowlark
STATE FLOWER: Bitterroot

MONTANA
Admitted to the Union in 1889

FOR FURTHER INFORMATION WRITE:

- Montana State Liason Officer
  U.S. Travel Service
  Montana Department of Highways
  Helena, Montana 59601

- U.S. National Forest Service
  Federal Building
  Missoula, Montana 59801

- Montana State Fish and Game Commission
  Helena, Montana 59601

Montana is known as the "Big Sky Country." Its clear, unpolluted air lets the blue come through to accent the mountains and plains of the nation's fourth largest state. It averages 550 miles in length and 275 miles in width. The Rocky Mountains dominate the western third of the state, the Continental Divide runs north and south in this area, and it was here that gold prospectors struck it rich in Bannack in 1862, with later strikes in Virginia City and in Last Chance Gulch, now the main street of Helena.

When the Lewis and Clark Expedition returned to St. Louis in 1806 with news of the lush prairies, wide rivers and abundant game in the new land, it wasn't long before trappers, prospectors, missionaries and families in wagon trains began their long, dangerous trek to the West. The first herd of Longhorn cattle was trailed from Texas to Montana in 1866. This opened an era of violence marked by range wars between sheepmen and cattlemen, stockmen and homesteaders. Vigilante committees formed to protect stage coaches carrying gold shipments. The Indian Wars ended with Custer's Last Stand in 1876, and a year later with Chief Joseph's surrender in the Battle of the Bearpaws. Law and order gradually took over, Montana became a territory in 1864, and the 41st state in 1889.

Many lakes, rivers, wilderness and primitive areas, and forest recreation lands offer the vacationer a great variety of pleasures. Glacier Park has some of the most spectacular scenery in the world. Yellowstone Park has many natural wonders, interesting geysers and abundant wildlife. The Gallatin, Jefferson and Madison Rivers join at Three Forks to form the Missouri River which flows through north-central Montana. The eastern two-thirds of the state is mostly rolling prairie lands, with large cattle ranches, wheat farms and strip mines. Six railroads, ten bus lines and four airlines serve Montana.

Montana's Glacier National Park is family fun country whether your inclination is a hike beside a sparkling lake or a leisurely trail ride over thousands of miles of rugged trails.

Photographs furnished by the Travel Promotion Unit.

treasure trails / page 105

Key:

① relates to number 1 on the following page.

page 106 / treasure trails

MONTANA POINTS OF INTEREST

1. BIG FORK - Summer Theatre
2. BIG TIMBER - Natural Bridge & Falls, 90 foot cascade in Boulder River
3. BILLINGS
   Great Western Sugar, factory;
   Yellowtail Sam, on Bighorn River, recreational center;
   Oil refineries;
   Yellowstone Art Center, historical center
4. BOZEMAN - Big Sky, ski center
5. BROWNING - Blackfoot Indian Reservation, museum of the Plains Indians
6. BUTTE
   Clark's Mansion, home of copper king;
   World Museum of Mining;
   Montana College of Mineral Science & Technology, tours;
   Kelly Mine, tours in summer;
   Richest Hill on Earth, gold, silver, copper, zinc;
   Berkeley Open-pit Copper Mine
7. CHINOOK - Chief Joseph Battlefield State Monument, final battle of Chief Joseph of Nez Perce Tribe
8. COLSTRIP - Strip coal mining, largest strip coal mine in the world
9. DILLON - Famous ski area
10. FORT BENTON
    One of the last stretches of the Missouri River that is free flowing, float trips;
    Grand Union Hotel, museum, last boat to come up the Missouri on display;
    National Historic Landmark, steamboat levee
11. FORT PECK - largest earthfill dam, recreational center
12. GLACIER NATIONAL PARK
13. GLENDIVE - Makoshika State Park, colorful badlands
14. GREAT FALLS
    Oil refineries;
    Flour mills, huge grain elevators and mills;
    Great Falls, discovered by Lewis & Clark in 1805;
    Giant Springs, discovered by Lewis & Clark, one of world's largest fresh-water springs;
    Square Butte, appears in many of Charles M. Russell's pictures;
    Home of Charles M. Russell, world famous cowboy artist, National Historic Site;
    Russell Gallery, original log cabin studio;
    C. M. Russell Western Art Auction, March;
    Mehmke Steam Museum, largest privately owned collection of gas and steam engines in the world
15. HARDIN - Custer Battlefield National Monument, General George Custer and 7th Cavalry slain here in 1886
16. HELENA
    Berkeley Pit, open-pit copper mine Anaconda Company, copper and zinc refineries;
    American Smelting and Refining;
    Gates of the Mountains, discovered by Lewis and Clark in 1805;
    Capitol Building, Charles Russell mural;
    State Historical Museum and Library;
    Last Chance Gulch Tour Train
17. KALISPELL - Flathead Lake, water sports center
18. LEWIS AND CLARK TRAIL - Modern highway paralleling much of the trail
19. LIBBY - Ross Creek Giant Cedars, walking tour, U.S. Forest Service
20. MADISON CANYON EARTHQUAKE AREA & QUAKE LAKE - earthquake created Quake Lake, August, 1959
21. MARSHALL SKI AREA
22. MISSOULA
    Ski area;
    Lumber mills and processing plants;
    Bonner Christmas tree farms
23. NATIONAL BISON RANGE - buffalo herds
24. OLD WEST TRAIL
25. POLSON - Flathead Valley Cherries, shipped nation-wide
26. RED LODGE
    Ski area;
    Beartooth Highway, #212, rises to 10,940 feet, spectacular scenery;
    Festival of Nations, each summer
27. SAINT IGNATIUS - St. Ignatius Mission, 58 hand-painted murals
28. STANFORD - Judith Basin County, named in 1805 by Captain William Clark. Gold, silver, iron and sapphires mined since 1865
29. STEVENSVILLE - St. Mary's Mission, first mission church in Montana, 1841
30. TETON PASS - ski area near Choteau
31. THREE FORKS
    Lewis & Clark Caverns, one of the nation's largest limestone caves;
    Missouri River Headwater, state park
32. YELLOWSTONE NATIONAL PARK - largest national park, contains Old Faithful Geyser

treasure trails / page 107

Montana means high country; a chance to escape the cares of everyday into a pristine setting like Nana Lake in the Hillgard Area.

Whitefish Lake in the tree-clad setting of northwestern Montana, where the Aluminum Cup regatta is held each summer and sails grace the lake from dawn til dark.

Dogs, kids, horses and summer add up to magic in the still-young world of Montana.

page 108 / treasure trails

Photographs furnished by the U.S. Forest Service, Missoula, Montana 59801.

STATE MOTTO: Equality Before The Law
STATE BIRD: Western Meadowlark
STATE FLOWER: Goldenrod

NEBRASKA
Admitted to the Union in 1867

FOR FURTHER INFORMATION:

- Game and Parks Commission
  2200 North 33rd Street
  P.O. Box 30370
  Lincoln, Nebraska 68504

- Director of Travel and Tourism
  Department of Economic Development
  P.O. Box 94666 - State Capitol
  Lincoln, Nebraska 69509

The name Nebraska is derived from the Indian terminology for the Platte River. The Platte was called "Nebthaska" by the Omahas and "Nibratha" by the Otoes. Both names signify "flat river" and refer to the wide, flat valley through which the shallow river flows.

It is difficult to determine the exact date of the settlement of the area which is now Nebraska. It is believed that prehistoric Indians who hunted big game roamed the area some ten thousand years ago. These were followed by Indians who raised crops.

Nebraska was organized into a territory in 1854 when the Kansas-Nebraska Act was passed by Congress. This opened the lands west of the Missouri to settlement. When the Homestead Act of 1863 gave 160 acres of land free in eastern Nebraska, further impetus for settling the territory was given. On March 1, 1867, Nebraska was granted statehood. The capital is Lincoln.

Once known as a desert, Nebraska actually has a large supply of water. Along with the climate and fertile soil, this abundant surface and groundwater has made agriculture the state's number one industry.

Nebraska ranks seventh among all states in the value of crops marketed. It has 22,000,000 acres of land under cultivation; 4,000,000 are irrigated. It ranks second in the nation in the number of cattle and calves fed.

Many industries are coming to the state and those in existence are expanding. Food processing is its largest industry.

Nebraska boasts 11,000 miles of streams and over 3,000 lakes. Nebraska offers abundant hunting of duck, geese, deer, antelope, and fishing of everything from sunfish to northern pike and rainbow trout.

Nebraskans believe in their state, its opportunities for health, prosperity and happiness. Therefore, their newly adopted slogan seems most appropriate—"Nebraska—The Good Life".

Chimney Rock, near Bayard, prominent landmark along the Oregon Trail designated as a national historic site.

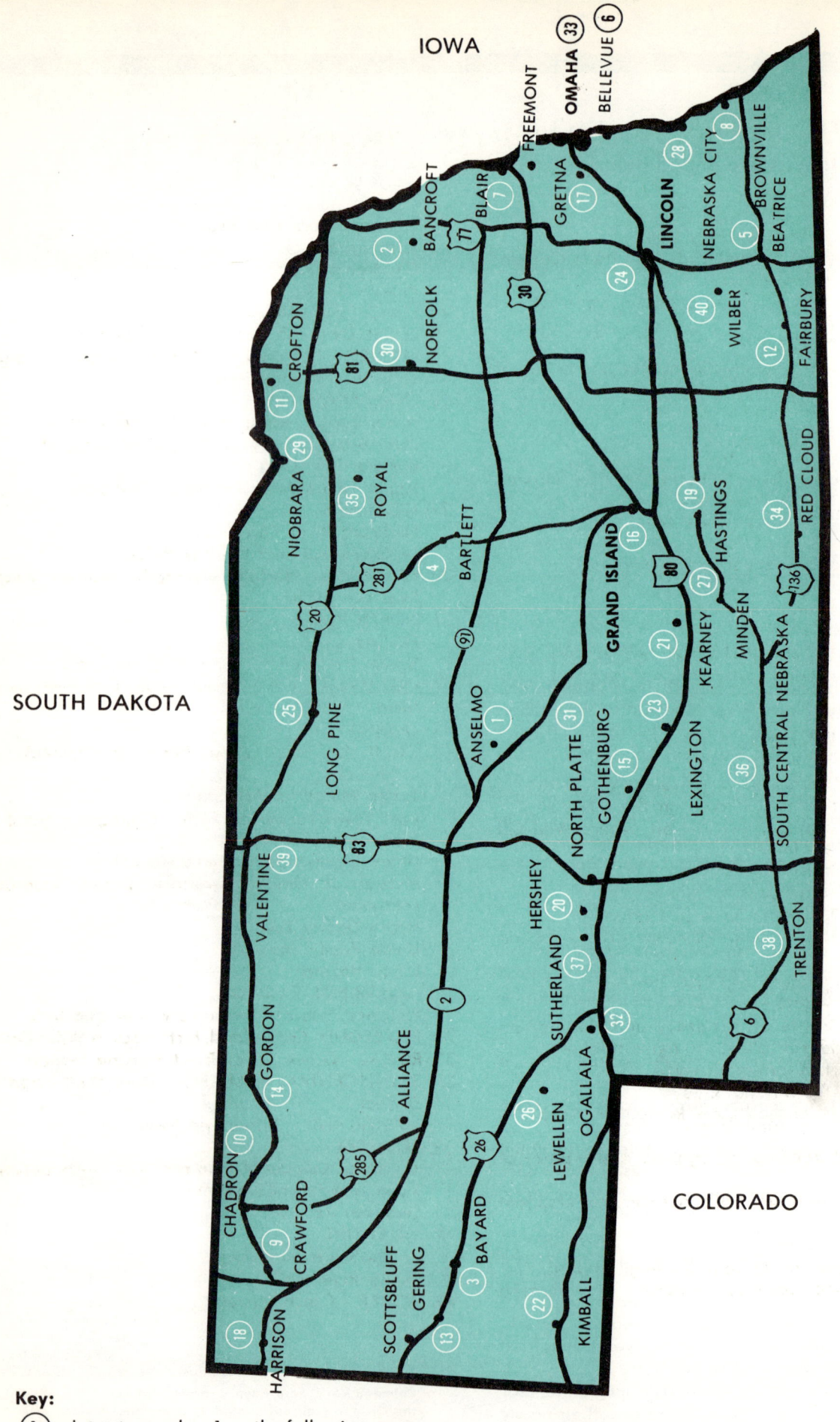

Key:
① relates to number 1 on the following page.

page 110 / treasure trails

NEBRASKA POINTS OF INTEREST

1. ANSELMO - Victoria Springs Park
2. BANCROFT - John G. Neilhardt Home and Garden, Nebraska's Poet Laureate
3. BAYARD - Chimney Rock, pioneer landmark on Oregon Trail
4. BARTLETT - Pibel Lake
5. BEATRICE - Homestead National Monument, site of first homestead in Nebraska
6. BELLEVUE
   Aerospace Museum;
   Old Presbyterian Church
7. BLAIR - DeSoto Bend National Wildlife Refuge, excavated steamer "Bertrand"
8. BROWNVILLE - restored river town
9. CRAWFORD
   Toadstool Park, unusual rock formations;
   Smiley Canyon;
   Trailside Museum;
   Nebraska Badlands;
   Ft. Robinson State Park, restored cavalry post where Indian Chief Crazy Horse was killed
10. CHADRON
    Chadron State College Museum;
    Museum of Fur Trade
11. CROFTON
    Devil's Nest Resort Area, recreational center;
    Gavins Point Dam, last dam on the Missouri
12. FAIRBURY - Pony Express Station, where Wild Bill Hickok became famous
13. GERING - Wildcat Hills Refuge
14. GORDON - Marie Sandoz Museum
15. GOTHENBURG - Pony Express Station
16. GRAND ISLAND - Stuhr Museum of the Prairie Pioneer
17. GRETNA - Aquarium and Fish Hatchery
18. HARRISON - Agate Fossil Beds
19. HASTINGS - House of Yesterday and Planetarium
20. HERSHEY - Chain of Lakes, 160 miles of lakes
21. KEARNEY - Ft. Kearney Museum
22. KIMBALL - Titan Missile Sites
23. LEXINGTON - Johnson Lake Recreation Area
24. LINCOLN
    State Capitol Building, recognized masterpiece of architecture;
    Morrill Hall, museum with outstanding elephant collection;
    Sheldon Art Gallery;
    Fairview, home of William Jennings Bryant;
    State Historical Society, University of Nebraska Campus;
    Antelope Park and Zoo;
    Kennard House;
    Children's Zoo;
    Pioneer Park
25. LONG PINE - Hidden Paradise
26. LEWELLEN - Ash Hollow Historical Park
27. MINDEN - Pioneer Village, nation's largest collection of Americana
28. NEBRASKA CITY
    Arbor Lodge, home of J. Sterling Morton;
    John Brown's Cave, underground railroad;
    Buffalo City U.S.A.;
    Apple Orchards and Processing Plants
29. NIOBRARA
    Niobrara River Ferryboat;
    Niobrara National Wildlife Refuge
30. NORFOLK - Norfolk Livestock, world's largest livestock auction
31. NORTH PLATT
    Ft. Cody;
    Scouts Rest Ranch, home of Buffalo Bill
32. OGALLALA - Front Street, replica of early cattle town
33. OMAHA
    Offutt Air Force Base, home of Strategic Air Command;
    Joslyn Memorial Art Gallery;
    Boys Town, renowned Father Flanagan's home for boys;
    Union Stockyards, nation's largest;
    Mutual of Omaha, world's largest insurance company;
    Henry Doorly Zoo;
    Union Pacific Museum;
    U.S.S. Hazard;
    AK-SAR-BEN, Racetrack,
    Florence, site of Mormon's winter quarters
34. RED CLOUD - Catherland, birthplace of Willa Cather
35. ROYAL - Grove Lake, Trout Rearing Station
36. SOUTH CENTRAL NEBRASKA - Deep Well Irrigation District
37. SUTHERLAND - Sutherland Reservoir
38. TRENTON
    Massacre Canyon Monument, last clash between Sioux and Pawnee Indians;
    Swanson Reservoir
39. VALENTINE
    Ft. Niobrara Museum;
    Snake River Falls
40. WILBER - Czech Museum

treasure trails / page 111

Wierd rock faces and eerie shadows result in a haunted atmosphere in Toadstool Park north of Crawford. Region is known for its rich fossil beds.

Main Museum Building in Grand Island stands as a memorial to the pioneers who settled the Nebraska prairies.

Nebraska State Capitol at Lincoln. This 400-foot structure is recognized as one of the world's architectural masterpieces.

A day on the trail in the Pine Ridge of northwest Nebraska includes pleasant hours spent in the pine-covered hills, inspiring vistas, regular sightings of deer and other wildlife.

Photographs furnished by Nebraska Game and Parks Commission.

page 112 / treasure trails

50 STATE FLAGS and the stories behind them

IN THE FOLLOWING TEXT the states are arranged in the order in which they were admitted to the Union. The date after the name of each state refers to the official adoption of its present flag. The 51st flag is, of course, that of the District of Columbia. It appears at the end of the text.

DELAWARE—1913—"December 7, 1787" on this flag is the day on which Delaware ratified the Federal Constitution. Because it was the first state to do so, it is given the first position in such national events as presidential inaugurations.

PENNSYLVANIA—1907—The Keystone State's coat of arms, carried by its flag, shows a sailing ship, a plow and three sheaves of grain over the motto, "Virtue, Liberty and Independence." The emblem on the flag dates from the latter part of the 18th century.

NEW JERSEY—1896—The buff background of this banner was derived from the buff facings on the Revolutionary War uniforms of the New Jersey Continental Regiments, specified by orders from General Washington. The flag was displayed at the surrender of Cornwallis' army at Yorktown.

GEORGIA—1956—The Georgia flag, one of the newest of all, combines the Battle Flag of the Confederacy and the state seal. Its thirteen stars correspond in number to the states recognized by the Confederate States Congress.

CONNECTICUT—1897—The three grape vines displayed on the state seal which decorates the Connecticut flag represent the three original settlements of the Nutmeg State—Hartford, Windsor and Wethersfield.

MASSACHUSETTS—1915—With an Indian warrior on one side and a green pine tree (not shown) on a blue shield upon the other, the Commonwealth of Massachusetts has one of the few state flags with two distinctly different sides. The Latin motto is translated, "With the sword she seeks peace under liberty."

MARYLAND—1904—One of the oldest flags in the world, the Maryland standard bears the arms of the Calvert and Crossland families. Calvert was the family name of the Lords of Baltimore who founded the state, while Crossland was the family of the mother of the first Lord Baltimore.

SOUTH CAROLINA—1861—The Palmetto State adopted its banner when it withdrew from the Union in 1861. It is the second oldest unchanged official state flag in existence.

NEW HAMPSHIRE—1931—This flag, first adopted in 1909, carried the Granite State's seal, in use since 1784. The seal was redrawn and the flag with the new seal approved in 1931.

VIRGINIA—1930—The flag adopted by Virginia in 1930 has been essentially unchanged since 1831 when it was first raised by Governor John Floyd at the head of a militia force called to quell the Nat Turner insurrection in Southampton County.

NEW YORK—1901—The Great Seal of New York, which decorates its banner, has changed little since its original design in 1777, though there have existed at least six slightly modified official versions since that date.

NORTH CAROLINA—1885—Because of its two dates, this flag carries special interest. The uppermost refers to the Mecklenburg Declaration of Independence, while the lower one commemorates the Halifax Resolves which empowered delegates from North Carolina "to concur with the delegates of the other Colonies in declaring Independency. . . ."

RHODE ISLAND—1897—The anchor was first used as a Colony symbol on the official seal adopted in 1647, and the motto "Hope" was added in 1664 when the government was organized under a charter from King Charles II.

VERMONT—1923—The 14th state in the Union, Vermont has had three state banners since 1803. The first two were originally patterned after the national emblem with alternating red and white stripes. The present flag carries the state's coat of arms.

KENTUCKY—1918—Though authorized in 1918, an actual Blue Grass State banner was not made until some ten years later by an art teacher in the Frankfort schools. The lower portion of the seal is encircled by goldenrod, the state flower.

TENNESSEE—1905—Tennessee's three stars denote the fact that it was the third state to enter the Union after the first thirteen colonies. They also represent the three political divisions of the state which were organized at different times in its history.

OHIO—1902—Ohio is the only state with a pennant-shaped flag, or "burgee," as it is correctly called. The Buckeye banner was originally designed to fly over the Ohio building at the Pan-American Exposition in Buffalo, New York in 1901.

LOUISIANA—1912—The Louisiana flag with its group of pelicans has been used since the War of 1812, though not officially adopted until 100 years later. At least ten different flags have flown over the territory.

INDIANA—1917—A prize-winning design in D.A.R. contest, the Indiana flag was adopted as part of the state's Centennial celebration. The outer circle of thirteen stars represents the original states; the inner semi-circle of five stars, the next five states admitted to the Union. Indiana was the nineteenth state.

MISSISSIPPI—1894—The Mississippi banner is one of six state flags that use only the red, white and blue of the national emblem. Its thirteen stars stand for the original states of the Union.

ILLINOIS—1915—The Illinois flag was the winning design selected from 35 entries submitted in a contest by various D.A.R. chapters within the state.

(continued on page 116)

treasure trails / page 113

FLAGS OF THE STATES

THE 50 STATES AND THE DISTRICT OF COLUMBIA

ALABAMA	ALASKA	ARIZONA
ARKANSAS	CALIFORNIA	COLORADO	CONNECTICUT
DELAWARE	DISTRICT of COLUMBIA	FLORIDA	GEORGIA
HAWAII	IDAHO	ILLINOIS	INDIANA
IOWA	KANSAS	KENTUCKY	LOUISIANA
MAINE	MARYLAND	MASSACHUSETTS	MICHIGAN
MINNESOTA	MISSISSIPPI	MISSOURI	MONTANA

FLAGS OF THE STATES (Continued)

NEBRASKA	NEVADA	NEW HAMPSHIRE	NEW JERSEY
NEW MEXICO	NEW YORK	NORTH CAROLINA	NORTH DAKOTA
OHIO	OKLAHOMA	OREGON	PENNSYLVANIA
RHODE ISLAND	SOUTH CAROLINA	SOUTH DAKOTA	TENNESSEE
TEXAS	UTAH	VERMONT	VIRGINIA
WASHINGTON	WEST VIRGINIA	WISCONSIN	WYOMING

Flags reprinted from Compton's Encyclopedia, by permission of F. E. Compton Company, a Division of Encyclopaedia Britannica.

treasure trails / page 115

ALABAMA—1895—The Cross of St. Andrew appears on Alabama's present flag. An earlier version carried a cotton plant in flower with a rattlesnake at its roots about to spring into action. Beneath the plant were the Latin words, "Noli Me Tangere"—"Don't Tread on Me."

MAINE—1909—The Maine flag is unusual in at least one respect. Though not shown in this illustration, the law prescribed a fringe for the flag to be two and one-half inches wide. "Dirigo" means "I direct."

MISSOURI—1913—A flag, of the design finally adopted, was made and submitted to the state legislature in 1909, but failed to gain immediate approval. Although this first flag was destroyed in a fire at the capitol in 1911, its features were accepted two years later.

ARKANSAS—1913—The three blue stars below the name "Arkansas" represent the three nations, Spain, France and the United States, to whom Arkansas has successively belonged.

MICHIGAN—1911—The first official flag of Michigan, similar to the present emblem, was adopted in 1865 and unfurled for the first time at the laying of the cornerstone of the monument in the Soldiers' National Cemetery, Gettysburg, on July 4, 1865.

FLORIDA—1900—The state seal in the center of Florida's banner pictures a cocoa tree, a steamboat, and an Indian maiden scattering flowers. The seal was adopted in 1868.

TEXAS—1839—The Lone Star banner is the oldest of the official state flags, adopted in the first half of the 19th century and unchanged since then.

IOWA—1921—"Our Liberties We Prize and Our Rights We Will Maintain," reads the motto on Iowa's flag, an adaptation of a design made during the First World War for use by state regiments.

WISCONSIN—1913—The Wisconsin legislature in 1863 adopted a state flag with the Badger State coat of arms on one side and the U.S. coat of arms on the other. After the Civil War the Wisconsin National Guard used a different flag, and the legislature in 1887 inadvertently repealed the 1863 law. The present standard was made official 26 years later.

CALIFORNIA—1911—The Californian flag was born from the "Bear Flag Revolt" of settlers against the Mexican government at the Cosumnes River in 1846. The early flag, similar to its modern cousin, first replaced the Mexican standard at the pueblo of Sonoma.

MINNESOTA—1957—Minnesota boasts the newest design of all the state flags. The 1893 version was discarded because its bulk and two separate sides (each of a different color) made it liable to wind damage and too expensive to manufacture.

OREGON—1925—Oregon is another of those few states whose banners have a different design on each side. Not shown here is the reverse side with its Oregon beaver, symbol of the fur trade which opened the great northwest. 1859 is the year Oregon came into the Union.

KANSAS—1927—The flower on Kansas' flag is a sunflower. The motto, "Ad Astra Per Aspera," means "To the stars through difficulties." The scene is representative of early Kansas history.

WEST VIRGINIA—1929—Typifying the independent spirit that was responsible for forging the state from the chaos of the Civil War, the West Virginia flag carries the motto, "Montani Semper Liberi," which means "Mountaineers always freemen."

NEVADA—1929—Showing its name in an unusual design around a star, Nevada's banner displays two sprays of sagebrush. "Battle Born" refers to the state's entry to the Union during the Civil War.

NEBRASKA—1925—The date on the flag of the Cornhusker State, March 1, 1867, is the date Nebraska was admitted to the Union. The motto on its seal is "Equality Before Law."

COLORADO—1911—The present flag of Colorado does not conform exactly to the state laws which authorize it. The law stipulated a "C" of smaller size than that actually in use. "C" stands, not only for Colorado, but also for Centennial State, its nickname due to its admission to the Union in 1876.

NORTH DAKOTA—1911—Of unknown origin, this banner was carried through thirty-seven engagements by the First North Dakota Infantry during the Spanish-American War and the Philippine Insurrection.

SOUTH DAKOTA—1909—South Dakota's nickname can be read from its flag, which carries the state seal on its reverse side. Design of this flag was started by a Black Hills pioneer, a member of Teddy Roosevelt's "Rough Riders."

MONTANA—1905—The state seal carried by the Montana flag shows mining equipment, a gold pan and a plow, while the background shows the mountains from which the state derives its name. "Oro y Plata" refers to the gold and silver found in the state.

WASHINGTON—1923—The only state flag with a green background, Washington's flag was designed by that state's D.A.R. organization eight years before its official adoption.

IDAHO—1927—State law forbids all military organizations within the Idaho boundaries from carrying any flag except the national and state banners. The flag shows the state coat of arms.

WYOMING—1917—Once monarch of the Great Plains, the bison or buffalo still reigns supreme on the Wyoming banner. The flag design was the result of a D.A.R. contest, and, appropriately enough, was submitted by a woman from Buffalo, Wyoming.

UTAH—1913—The state flag of Utah was presented to the battleship *Utah* the year before its official adoption. Its two dates commemorate the year in which the Mormon pioneers entered Salt Lake Valley, 1847 and the year that Utah became a state, 1896.

OKLAHOMA—1925—The present Oklahoma flag with its buckskin Indian war shield, peace pipe and olive branch, is the fourteenth emblem to fly over Oklahoma soil.

NEW MEXICO—1925—The ancient sun symbol of a forgotten southwestern Indian tribe gives the New Mexican flag a striking appearance. Its colors are the red and yellow of old Spain.

ARIZONA—1917—Arizona took its flag from one originally flown by the battleship *Arizona*, sunk at Pearl Harbor in 1941. Ironically, the banner shows the rays of the setting sun, while the *Arizona* was sunk by a nation whose flag represents the rising sun.

ALASKA—1927—Resulting from a public school contest conducted by the American Legion, The Alaska flag was designed by a 13-year-old orphan boy. He described the North Star in his design as standing "for the future State of Alaska."

HAWAII—1898—The Hawaiian flag, though not adopted as its Territorial flag until the annexation in 1898, was originally designed for King Kamehameha I in 1816. The stripes stand for the eight major islands, while the British Union Jack is included as a reminder of Captain Vancouver, who on his voyage around the world in 1794, gave Kamehameha a British flag.

DISTRICT OF COLUMBIA—1938—Until this flag was adopted the District of Columbia had no official flag other than that carried by the District Militia.

STATE MOTTO: All For Our Country
STATE BIRD: Blue Bird
STATE FLOWER: Sagebrush

NEVADA
Admitted to the Union in 1864

FOR FURTHER INFORMATION WRITE:

- Intermountain Region
  324 25th Street
  Ogden, Utah 84401

- Nevada Fish and Game Commission
  P.O. Box 678
  Reno, Nevada 89504

- Nevada Department of Economic Development
  Carson City, Nevada 89701

Nevada is the seventh largest state with the second smallest population. Twenty minutes from the clatter of Reno and Las Vegas, the only sound is wind brushing across miles of sage. Not far above alkaline deserts, ski trails hairpin down forested mountainsides. While the skeletal buildings of old mining towns stare back at their boom-and-bust yesterdays, students and ideas at the University of Nevada maintain a steady tread toward tomorrow.

The first official explorations were those of Captain John C. Fremont, in 1843-45. The discovery of gold at Carson City in 1850 only began a long overturning of gold and silver throughout the state, resulting in a more stable economy. Nevada became a state in 1864, mainly because two more votes were needed to propose the 13th amendment abolishing slavery.

Nevada's greatest boom was the legalization of gambling in 1931. Along with the liberalization of the marriage and divorce laws, this legislation paved the way for the state's becoming one of the busiest all-year resorts in the country.

Except for its northeast corner, Nevada lies within the Great Basin. Rivers here do not reach the sea, but flow inward and evaporate in alkaline sinks.

Nevada produces crops of alfalfa, hay, wheat, barley, plus potatoes, sugar beets, orchard fruits and cantaloupe. Cattle and sheep graze on more than 50 million acres.

Although mineral production has declined in the past several years, it is still a multimillion dollar source of income.

Ruby Mountains, Elko County

treasure trails / page 117

Key:
① relates to number 1 on the following page.

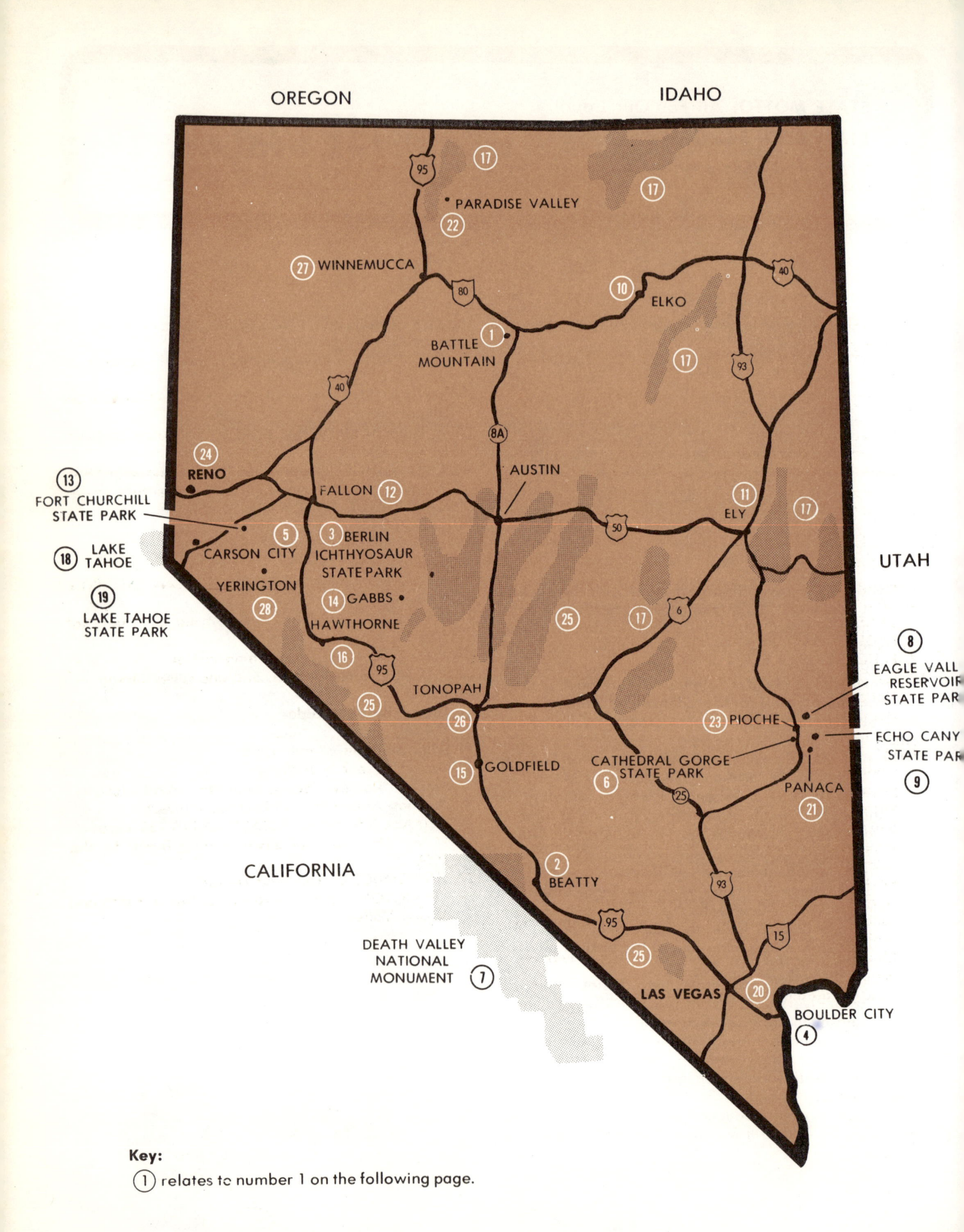

page 118 / treasure trails

NEVADA POINTS OF INTEREST

1. BATTLE MOUNTAIN - open copper mining in nearby Copper Canyon
2. BEATTY - picturesque mining town in Amargosa River Valley
3. BERLIN-ICHTHYOSAUR STATE PARK - historic sites
4. BOULDER CITY
   Hoover Dam, one of the highest dams ever constructed and greatest engineering project in the world;
   Lake Mead National Recreation Area
5. CARSON CITY
   Genoa, first permanent settlement of Nevada;
   Virginia City, historical ghost town;
   Gold Hill, historical sites;
   Bowers Mansion, museum and county park
6. CATHEDRAL GORGE STATE PARK - 1,608 acres
7. DEATH VALLEY NATIONAL MONUMENT
8. EAGLE VALLEY RESERVOIR STATE PARK
9. ECHO CANYON STATE PARK
10. ELKO
    National Basque Festival, held annually;
    Hunting and fishing area;
    Northeastern Nevada Museum
11. ELY
    Liberty Copper Pit, one of the world's largest open pit mines;
    Ward Charcoal Ovens, historic state monument, Site of six 30-foot high stone ovens, built 1870;
    Wheeler Peak: Lehman Caves National Monument, colorful formations of limestone
12. FALLON
    Agricultural center for western Nevada;
    Lahontan Dam Reservoir, first major reclamation project;
    Churchill County Museum, National Award winning historical museum;
    Sand Mountain, U.S. Naval Air Station
13. FORT CHURCHILL STATE PARK - historic sites
14. GABBS - Reptile fossils
15. GOLDFIELD - famed gold and silver mining town of early 1900
16. HAWTHORNE - site of U.S. Naval Ammunition Depot
17. HUMBOLDT NATIONAL FOREST - 5 million acres of forest reserve
18. LAKE TAHOE - clear deep blue waters, 1/3 in Nevada, remainder in California, recreation center
19. LAKE TAHOE STATE PARK
20. LAS VEGAS
    Entertainment capital of the world;
    University of Nevada;
    Valley of Fire State Park, Elephant Rock Formation
21. PANACA - Cathedral Gorge Formations, unusual clay formations
22. PARADISE VALLEY - ranching center
23. PIOCHE - center for lead, zinc, and silver mining
24. RENO
    University of Nevada;
    Mackey School of Mines;
    Atmospherium Planetarium;
    Desert Research Institute;
    Washoe County Library, beautiful architecture;
    Harrahs Automobile Collection, museum
25. TOIYABE NATIONAL FOREST - 3,118,966 acres
26. TONOPAH - start of silver mining boom in the 1900's
27. WINNEMUCCA - ranching center
28. YERINGTON - noted rich ranching area of Smith and Mason Valleys

treasure trails / page 119

Reno

Las Vegas Strip

Lake Tahoe

Virginia City

Photographs furnished by Nevada Dept. of Economic Development.

Valley of Fire, State Park, Clark County

Hoover Dam

page 120 / treasure trails

STATE MOTTO: Live Free Or Die
STATE BIRD: The Purple Finch
STATE FLOWER: The Purple Lilac

NEW HAMPSHIRE
Admitted to the Union in 1788

FOR FURTHER INFORMATION WRITE:

- Department of Resources and Economic Development
  Concord, New Hampshire 03301

- New Hampshire Fish & Game Department
  Concord, New Hampshire 03301

- U.S. Travel Service
  Liaison Officer,
  New Hampshire Office of Vacation Travel
  Box 856
  Concord, New Hampshire 03301

New Hampshire was first settled in 1623 by David Thompson at Odiorne's Point, Rye Beach. On January 5, 1776 a provisional constitution was adopted, the first by any of the states, and before the Continental Congress recommended such action in May, 1776. John Langdon and Nicholas Gilman signed the Federal Constitution for New Hampshire, which was the ninth and decisive state to ratify it, on June 21, 1788.

In the early nineteenth century, farming, fishing and lumbering were the chief sources of income but were gradually replaced by manufacturing, chiefly of textiles and shoes. Turnpikes, locks and canals on the Merrimack River to connect with the Middlesex Canal, and then railroads provided the means of transportation. Interest in the White Mountains, which increased after the Civil War, attracted many tourists. Anti-slavery and temperance organizations were formed the first part of the nineteenth century and the state had a prohibition law in 1855. The second half of the century was marked by industrial expansion, the growth of cities, more state responsibility for public health and public education, and better means of communication and transportation.

A cotton mill established at New Ipswich about 1804, the introduction of a power loom in 1819, and the opening of a shoe factory at Weare in 1823, marked the beginning of expanded employment opportunities for New Hampshire residents and the start of the largest cotton industry in the world.

At summer's end the spectacular autumn foliage lures visitors from all over the nation. Hunting and fishing is also famous.

Silver Cascade, Crawford Notch, New Hampshire.

treasure trails / page 121

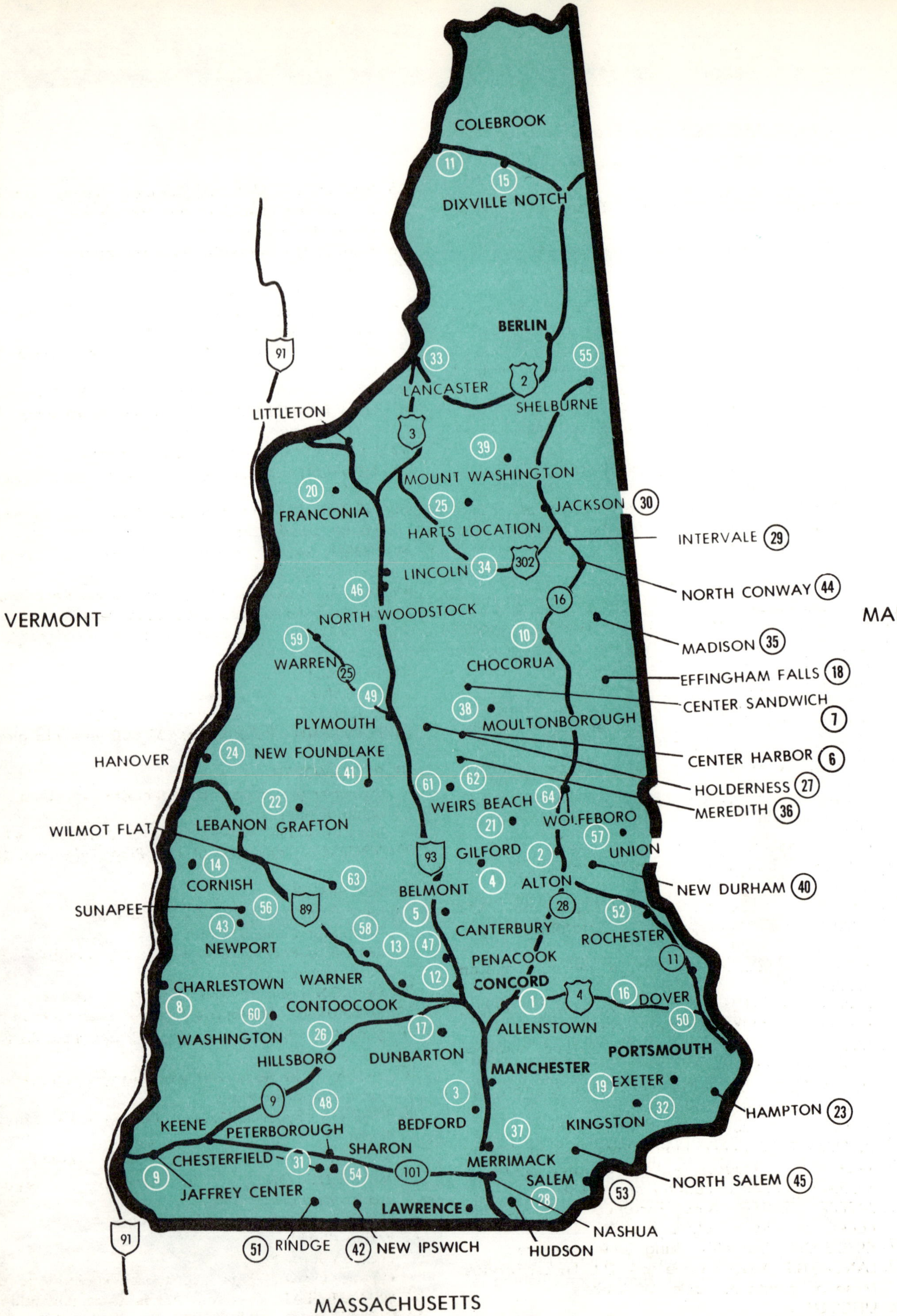
COLEBROOK
11
15
DIXVILLE NOTCH
BERLIN
91
33
55
2
LANCASTER
SHELBURNE
LITTLETON
3
39
MOUNT WASHINGTON
20
FRANCONIA
25
JACKSON 30
HARTS LOCATION
INTERVALE 29
LINCOLN
34
302
NORTH CONWAY 44
46
16
VERMONT
NORTH WOODSTOCK
MAINE
59
10
MADISON 35
WARREN
25
CHOCORUA
EFFINGHAM FALLS 18
49
CENTER SANDWICH
7
38
PLYMOUTH
MOULTONBOROUGH
HANOVER
24
NEW FOUNDLAKE
CENTER HARBOR 6
41
61
62
HOLDERNESS 27
22
WEIRS BEACH
64
MEREDITH 36
WILMOT FLAT
LEBANON
GRAFTON
21
WOLFEBORO
57
UNION
93
GILFORD
2
14
CORNISH
63
4
ALTON
NEW DURHAM 40
BELMONT
28
SUNAPEE
56
89
5
52
43
58
CANTERBURY
NEWPORT
13
47
ROCHESTER
PENACOOK
11
CHARLESTOWN
WARNER
12
CONCORD
16
1
4
DOVER
8
CONTOOCOOK
60
50
17
ALLENSTOWN
WASHINGTON
26
HILLSBORO
DUNBARTON
PORTSMOUTH
MANCHESTER
19
EXETER
9
48
3
32
HAMPTON 23
KEENE
PETERBOROUGH
BEDFORD
37
KINGSTON
SHARON
CHESTERFIELD
31
54
101
MERRIMACK
9
SALEM
NORTH SALEM 45
JAFFREY CENTER
28
53
LAWRENCE
NASHUA
91
51 RINDGE
42 NEW IPSWICH
HUDSON
MASSACHUSETTS

Key:

(1) relates to number 1 on the following page.

NEW HAMPSHIRE POINTS OF INTEREST

1. ALLENSTOWN
   Mary Baker Eddy's Birthplace, founder of Christian Science;
   Bear Brook State Park, audibon center
2. ALTON - Alton Bay, vacation center
3. BEDFORD - Horace Greeley Birthplace
4. BELMONT - Schuller Million Dollar Museum, medieval arms and armor, palace furnishings
5. CANTERBURY - Shaker Village & Museum
6. CENTER HARBOR - New Hampshire Music Festival
7. CENTER SANDWICH - Ayotte's Designery, handweaving studio
8. CHARLESTOWN - Old Fort #4, built 1740
9. CHESTERFIELD
   Antique Carriage & Sleigh Museum;
   Museum of Dolls & Toys
10. CHOCORUA - Old Village Barn, historical
11. COLEBROOK - State Fish Hatchery, salmon and brook trout farm
12. CONCORD
    New Hampshire Historical Society;
    Rumford Press
13. CONTOOCOOK - Mildred I. Reid Writers Colony
14. CORNISH - Saint Gaudens National Historic Site, home of Augustus Saint Gaudens, 1848
15. DIXVILLE NOTCH - State Reservation, scenic
16. DOVER - Woodman Institute, historical articles
17. DUNBARTON - Pinecroft, Juniper Ridge Fabrics, handweaving, custom clothing
18. EFFINGHAM FALLS - The Textile House, exclusive fabrics
19. EXETER - Exeter Historic Houses
20. FRANCONIA
    Cannon Mountain Tramway & Ski Area;
21. GILFORD - Gunstock Recreation Area, leading ski area
22. GRAFTON - Ruggles Mine, first Mica mine, 1803
23. HAMPTON - Winnacunnett Plantation, historic restoration, 1638
24. HANOVER - Dartmouth College, museum, Indian display
25. HARTS LOCATION - Bemis Museum, colonial furnishings, White Mountain books
26. HILLSBORO - Franklin Pierce Homestead, home of 14th president
27. HOLDERNESS - Squam Lakes Science Center, 250 acres of natural woodland
28. HUDSON - Benson's Wild Animal Farm
29. INTERVALE - Abenaki Indian Shop, Indian display
30. JACKSON - Wildcat Valley Country Store & Museum, authentic country store, 1880
31. JAFFREY CENTER - Amos Fortune Forum, meeting house, lectures in July & August
32. KINGSTON - Darrell's Thing, junk sculpture
33. LANCASTER - Weeks State Park, U.S. Forest Service Museum, estate of John W. Weeks
34. LINCOLN
    Loon Mountain Summer Theater;
    Clark's Trading Post, museum
35. MADISON - Madison Boulder, largest glacially transported boulder on the North American continent
36. MEREDITH - Meredith Auto Museum
37. MERRIMACK - Anheuser-Bush Brewery, famous Clydesdale Horses
38. MOULTONBOROUGH - Castle In The Clouds, 7 million dollar estate, built 1910
39. MOUNT WASHINGTON - Bretton Woods Cog Railway
40. NEW DURHAM - Powder Hill Fish Hatchery
41. NEW FOUNDLAKE - Wellington State Park, bird sanctuary
42. NEW IPSWICH - Baret House, mansion
43. NEWPORT - Clock Museum, 400, 16-17 century clocks
44. NORTH CONWAY - Echo Lake State Park, Cathedral Lodge, scenic area
45. NORTH SALEM - Mystery Hill, sacrificial temples, from 2,000 B.C.
46. NORTH WOODSTOCK - Lost River Reservation, Paradise Falls, nature gardens, museum
47. PENACOOK - Hannah Duston Monument, to pioneer woman
48. PETERBOROUGH
    Tewksbury's art studio;
    MacDowell Colony, colony for artists
49. PLYMOUTH - Polar Caves, 50,000 year old glacial caves
50. PORTSMOUTH
    Strawberry Banke, architectural museum, 30 colonial houses;
    Isles of Shoals, ocean trip to historic Star Island
51. RINDGE - Cathedral of the Pines, National War Memorial
52. ROCHESTER
    New English Art Gallery & Studio;
    Rochester Music Theater
53. SALEM - Rockingham Park, thoroughbred and harness racing
54. SHARON - Sharon Arts Center, art classes
55. SHELBURNE - Shelburne Birches, scenic grove
56. SUNAPEE - Mt. Sunapee State Park, gondola lifts, ski area
57. UNION - Poke About Hill, woodturning mill arts and crafts demonstrations
58. WARNER - Bygones Museum Post Office & General Store
59. WARREN - Morse Museum, mounted animals
60. WASHINGTON - Washington museum, transportation
61. WEIRS - Animal Forest Park, loose animals
62. WEIRS BEACH
    Endicott Rock Park;
    Funspot Indian Village, reproductions of village life
63. WILMOT FLAT - Freedom Acres, jams and jellies
64. WOLFEBORO - Clark House, early American furnishings

treasure trails / page 123

Lake Winnipesaukee from Alton Bay, New Hampshire, with a view of Mt. Washington Boat.

The Governor John Langdon Mansion, one of many elegant old homes in Portsmouth, New Hamshire, was built in 1784.

This is the celebrated 100 year old Mt. Washington Cog Railroad with an excursion train huffin' and puffin'.

page 124 / treasure trails

STATE MOTTO: Liberty And Prosperity
STATE BIRD: Eastern Goldfinch
STATE FLOWER: Purple Violet

NEW JERSEY
Admitted to the Union in 1787

FOR FURTHER INFORMATION WRITE:

- New Jersey Bureau of Parks
  P.O. Box 1420
  Trenton, New Jersey 08625

- Division of Fish and Game
  Labor and Industry Building
  P.O. Box 1809
  Trenton, New Jersey 08625

- State Promotion Office
  P.O. Box 400
  Trenton, New Jersey 08625

New Jersey, compact in land size, provides a wide diversity in terrain and industry. It is located on the Atlantic Ocean, bordered on the northeast by New York, on the south by the Delaware Bay and on the west by the Delaware River separating it from Pennsylvania and Delaware.

New Jersey was originally settled by the Dutch. In 1664, it became a British colony. It was named after the Isle of Jersey, which was governed by Sir George Carteret. John Fenwick purchased part of Berkeley's share in the western part of the state to begin the first Quaker colony in America.

During the Revolutionary War, New Jersey's geographical location between New York and Philadelphia, made it the battleground for the British and Continental Armies. About one hundred engagements were fought on New Jersey soil.

Today, manufacturing is the most important industry in the state. Principal industries include: pharmaceuticals, clothing, textiles, metal goods, stone clay and glassware and medical instruments.

Rich in mineral and clay deposits, particularly zinc and iron, New Jersey also has extensive quarries that yield limestone, granite and sandstone.

The nickname, "Garden State" is indicative of the variety of agricultural products offered by New Jersey. Vegetable and fruit growing along with dairy and poultry farming make up the backbone of the state's agriculture industry.

New Jersey is also rich in porgy, fluke, sea bass, bluefish, cod, clams and oysters. Numerous rivers, streams and mountain lakes make camping, hunting, and skiing great fun in New Jersey.

Rutgers—the state university located in New Brunswick, New Jersey.

treasure trails / page 125

NEW JERSEY MAP

NEW YORK

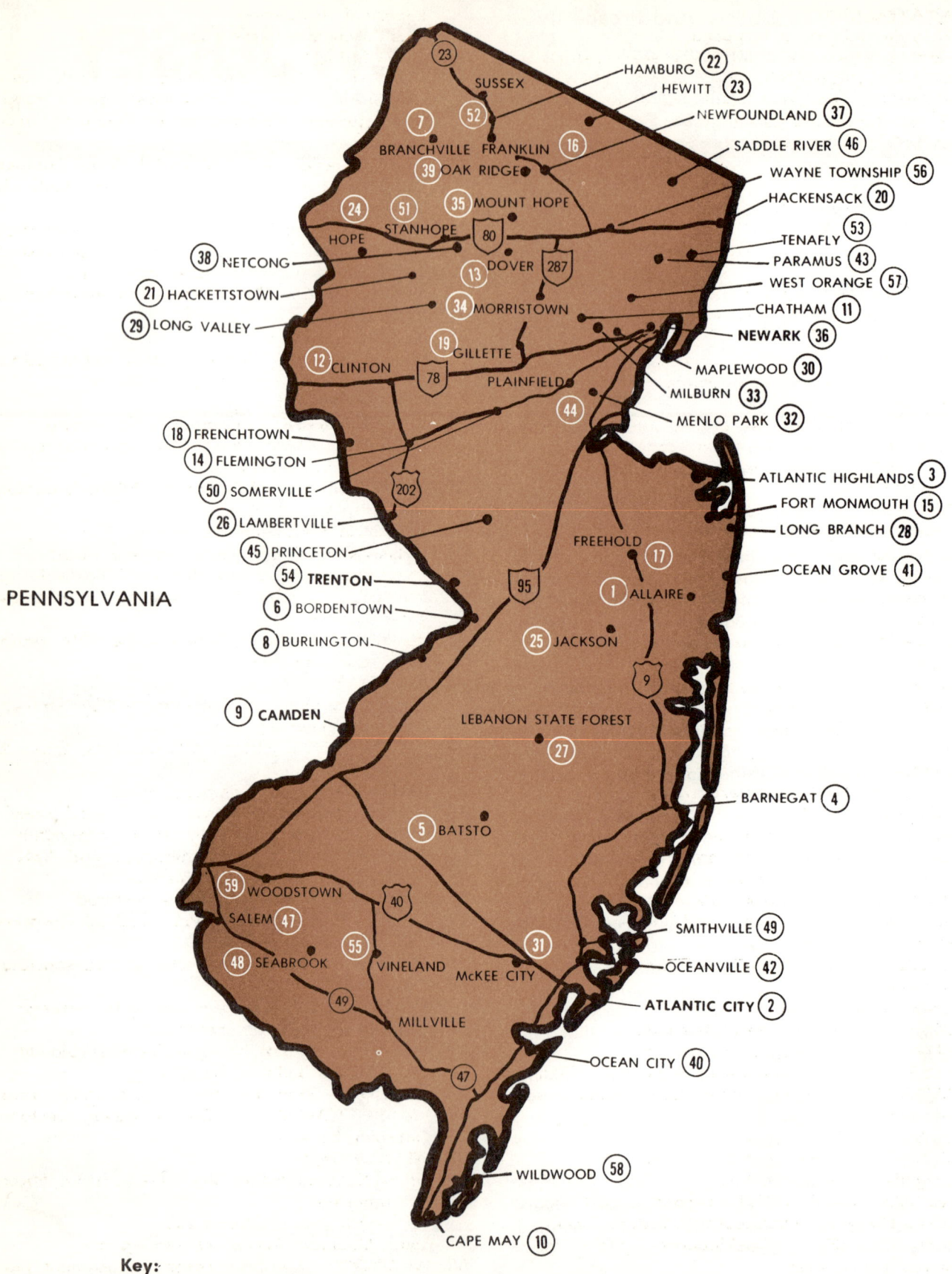

- ② 23
- SUSSEX ⑤2
- HAMBURG ㉒
- HEWITT ㉓
- ⑦ BRANCHVILLE
- FRANKLIN ⑯
- NEWFOUNDLAND ㊲
- ㊴ OAK RIDGE
- SADDLE RIVER ㊻
- WAYNE TOWNSHIP ㊶
- ㉔ ㊶ ㉟ MOUNT HOPE
- HACKENSACK ⑳
- STANHOPE ⑧⓪
- TENAFLY ㊼
- ㊳ NETCONG HOPE
- ⑬ DOVER ②87
- PARAMUS ㊸
- ㉑ HACKETTSTOWN
- ㉞ MORRISTOWN
- WEST ORANGE ㊼
- ㉙ LONG VALLEY
- CHATHAM ⑪
- ⑫ CLINTON
- ⑲ GILLETTE
- NEWARK ㊱
- ⑦8 PLAINFIELD
- MAPLEWOOD ㉚
- MILBURN ㉝
- ㊹
- MENLO PARK ㉜
- ⑱ FRENCHTOWN
- ⑭ FLEMINGTON
- ATLANTIC HIGHLANDS ③
- ㊿ SOMERVILLE
- ②02
- FORT MONMOUTH ⑮
- ㉖ LAMBERTVILLE
- LONG BRANCH ㉘
- ㊺ PRINCETON
- FREEHOLD ⑰
- OCEAN GROVE ㊶
- ㊼ TRENTON
- ⑨⑤ ALLAIRE ①
- ⑥ BORDENTOWN
- ⑧ BURLINGTON
- ㉕ JACKSON
- ⑨
- ⑨ CAMDEN
- LEBANON STATE FOREST
- ㉗
- BARNEGAT ④
- ⑤ BATSTO
- ㊾ WOODSTOWN
- ④0
- SALEM ㊼
- SMITHVILLE ㊾
- ㊽ SEABROOK
- ㉟ VINELAND
- OCEANVILLE ㊷
- ㉛ McKEE CITY
- **ATLANTIC CITY** ②
- ㊾ MILLVILLE
- OCEAN CITY ㊵
- ㊼
- WILDWOOD ㊽
- CAPE MAY ⑩

PENNSYLVANIA

Key:
① relates to number 1 on the following page.

page 126 / treasure trails

NEW JERSEY POINTS OF INTEREST

1. ALLAIRE - Allaire State Park, restored village and iron works
2. ATLANTIC CITY
   Absecon Lighthouse, restored;
   Piers, amusements, boardwalks, shore resorts
3. ATLANTIC HIGHLANDS - Twin Lights, light towers
4. BARNEGAT - Barnegat Lighthouse State Park, site of 200 shipwrecks during sailing days
5. BATSTO - Wharton State Forest, iron works sawmill, grist mill
6. BORDENTOWN
   Patience Wright House, home of first American sculptor;
   Thomas Paine House, home of famous American writer
7. BRANCHVILLE - Stokes Forest, scenic country
8. BURLINGTON - Birthplace of James Fenimore Cooper, author
9. CAMDEN
   Cherry Hill Mall, shopping center;
   Garden State Race Track;
   Home of Walt Whitman, original furnishings;
   Harleigh Cemetery, Whitman's tomb
10. CAPE MAY - resort area
11. CHATHAM
    The Pottery Shop (Old Bonnelle House), in operation;
    Nature Center
12. CLINTON
    Hunterdon County Arts Center, restored stone mills;
    Hunterdon Hills Playhouse, theatre
13. DOVER - Picatinny Arsenal
14. FLEMINGTON
    Lorlo's Glass Shop, glass blowing displays;
    Flemington Cut Glass Company, displays
15. FORT MONMOUTH - U.S. Army Signal Corps Museum, communications devices
16. FRANKLIN - Franklin Mineral Dump, rock museum
17. FREEHOLD - Freehold Raceway, harness racing
18. FRENCHTOWN - Kerr Chickeries Corporation, tours
19. GILLETTE - Phifer's Animal Farm, training center for stage, movie and T.V. animals
20. HACKENSACK - Zabriskie (Von Steuben) House, occupied by British and Americans in Revolutionary War
21. HACKETTSTOWN - State Fish Hatchery, tours
22. HAMBURG
    Great Gorge Ski Area;
    Gingerbread Castle, fairytale castle
23. HEWITT - Greenwood Lake, fishing
24. HOPE - Land of Make Believe, displays for children
25. JACKSON - Great Adventure, safari and amusement park
26. LAMBERTVILLE
    Music Circus, theatre under a tent;
    Coryell's Ferry, scenic trip
27. LEBANON STATE FOREST - second largest
28. LONG BRANCH - Monmouth Park Race Track
29. LONG VALLEY - Hacklebarney State Park, recreational center
30. MAPLEWOOD - Deer Preserve, tame deer
31. McKEE CITY - Atlantic City Racecourse
32. MENLO PARK - Edison State Park, Edison Memorial Tower, Edison's early inventions
33. MILBURN
    Papermill Playhouse;
    South Mountain Reservation
34. MORRISTOWN
    Morristown National Historical Park, commemorates encampment of Washington's troups;
    Ford Mansion, museum at Washington's headquarters;
    Jocky Hollow, site Continental Army camped;
    Fort Nonsense, remains of fort built by Washington's men, 1777;
    Wick House and Farm, restored and refurnished;
    McCullock Hall Museum, restored and refurnished;
    Seaton-Hackney Stable, horseback riding
35. MOUNT HOPE - Mount Hope Shammon Indians Mine, Inc., mine and quarry
36. NEWARK
    Newark Museum, historical and contemporary paintings, sculptures and planetarium;
    Anheuser-Busch brewery
37. NEWFOUNDLAND - Craigmur Lodge, skiing
38. NETCONG - Wild West City, reproduction of western frontier town
39. OAK RIDGE - Fairy Tale Forest, children's outdoor story displays
40. OCEAN CITY - commercial fishing
41. OCEAN GROVE - religious seashore resort
42. OCEANVILLE - Brigantine National Wildlife Refuge
43. PARAMUS - Garden State Plaza Civic Auditorium, entertainment
44. PLAINFIELD - Nathaniel Drake House, 18th century Early American style
45. PRINCETON
    Morven, residence of Governor of New Jersey;
    Princeton University
46. SADDLE RIVER - Trickers Water Gardens, America's oldest water garden
47. SALEM - H.J. Heinz Company, tours
48. SEABROOK—Seabrook Farms, frozen food plant
49. SMITHVILLE - restored 18th century community
50. SOMERVILLE - Old Dutch Parsonage and Wallace House, Dutch colonial architecture
51. STANHOPE - Waterloo Village, restored
52. SUSSEX - High Point State Park, highest elevation, park and campgrounds
53. TENAFLY - Greenbrook Sanctuary, bird sanctuary
54. TRENTON
    New Jersey State Museum, concerts, lectures;
    Old Barracks, colonial barracks;
    Trent House, oldest home in Trenton, colonial;
    State Capitol Building, battle flags
55. VINELAND - Vineland Speedway, sportscar races
56. WAYNE TOWNSHIP - Dey Mansion, restored Georgian home
57. WEST ORANGE
    Edison National Historic Site, Edison's home, library and laboratory;
    Turtleback Zoo, children's zoo;
    South Mountain Arena, ice skating rink
58. WILDWOOD - seashore resort, amusement park
59. WOODSTOWN - Richman's Ice Cream Company, tours

treasure trails / page 127

A picturesque country scene—Warren County farm.

Port Newark—a large commercial port (ship, rail, truck and barge traffic in international trade).

Horse farm—Monmouth County.

page 128 / treasure trails

STATE MOTTO: It Grows As It Goes
STATE BIRD: Roadrunner
STATE FLOWER: Yucca

NEW MEXICO
Admitted to the Union in 1912

FOR FURTHER INFORMATION WRITE:

- Department of Game and Fish
  State Capitol
  Santa Fe, New Mexico 87501

- New Mexico Tourist Division
  State Capitol Building
  Santa Fe, New Mexico 87501

New Mexico has had a long and eventful history. It was the scene of a very large population in prehistoric times, and many Indians made it their home before the Spaniards came in 1541. A sizable number of Hispanic people made it their home when the Anglos came in 1846.

The Spanish influence is evident in a variety of phases of New Mexican life. From the publication of Spanish-language newspapers and magazines to Spanish-language plays and motion pictures. For many years the business of the New Mexican government was carried on in both English and Spanish. But today, only English is used for official government business. The courts must still use an interpreter in the event of a defendant or juror who does not understand English.

New Mexico is the fifth largest state in the Union. Yet within its boundaries live only a million people, a population so uncrowded that there is a square mile of land for every eight people.

Sunshine, dry climate and a scenic wonderland are the lures that bring people to New Mexico to vacation and to live.

Among the valuable natural resources in New Mexico are oil and gas, with their development concentrated in the southeast and northwest sections. Potash, found in the Carlsbad vicinity, ranks second while copper, in the Santa Rita district stands third.

Giant ranches are probably more common in New Mexico than elsewhere with several running in excess of 100,000 acres.

Here is the "Great Dome" in the Carlsbad Caverns near Carlsbad, New Mexico. The Caverns are the world's largest and one of the wonders of the world.

treasure trails / page 129

Key:

① relates to number 1 on the following page.

page 130 / treasure trails

NEW MEXICO POINTS OF INTEREST

1. **ALAMOGORDO**
   White Sands National Monument, rare gypsum deserts;
   Guided Caravan Tours, tour to Trinity Site;
   The Petroglyphs, 800 years old
2. **ALBUQUERQUE**
   Old Town, early Albuquerque, 1706;
   Ernie Pyle House, residence of war correspondent killed in World War II;
   Church of San Felipe de Neri, stands as originally built;
   Madonna of the Trail Monument, honoring pioneer women;
   Rio Grande Park, baseball stadium, zoo
3. **AZTEC** - Aztec Ruins National Monument, Pueblo ruins
4. **CAPITAN** - Home of Smokey the Bear
5. **CAPULIN** - Capulin Mountain National Monument, extinct volcanic cinder cone
6. **CARLSBAD** - Carlsbad Museum, exhibits of potash and other minerals, archeological relics;
   Carlsbad Caverns National Park, one of the world's largest caves
7. **CARRIZOZO** - Valley of Fires State Park, ancient lava flow
8. **CHACO CANYON NATIONAL MONUMENT** - ruins of 12 major cities
9. **CIBOLA NATIONAL FOREST** - Sandia Peak Tramway and Ski Area, museum, gardens
10. **CIMARRON** - Raton Pass, follows original Santa Fe Trail
11. **CLAYTON**
    Fort Jordon, reproduction of frontier stockade;
    Clayton Lake State Park, fishing
12. **COLUMBUS** - City of Rocks State Park, unusual rock formations
13. **ESPANOLA**
    Ghost Ranch Museum;
    Beaver National Forest;
    Puye Cliff Dweller and Communal House Ruins, example of Ancient Pajaritan culture
14. **FORT SUMNER**
    Grave of Billy the Kid;
    Alamogordo Lake State Park, recreational area
15. **GALLUP** - Museum of Indian Arts and Crafts
16. **GRANTS** - Mount Taylor, nearly 12,000 feet
17. **HURLEY** - The Kennecott Copper Corporation, reduction plant, mill and smelter
18. **LAS CRUCES** - White Sands Missile Range, research center for Apollo moon projects
19. **LINCOLN** - The Old Courthouse, site where Billy the Kid was held in 1881 and from which he escaped, restored museum
20. **LOS ALAMOS**
    Science Museum, research programs dating from the origination of nations first nuclear weapons;
    Bandelier National Monument, unique man-made cave rooms
21. **MESCALERO** - Mescalero Apache Reservation
22. **MORIARITY** - Longhorn Ranch and Museum of the Old West, includes country store, Wells Fargo Office, old automobiles
23. **MOUNTAINAIR**
    ABO State Monument, ruins of a Spanish mission and an Indian pueblo;
    Quarai State Monument, ruins of The Mission Church of the Immaculate Conception, built in 1630
24. **PECOS** - Pecos National Monument, Pueblo ruins and crumbling walls of old Pecos Mission
25. **PORTALES** - Oasis State Park, remains of five mammoths, discovered in a gravel pit
26. **RED RIVER** - Jeep tours to ghost towns and old mines
27. **ROSWELL**
    Bitter Lake National Wildlife Refuge, contains over 200 species of birds;
    Roswell Museum and Art Center, historical, archeological and geological displays;
    Bluewater Lake State Park, recreational center;
    Bottomless Lakes State Park, recreational center
28. **SAN ANTONIO** - birthplace of Conrad Hilton
29. **SANTA FE**
    Capitol Building, Spanish Colonial architecture;
    Cathedral of St. Francis of Assisi;
    Museum of New Mexico, units dealing with various phases of southwestern culture;
    Hall of the Modern Indian, utensils and handicrafts of contemporary Indians;
    Cristo Rey Church, largest adobe structure in the U.S.;
    Santa Fe National Cemetery;
    Scottish Rite Temple, replica of the Alhambra in Granada, Spain;
    Our Lady of Light Church, spiral staircase constructed without nails or visible support
30. **SANTA RITA** - open-pit copper mine
31. **SHIPROCK** - Four Corners Monument, only place in the country where four states meet
32. **SILVER CITY** - Gila Cliff Dwellings National Monument, prehistoric dwellings
33. **SOCORRO** - San Miguel Church, erected in 1620
34. **TAOS**
    Harwood Foundation, display of early Tao artists;
    Kit Carson House and Museum, home of the famous frontiersman, 1843-1868;
    Kit Carson Memorial State Park, cemetery where Kit Carson was buried;
    Millicent Rogers Foundation, authentic Spanish, Indian and pioneer articles;
    The Stables Gallery, art gallery;
    Pueblo De Taos, two terraced communal dwellings five stories high;
    Mission of St. Francis of Assisi, one of the Southwest's most splendid Spanish churches
35. **TUCUMCARI** - Tucumcari Historical Museum, displays Indian western frontier articles
36. **TRUTH OR CONSEQUENCES** - Caballo Lake State Park, recreational area
37. **ZUNI** - only surviving settlement of the Seven Cities of Cibola sought by Coronado in his quest for gold

These brave adventurers head downstream through the churning rapids of the Rio Grande in New Mexico.
Photographs furnished by New Mexico State Tourist Bureau.

The village of San Juan, on the banks of the Rio Grande near the site of San Gabriel is where New Mexico's first permanent Spanish settlement was established in 1598.

Pueblo Bonito, the "City of Mystery" was occupied long before Columbus reached the New World. The ruins are found in Chaco Canyon National Monument in northwestern New Mexico.

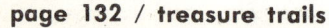

Frenchy's Cabin, once the abode of a mysterious recluse, is wedged in Dog Canyon near Alamogordo, New Mexico.

STATE MOTTO: Higher
STATE BIRD: Eastern Bluebird
STATE FLOWER: Rose

NEW YORK
Admitted to the Union in 1788

FOR FURTHER INFORMATION WRITE:

- Department of Parks & Recreation
  South Swan Street Building
  Empire Street Plaza
  Albany, New York 12223

- Department of Commerce
  99 Washington Avenue
  Albany, New York 12210

- Mrs. Cherry Sumner, Director
  Capital Guide Desk
  Albany, New York 12224

For years before the white men came to the area now known as New York State, the Iroquois Indians dominated that part of the country. In 1664 an English fleet took what was then called New Amsterdam, the name soon changed to New York since the area had been granted to the Duke of York, the brother of Charles II. Much Revolutionary action took place in New York, the British held it until the end of the war. After the new nation was formed, New York City was the nation's capital from 1789-1791. The opening of the Erie Canal in 1825 opened the western part of the state and other western areas to use as a commercial oasis. Soon New York City became the nation's financial center and for years its greatest metropolis.

The northeast is dominated by the circular Adirondack Mountains. Fertile river valleys, plains and coast land give a diversity of soils and types of vegetation. Lakes abound. The average temperature is about 45 degrees F. Precipitation is fairly uniform. The soil is typical of glacial area, having both shallow and deep top soil.

Residents of New York have enjoyed the highest standards of living in the world for many years, yet as late as 1968 over 13 per cent of the state's finances went to welfare. The percentage of people engaged in clerical and sales work exceeds all other states while farm works involve a much lower percentage. By 1840 New York City was the largest wholesale center in the country. Transportation is a major factor in New York's economy.

Luna Island, Niagara Falls.

treasure trails / page 133

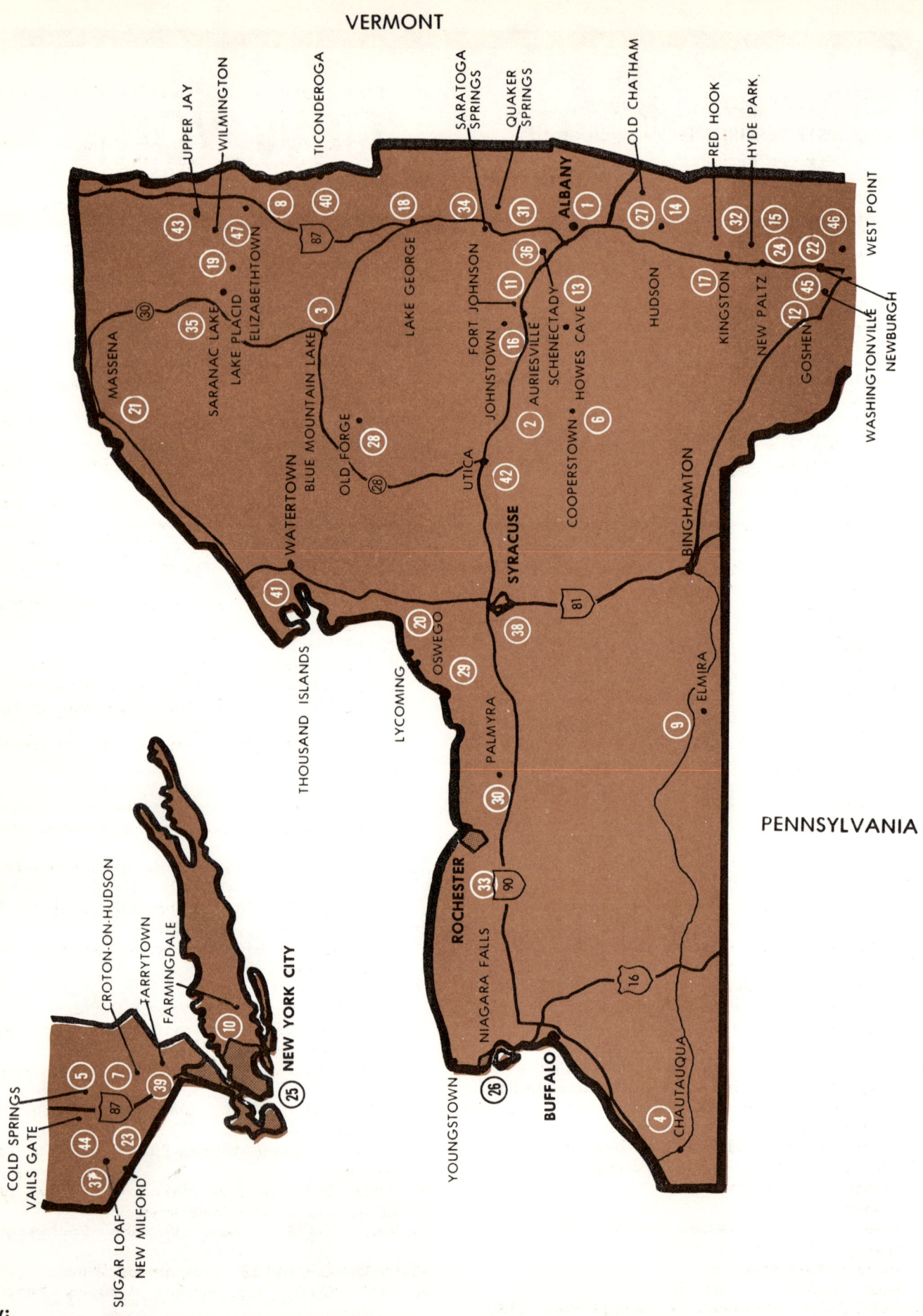

Key:
① relates to number 1 on the following page.

page 134 / treasure trails

NEW YORK POINTS OF INTEREST

1. ALBANY
   State Capitol Building, million dollar staircase;
2. AURIESVILLE - Auriesville Shrine, where Father Isaac Jogues was slain
3. BLUE MOUNTAIN LAKE - Adirondack Museum, exhibits of life in the Adirondacks
4. CHAUTAUQUA - Chautauqua Institute, drama, music and religious programs
5. COLD SPRING - Boscobel House, "Sound and Light" shown in summer
6. COOPERSTOWN
   Baseball Hall of Fame, mementos of game's immortals;
   Farmers' Museum, recreated village of 1790;
   Fenimore House, James Fenimore Cooper memorabilia;
   Busch Woodlands and Museum, featuring Clydesdale horses
7. CROTON-ON-HUDSON - Van Cortlandt Manor, furnished in 18th century style
8. ELIZABETHTOWN - Adirondack Center Museum, exhibits of early Adirondack life
9. ELMIRA
   National Soaring Museum, "soaring capital" of the United States;
   Mark Twain Study, Elmira College, where author wrote some of his works
10. FARMINGDALE - Old Bethpage Village, museum of rural life of the 1800's
11. FORT JOHNSON - Old Fort Johnson, built in 1749 by Sir William Johnson
12. GOSHEN - Hall of Fame of the Trotter, historic center for harness racing
13. HOWES CAVE - Howe Caverns, 200 feet underground, rides
14. HUDSON
    American Museum of Firefighting, one of the finest collections of memorabilia; Olana, castle-like home of F.E. Church, landscape artist
15. HYDE PARK
    Vanderbilt Mansion, 19th century home of Fredrick W. Vanderbilt;
    Roosevelt Home, home is as when Franklin Roosevelt lived
16. JOHNSTOWN - Johnson Hall, residence of British Superintendent of Indian Affairs
17. KINGSTON - Senate House and Museum, first meeting of New York State Senate, 1777
18. LAKE GEORGE
    Lake George, daily scenic trips aboard "Ticonderoga" and "The Mohican";
19. LAKE PLACID
    Olympic Arena, year-round sports area;
20. LYCOMING - Niagara Mohawk Progress Center, model of atomic power plant
21. MASSENA
    Eisenhower Lock, vessels passing through St. Lawrence Seaway;
    Antique Auto Museum;
    Boat trip down the canyon
22. NEWBURGH - Washington's Headquarters, 1782-1783, built 1750
23. NEW MILFORD - Sterling Forest Gardens, 125 acre garden
24. NEW PALTZ - Hasbrouck Memorial House, erected by French Huguenots, 1692-1712
25. NEW YORK CITY
    Rockefeller Center, 70th floor observatory;
    United Nations Headquarters, tours;
    American Museum of Natural History;
    Metropolitan Museum of Art;
    Empire State Building, observation areas on 86th and 102nd floors;
    Statue of Liberty
26. NIAGARA FALLS - Niagara Falls, one of the world's outstanding wonders
27. OLD CHATHAM - Shaker Museum, over 17,000 Shaker items
28. OLD FORGE - Enchanted Forest, re-created storybook characters
29. OSWEGO - Fort Ontario, dating to 1755, early English stronghold
30. PALMYRA - "America's Witness for Christ", early Mormon history
31. QUAKER SPRINGS - Saratoga National Historical Park, decisive American victory over British in 1777.
32. RED HOOK - Old Rhinebeck Aerodrome, antique airplanes and engines
33. ROCHESTER
    Highland Park, flower city, famed for lilacs;
    Campbell-Whittlesey House, period elegance;
    Eastman Kodak, Kodak Park Division and Hawkeye Works;
    George Eastman House, museum of photography and movies
34. SARATOGA SPRINGS
    Saratoga Race Track, nation's oldest;
35. SARANAC LAKE - Robert Louis Stevenson Cottage, in resort area
36. SCHENECTADY - Stockade Area, old building dates from the 1700's
37. SUGAR LOAF - Old Museum Village of Smith's Clove, 19th century America
38. SYRACUSE - French Fort, reproduction of Fort Ste. Marie de Gannentaha
39. TARRYTOWN
    Sunnyside, home of Washington Irving;
    Phillipsburg Manor, 18th century restoration, grist mill in use
40. TICONDEROGA - Fort Ticonderoga, built by French in 1755-58
41. THOUSAND ISLANDS - Boldt Castle, replica of German castle
42. UTICA - Munson-Williams-Proctor Institute, art exhibits
43. UPPER JAY - Land of Make-Believe, fairy tale village and western style town
44. VAILS GATE - New Windsor Cantonment,
45. WASHINGTONVILLE - Brotherhood Winery,
46. WEST POINT - U.S. Military Academy, chapel, museum
47. WILMINGTON - High Falls Gorge, scenic area

treasure trails / page 135

Visitors witness a demonstration of eighteenth century ordnance at Fort Ticonderoga.

Trophy Point, on the grounds of the United States Military Academy at West Point, overlooks Hudson River.

Water-powered grist mill at Philipsburg Manor in Tarrytown, trading center of a 90,000-acre complex.

United Nations Building in New York City.

Photographs furnished by New York State Department of Commerce.

page 136 / treasure trails

NORTH CAROLINA
Admitted to the Union in 1789

STATE MOTTO: To Be Rather Than To Seem
STATE BIRD: Cardinal
STATE FLOWER: Dogwood

FOR FURTHER INFORMATION WRITE:

- Forest Service
  Southern Region
  50 Seventh Street Northeast
  Atlanta, Georgia 30323

- North Carolina Wildlife
  Resources Commission
  P.O. Box 2919
  Raleigh, North Carolina 27602

- Travel and Promotion Division
  Department of Conservation & Development
  Raleigh, North Carolina 27611

The first attempt of English colonization of the area that is now North Carolina was in 1585. Carolina means "The Land of Charles," reflecting the fact that King Charles II of England gave the original land grants. In 1660 the English had their first permanent settlement in the area. North Carolina entered the Union in November, 1779 as the 12th state. In 1903 the "Air Age" was ushered in by Wilbur and Orville Wright with their first powered flight at Kill Devil Hills.

North Carolina is geographically three states since it has three distinct types of topography. The Appalachian highlands in the west as "The Blue Ridge and the Great Smoky Mountain Ranges" converge, is an area of unique beauty. There, also is the highest point in the Eastern U.S., Mount Mitchell, elevation 6,684 feet above sea level. East of the mountains is the Piedmont Plateau, the largest of the three geographic states. The third geographic state is the coastal area with the offshore Outer Banks and infamous Cape Hatteras (infamous for its violent weather and attendant hazard to ships). The extreme southeastern part of the state has a subtropical climate.

North Carolina has a diversity of terrains and climates. There are more than 3,000 square miles of inland water which tantalizes any fisherman.

North Carolina leads the southeastern states in manufacturing. The main industries are textiles, hosiery, tobacco products, furniture, wood products, electrical machinery, and chemicals. Despite this, the economy is basically agricultural. Tobacco, corn, cotton, fruits and vegetables are grown in this area and poultry and livestock are raised. Commercial fishing also plays a part in the economy. A portion of the economy is supported by the mining of clays, feldspar, mica, phosphates, sand gravel and stone. Finally, part of North Carolina's economy is supported by tourism.

Linville Gorge in Pisgah National Forest near Linville, North Carolina.

page 138 / treasure trails

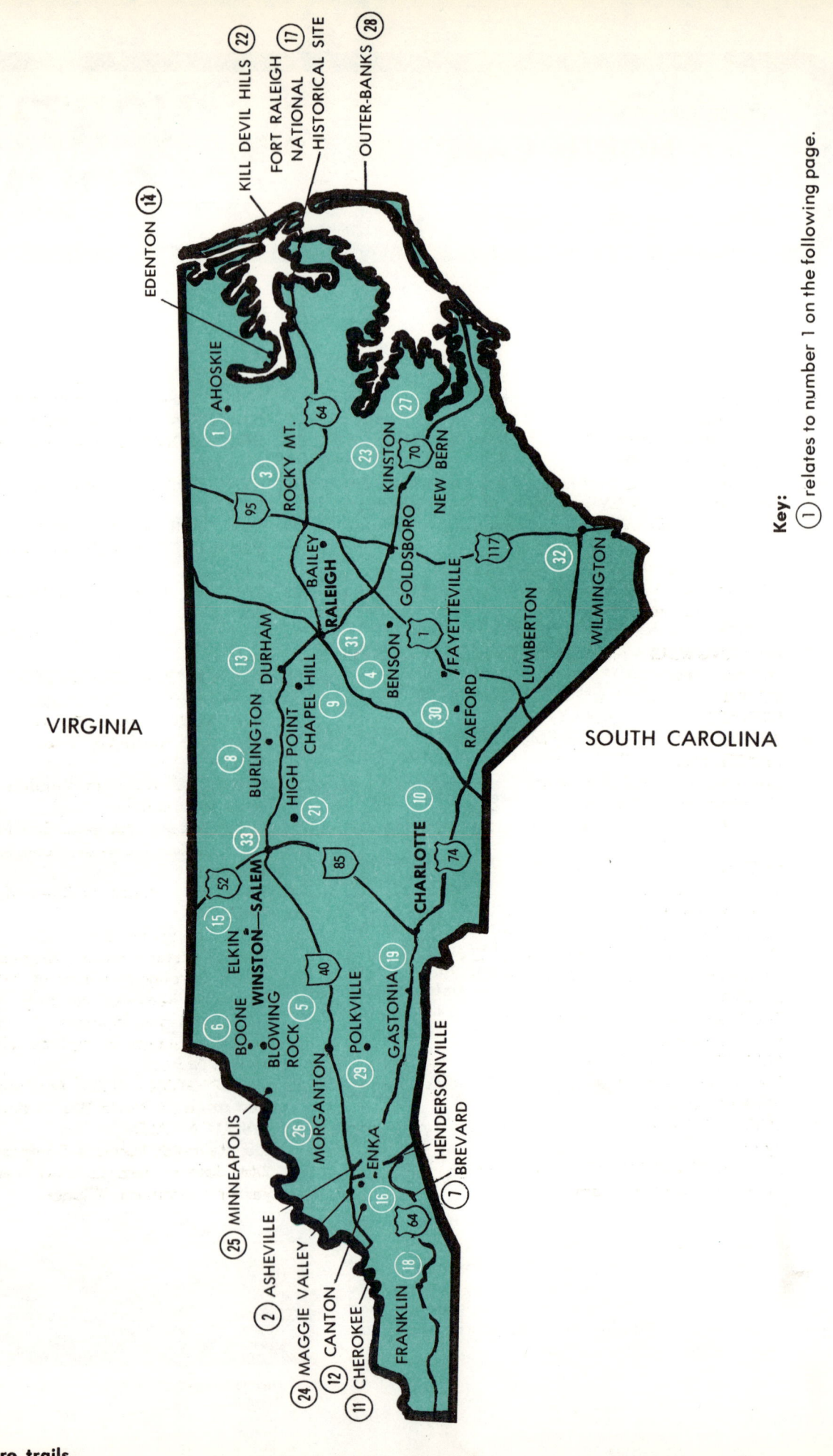

NORTH CAROLINA POINTS OF INTEREST

1. AHOSKIE - Tobacco Market
2. ASHEVILLE
   Mt. Mitchell State Park, highest elevation in eastern United States;
   Biltmore House & Gardens, Vanderbilt Mansion;
   Zabulon B. Vance Birthplace, Civil War Governor;
   Thomas Wolfe Memorial, novelist's childhood home;
   Colburn Mineral Museum;
   Biltmore Industries, old style weaving and finishing
3. BAILEY - Country Doctor Museum
4. BENSON - "Sweet Potato Capital of the World"
5. BLOWING ROCK - Tweetsie Railroad, narrow gauge railroad, restored
6. BOONE - "Horn in the West", Daniel Boone drama
7. BREVARD - Olin Industries, paper
8. BURLINGTON - Burlington Mills, textiles
9. CHAPEL HILL
   University of North Carolina;
   Morehead Planetarium
10. CHARLOTTE - Mint Museum of Art, remodeled U.S. Mint
11. CHEROKEE
    Ocenaluftee Indian Village, culture 200 years old;
    Frontierland Cherokee, western town replica;
    "Unto Those Hills" Indian history drama;
    Qualla Boundary, Eastern Band Cherokee home
12. CANTON - Champion Fibers, paper
13. DURHAM
    The Chapel of Duke University;
    Duke University
14. EDENTON - Site of North Carolina's "Tea Party"
15. ELKIN - Chatham Manufacturing Company, largest blanket factory in world
16. ENKA - Enka Manufacturing Company, rayon and nylon
17. FORT RALEIGH NATIONAL HISTORICAL SITE
    "The Lost Colony" drama
18. FRANKLIN - Cowee Ruby Mine
19. GASTONIA - Textile Center of the World
20. HENDERSONVILLE - General Electric Manufacturing Company
21. HIGH POINT - Southern Furniture Exposition Building
22. KILL DEVIL HILLS - Wright Brothers National Memorial, first flight of power driven airplane, 1903
23. KINSTON - Du Pont Manufacturing Plant, first with dacron
24. MAGGIE VALLEY - Ghost Town, western town replica
25. MINNEAPOLIS - Cannon Mills, household linen
26. MORGANTON - Drexel Furniture Company
27. NEW BERN - Tryon Palace Restoration, Colonial Capitol of North Carolina
28. OUTER-BANKS
    Pea Island National Wildlife Refuge, migratory birds winter home;
    Cape Hatteres National Seashore
29. POLKVILLE - James K. Polk Birthplace, 11th U.S. President
30. RAEFORD - House of Raeford, turkey processing
31. RALEIGH
    State Capitol Building;
    Hall of History, State Historical Museum;
    North Carolina Museum of Art;
    Nuclear Reactor Building, first facility for peacetime development of the atom;
    Andrew Johnson Birthplace, 17th President of the United States
32. WILMINGTON - U.S.S. Battleship North Carolina, dedicated to World War II dead
33. WINSTON-SALEM
    R.J. Reynolds Tobacco Company;
    Old Salem, Incorporated, restoration of 18th century Moravian Village

treasure trails / page 139

Reproduction of Wright Brothers' 1903 airplane, Wright Brothers National Memorial, Kill Devil Hills, North Carolina.

Photographs furnished by N.C. Department of Natural & Economic Resources.

Miksch Tobacco Shop, Old Salem, Winston-Salem, North Carolina.

Commercial fishing boats at Wanchese, North Carolina.

STATE MOTTO: Liberty And Union, Now And Forever, One And Inseparable
STATE BIRD: Western Meadowlark
STATE FLOWER: The Wild Prairie Rose

NORTH DAKOTA
Admitted to the Union in 1889

FOR FURTHER INFORMATION WRITE:

- North Dakota Outdoor Recreation Agency
  Mr. Gary Lepport
  Bismarck, North Dakota 58501

- State Game & Fish Department
  Mr. Russell W. Stuart, Commissioner
  Bismarck, North Dakota 58501

- North Dakota Travel Division
  North Dakota Highway Department
  Capitol Grounds
  Bismarck, North Dakota 58501

North Dakota lies in the center of the North American continent about 1,500 miles from the Atlantic, the Pacific, Gulf of Mexico, and the Arctic Ocean. It extends 210 miles north to south, 335 miles east to west. Four sovereign powers have claimed the area now included within North Dakota. In 1610 the explorer Hudson claimed this area; in 1682 La Salle claimed it for France; it was ceded to Spain in 1762, and then returned to France in 1800. North Dakota was sold by Napoleon to the United States in 1803 as part of the Louisiana Purchase. Title to the eastern part of the state was secured from Great Britain by the Treaty of 1818. The Dakota Territory officially was organized in 1860.

A bill known as the "omnibus bill" divided the Dakotas and enabled the formulation of a state constitution for North Dakota. It was voted upon and passed on February 22, 1889. A constitutional convention was held beginning July 4, and a constitution was submitted to the people at an election held October 1. November 2, 1889, President Harrison admitted North Dakota to statehood.

The first white man to explore the Dakota wilderness was the French adventurer, La Verendrye, in 1738. La Verendrye's sons explored what is now southwestern North Dakota in 1742. The Lewis and Clark expedition spent the winter of 1804-05 encamped near the Mandan Indians, a few miles west of present-day Washburn. It was here that Sakakawea, the Shoshone "Bird Woman," was employed as a guide.

Fort Abraham Lincoln near Mandan, was the site from which Lt. Col. George A. Custer and the Seventh Cavalry left from for their battle at Little Bighorn on May 7, 1876. During the 1880's Theodore Roosevelt and the Marquis De Mores, a French nobleman, ranched in the North Dakota Badlands.

Medora's fun loving "Teddy" greets visitors to one of the summer's many events.

treasure trails / page 141

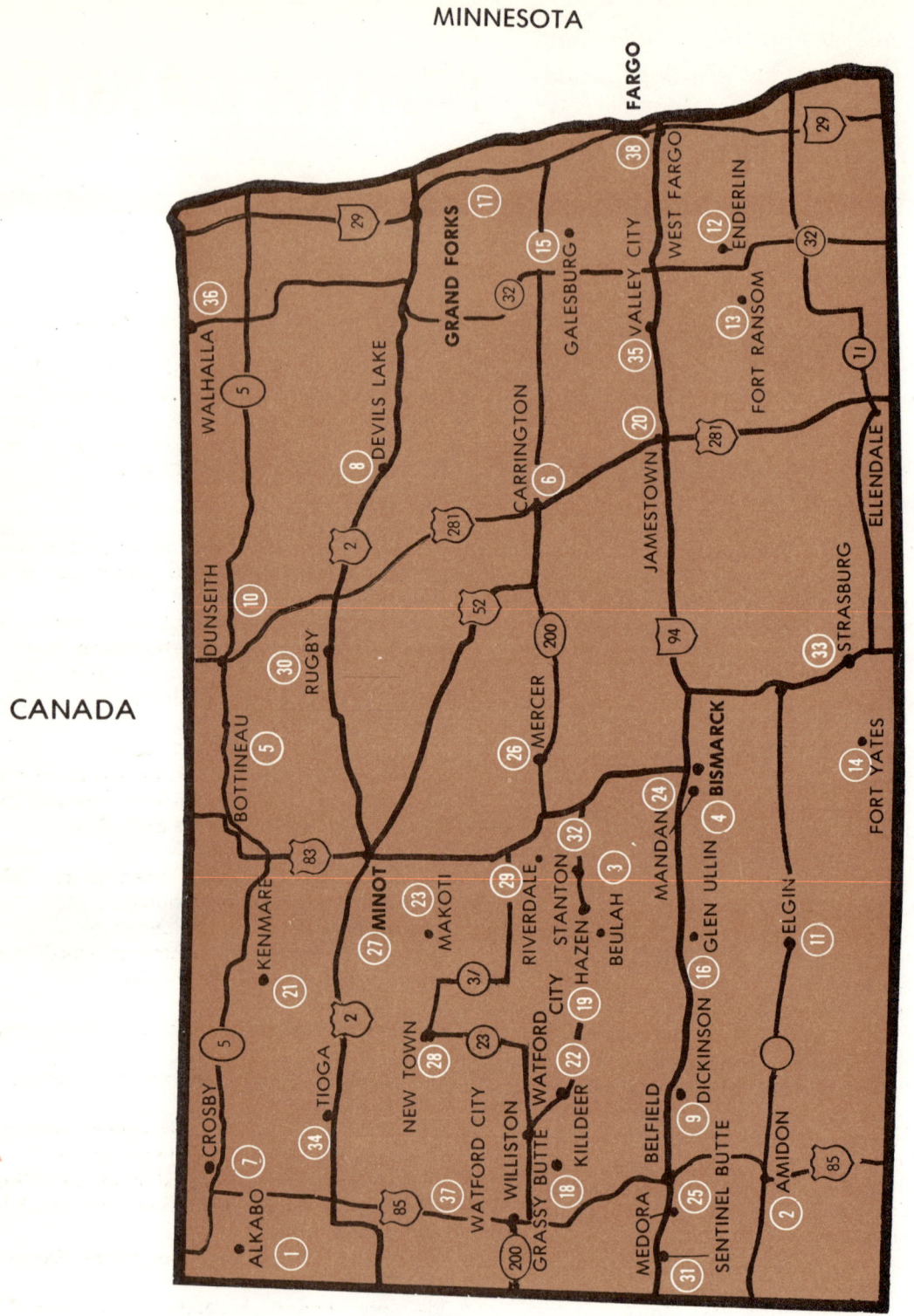

Key:
① relates to number 1 on the following page.

page 142 / treasure trails

NORTH DAKOTA POINTS OF INTEREST

1. ALKABO - Writing Rock Historic Site, ancient Indian picture carvings
2. AMIDON
   Burning coal vein, rare phenomena;
   Columnar junipers
3. BEULAH - Lignite Open Coal Mines, open-pit mining method
4. BISMARCK
   State Capitol building, skyscraper of the prairies;
   Dakota Zoo, features "Prairie Dog Town";
   State Historical Museum, Indian artifacts;
   Camp Hancock Museum, established 1872
5. BOTTINEAU
   Turtle Mountains;
   Lake Metigoshe State Park, recreational center;
   Sawmill Playhouse
6. CARRINGTON - Agricultural Experimental Field Station
7. CROSBY
   Divide County Pioneer Village and Museum, pioneer church and school;
   Annual Threshing Bee, October
8. DEVILS LAKE - Fort Totten Little Theater, Broadway productions
9. DICKINSON - Sosondowah Outdoor Theater, melodrama in natural amphitheatre
10. DUNSEITH - International Peace Garden, formal gardens developed as symbol of lasting friendship between Canada and the U.S.
11. ELGIN - Elgin Museum, model railroad, historical items
12. ENDERLIN - Sheyenne River Scenic Drive
13. FORT RANSOM - Little Yellowstone Park, scenic beauty
14. FORT YATES - Sitting Bull Burial Site, burial site of famed Sioux Indian leader
15. GALESBURG - World's tallest structures, two television towers, reach 2,000 feet
16. GLEN ULLIN - Heart Butte Reservoir, recreational center
17. GRAND FORKS - Grand Forks Air Base, SAC base
18. GRASSY BUTTE - Grassy Butte Post Office
19. HAZEN - Pioneer Village & Museum, historical mercantile store
20. JAMESTOWN - Frontier Fort and Village, with world's largest buffalo statue
21. KENMARE - Danish Mill, one of six such Danish mills in the nation
22. KILLDEER - Lost Bridge Road, scenic drive
23. MAKOTI - Makoti Threshing Association Museum
24. MANDAN
    Missouri River Valley and Oahe Impoundment;
    Slant Indian Village, restored earth-lodge;
    Indian village located at Fort Lincoln State Park, first military post built, 1872, reconstructed block houses used by General Custer
25. MEDORA
    Historic cowboy town;
    Native wildlife abounds, talks by park rangers;
    Outdoor musical, July and August, at Gold Seal Amphitheater;
    Chateau De Mores Historic Site, 25 room mansion, residence of early day cattle baron
26. MERCER - Schlafmann Museum, antique household items and musical instruments
27. MINOT
    Minot Air Force Base, SAC base;
    Dakota Boys Ranch, nondenominational home
28. NEW TOWN - Four Bears Motor Lodge and Museum, all Indian museum owned by Indians
29. RIVERDALE
    Garrison Dam and Lake Sakakawea, lake 200 miles long, recreational center;
    Federal Fish Hatchery, below dam
30. RUGBY - geographical center of North America, restored pioneer village at site
31. SENTINEL BUTTE
    Home on the Range for Boys, home for needy boys;
    professional rodeo, August
32. STANTON - United Power Association Plant, 2,000,000 kilowatts
33. STRASBURG - Birthplace of Lawrence Welk, famous orchestra leader, original farm home
34. TIOGA - Oil fields, site of first major oil strike, 1951
35. VALLEY CITY - Lake Ashtabula and Baldhill Dam, recreational area
36. WALHALLA - Pembina Valley Scenic Drive
37. WATFORD CITY
    Theodore Roosevelt National Memorial Park, beautiful badlands scenery;
    Native wildlife and Longhorn steers
38. WEST FARGO - Bonanzaville, U.S.A., restored frontier village, antique furnishings

treasure trails / page 143

Saddle bronc riding is the highlight of any North Dakota rodeo.

Teddy Roosevelt's Maltese Cross Ranch Cabin is located at the entrance to the south unit of Theodore Roosevelt National Park near Medora.

North Dakota's largest threshing bee is held annually in Makoti.

Parshall, North Dakota, is the site of Broste Rock Museum.

The International Peace Gardens, the only gardens dedicated to peace between two nations, is near Dunseith.

page 144 / treasure trails

Photographs furnished by North Dakota Travel Department.

STATE MOTTO: With God All Things Are Possible

STATE BIRD: Cardinal

STATE FLOWER: Scarlet Carnation

OHIO
Admitted to the Union in 1803

FOR FURTHER INFORMATION WRITE:

- Ohio Department of Community Development
  Box 1001
  Columbus, Ohio 43216

Ohio, with an area of 41,222 square miles ranks only 35th among the 50 states in size, while it is sixth in population and third in industry and manufacturing. Ohio leads the nation in exports of rubber and plastic products. Ohio's ideal geographical location combined with her production and consumption levels have established the state as "The Transportation Center of America". It is served by the greatest inland waterways in the world, Lake Erie, the St. Lawrence Seaway and the Ohio River. Some 75 percent of the nation's consumer markets are located within a 500 mile radius and within 600 miles are three-fourths of the people in the United States.

The state's climate is definitely on the cooler side of the temperate zone, with moderate precipitation. The land varies greatly in roughness and elevation, from rolling plains, flat lake plains to steep hilly plateaus.

In Ohio, farming is the largest single industry in the state, ranking eleventh among the states in gross value of farm production. The state raises more tomatoes under glass than any other.

Beneath her productive soil Ohio is a vast underground storehouse of mineral resources.

The name Ohio comes from the Indian word meaning "Great". It was the coveted hunting grounds of several tribes. The first inhabitants earned the name Mound Builders because they constructed more than 10,000 mounds and earth works. In 1772 the first white settlers, Moravian Missionaries, established a village on the banks of the Tusearawas River. In 1803 the population was large enough to gain recognition of the Congress. Ohio became the 17th state of the Union and the first to be carved out of the Northwest Territory.

Severance Hall

treasure trails / page 145

Ohio Map

MICHIGAN

- TOLEDO (50)
- SILICA (48)
- MAUMEE
- PORT CLINTON (44)
- LAKE ERIE (24)
- KELLY ISLAND (21)
- CHESTERLAND (9)
- CLEVELAND (47)
- MADISON (29)
- MENTOR (35)
- KIRTLAND (22)
- METALS PARK (36)
- AURORA (2)
- (90)
- DEFIANCE
- (24)
- SANDUSKY
- FREMONT (19)
- BELLEVUE (5)
- MILAN (37)
- BEREA (3)
- (12)
- PENINSULA (42)
- YOUNGSTOWN
- (11)
- (224)
- FINDLAY (18)
- (20)
- LAFAYETTE (23)
- AKRON (1)
- (76)
- COLUMBIANA (13)
- (30)
- (75)
- LIMA
- (31) MANSFIELD
- WOOSTER (55)
- CANTON (8)
- WAPAKONETA (51)
- (68)
- (33)
- (28) LOUDONVILLE
- BUTLER (7)
- DOVER
- (30) LIVERPOOL
- MAGNOLIA (17)
- (4) BELLEFONTAINE
- MARION
- (23)
- NEW PHILADELPHIA (40)
- TIPPECANOE (49)
- (127)
- WEST LIBERTY (52)
- (33)
- (71)
- COSHOCTON
- (36)
- (15)
- (77)
- MOUNT PLEASANT (38)
- WHEELING
- WEST MILTON (53)
- COLUMBUS (14)
- NEWARK (39)
- (40)
- (56)
- (70)
- DAYTON (16)
- BROWNSVILLE (6) ZANESVILLE
- (7)
- GERMANTOWN (20)
- (33)
- LANCASTER
- (25)
- WILLMINGTON
- (23)
- LOGAN (27)
- (41) NORTH BEND
- LEBANON (54)
- CHILLICOTHE (10)
- ATHENS
- MARIETTA (32)
- (50)
- CINCINNATI (11)
- LOCUST GROVE
- (52)
- POINT PLEASANT (43)
- (26)
- RIPLEY (46)
- PORTSMOUTH
- RIO GRANDE (45)
- (52)

INDIANA — **PENNSYLVANIA** — **WEST VIRGINIA** — **KENTUCKY**

Key:
① relates to number 1 on the following page.

page 146 / treasure trails

OHIO POINTS OF INTEREST

1. AKRON
   Jonathan Hale Homestead;
   Western Reserve Pioneer Village;
   Stan Hywer Gardens and Home, English Tudor Home, industrialist
2. AURORA - Sea World, 700 acres, sea life show
3. BEREA - Book Festival, in Baldwin Wallace College, extensive collection of books, May
4. BELLEFONTAINE - Zane Caverns, "Cave Pearls"
5. BELLEVUE - Seneca Caverns, "The Earthquake Crack", and artesian spring
6. BROWNSVILLE - Flint Ridge, rock collecting
7. BUTLER
   Clear Fork Valley Ski Area;
   Malabar Farm, home of Louis Bromfield, novelist
8. CANTON
   Professional Football Hall of Fame;
   William McKinley Tomb, Stark County Historical Society, adjacent
9. CHESTERLAND - Mont Chalet Ski Area, cross country and down hill
10. CHILLICOTHE
    Tecumseh, outdoor drama, Sugar Loaf Mountain;
    Adena Gardens, restored home and grounds of former Ohio Governor, Thomas Worthington
11. CINCINNATI
    Harriet B. Stowe House, author's home;
    William Howard Taft's birthplace;
    Garden Center of Greater Cincinnati, garden for the blind;
    King's Island, "Little Disney Land";
    Cincinnati Zoo;
    Showboat "Majestic" old time shows;
    Delta Queen, only overnight paddle wheeler in inland water
12. CLEVELAND
    Aviation Museum, 1895 to 1932;
    Auto Museum;
    Western Reserve Historical Society;
    Cleveland Zoo;
    Blossom Music Center, summer home of Cleveland Orchestra
13. COLUMBIANA - Therons Country Store
14. COLUMBUS
    State Capitol Building, tours;
    Center of Science and Industry, planetarium, and museum;
    Ohio Historical Center;
    Ohio State Fair, August, world's largest fair
15. COSHOCTON
    Canal Boat Rides;
    Roscoe Village Restoration, restored canal town
16. DAYTON - Air Force Museum, Wright Patterson Air Force Base
17. DOVER - Warther Museum, carver of working models
18. FINDLAY - Ghost Town Museum Park
19. FREMONT - Rutherford B. Hayes Estate and Tomb
20. GERMANTOWN - Mud Liek Mill and Museum, old covered bridge spans creek
21. KELLY ISLAND - Glacial Grooves, in Lake Erie, by plane
22. KIRTLAND - First Morman Temple in United States
23. LAFAYETTE - Red Brick Tavern, built in 1837
24. LAKE ERIE - Perry's Victory and International Peace Memorial
25. LEBANON - Golden Lamb Inn, oldest hotel in Ohio, 1803
26. LOCUST GROVE - Serpent Mound State Memorial
27. LOGAN - Hocking Hills State Park, caves, Cedar Falls, Roek House, Cantwell Cliffs
28. LOUDONVILLE - Mohican Wilderness Camp Grounds
29. MADISON - Chalet Debonne Vineyards, informal tours
30. MAGNOLIA - Elson Mill, continuous operation by same family since 1834
31. MANSFIELD - Kingwood Center and Gardens
32. MARIETTA - Campus Martin Museum, Ohio River Museum
33. MARION - Warren G. Garding Home and Tomb, most handsome tomb in the nation
34. MAUMEE - Old Plantation, built 1836
35. MENTOR
    James A. Garfield Home;
    Holden Arboretum, North America's largest arboretum, 2000 acres
36. METALS PARK - Geodesie Dome, largest in world, with rock garden, 350 specimens
37. MILAN - Thomas A. Edison Birthplace
38. MOUNT PLEASANT - Friends Meeting House, Quaker yearly meeting
39. NEWARK
    Great Circle Earthworks, museum of Indian Art;
    Dawes Arboretum, 1500 species of trees
40. NEW PHILADELPHIA
    First white settlement;
    "Trumpet in the Land", outdoor drama
41. NORTH BEND - William Henry Harrison's Tomb
42. PENINSULA - Boston Mills Ski Area
43. POINT PLEASANT - Ulysses S. Grant Birthplace
44. PORT CLINTON - African Safari, wild beasts roam freely, drive through tours
45. RIO GRANDE - Bob Evans Farm, farm festival in early October, open year-round
46. RIPLEY - Tobacco Auctions, November through January
47. SANDUSKY
    Meiers, winery;
    Cedar Point, amusement park
48. SILICA - Silicia Quarry
49. TIPPECANOE - Devils Den Park, caves, rocks waterfalls, glens
50. TOLEDO
    Museum of Health and Natural History;
    Toledo Zoological Park
51. WAPAKONETA - Neil Armstrong Museum, air space
52. WEST LIBERTY - Ohio Caverns, tours
53. WEST MILTON - Hoover Grist Mill, 125 years old
54. WILLMINGTON
    Stony Run Stream;
    Fort Ancient
55. WOOSTER - Ohio Agricultural Research and Development Center
56. ZANESVILLE - Bridge, only bridge on Main Street in the United States

treasure trails / page 147

Simulated hut scene at the Fort Laurens Museum, near Bolivar.

Pro Football Hall of Fame, located in Canton, Ohio.

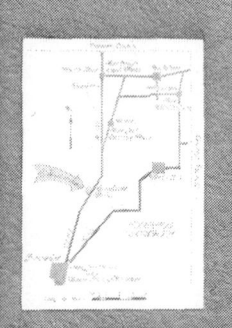

ANNIE OAKLEY
"LITTLE SURE SHOT"

This marker honors the memory of a beloved native of Darke County, the famous sharp-shooter, Annie Oakley. Within a radius of a few miles of this site Annie—

Was Born at Woodland (Willow Dell).
Spent her early childhood at North Star.
Enjoyed her last days at Greenville, and
Lies buried at Brock.

There are markers at North Star and Brock and at the Darke County "Garst Museum" in Greenville there may be seen the world's finest collection of Annie Oakley material.

Memorial marker to Annie Oakley, located in Brock.

Oldest stone house, Lakewood, Ohio, built 1838, restored as pioneer home.

page 148 / treasure trails

Photographs furnished by Department of Economic and Community Development.

STATE MOTTO: Labor Conquers All Things
STATE BIRD: Scissor-Tailed Flycatcher
STATE FLOWER: Mistletoe

OKLAHOMA
Admitted to the Union in 1907

FOR FURTHER INFORMATION WRITE:

- Chamber of Commerce
  Talihina, Oklahoma 74571

- U.S. Fish and Wildlife Service
  Federal Courthouse Building
  Oklahoma City, Oklahoma 73105

- Oklahoma Tourist Information
  500 Will Rogers Building
  Oklahoma City, Oklahoma 73105

The history of Oklahoma does not begin with the planting of a single colony. Oklahoma, a land of many peoples, is our 46th state. The greatest part of its history has been made within the past fifty years. Within its limits live the descendants of not less than fifty different tribes and nations of Indians. Practically every state in the union is represented by the people who settled in Oklahoma. In the space of a third of a century a mighty state has been built in what had been a wilderness. In Oklahoma, the Indian appears in the earlier history of the state, and remains to bear his part in its present and future history. April 22, 1889, saw the first land run for legal settlement. Her past has been filled with achievement, and her present is laden with opportunity, so the future is a challenge to all to rise to the possibilities that await honest effort.

Oklahoma covers 69,919 square miles, with over 374,769 acres of inland lakes, 22 state parks, and 250 public golf courses. It is bound on the south by the Red River, Great Plains in the west, broken by the Black Mesa in the Panhandle, the Wichita Mountains in the southwest, Quachita Mountains in the southeast, with the Ozark mountains in the northeast.

Oklahoma's climate is varied and changeable, its summers are dry with cool breezes at night. Autumn is golden and perfect, beginning in August and lasting through October. Winter can vary from warm sunny days to chilling winds, hail, snow and sleet.

Oklahoma is a great oil state, boasting the only state capitol building with oil wells on its grounds. It also has natural gas, lead, gypsum and zinc. Incomes are derived from farming of wheat, corn, cotton, grain, sorghums, cotton goods and packed meats. Many ranches and farms dot the landscape. Cattle of all breeds are raised and fed in feed lots and private undertakings.

Oklahoma has seven universities, thirty-three colleges and junior colleges and sixteen vocational technical schools.

The Pioneer Woman, a seventeen foot high bronze statue in Ponca City, displays the courage and fortitude of the early settlers.

treasure trails / page 149

Key:
① relates to number 1 on the following page.

page 150 / treasure trails

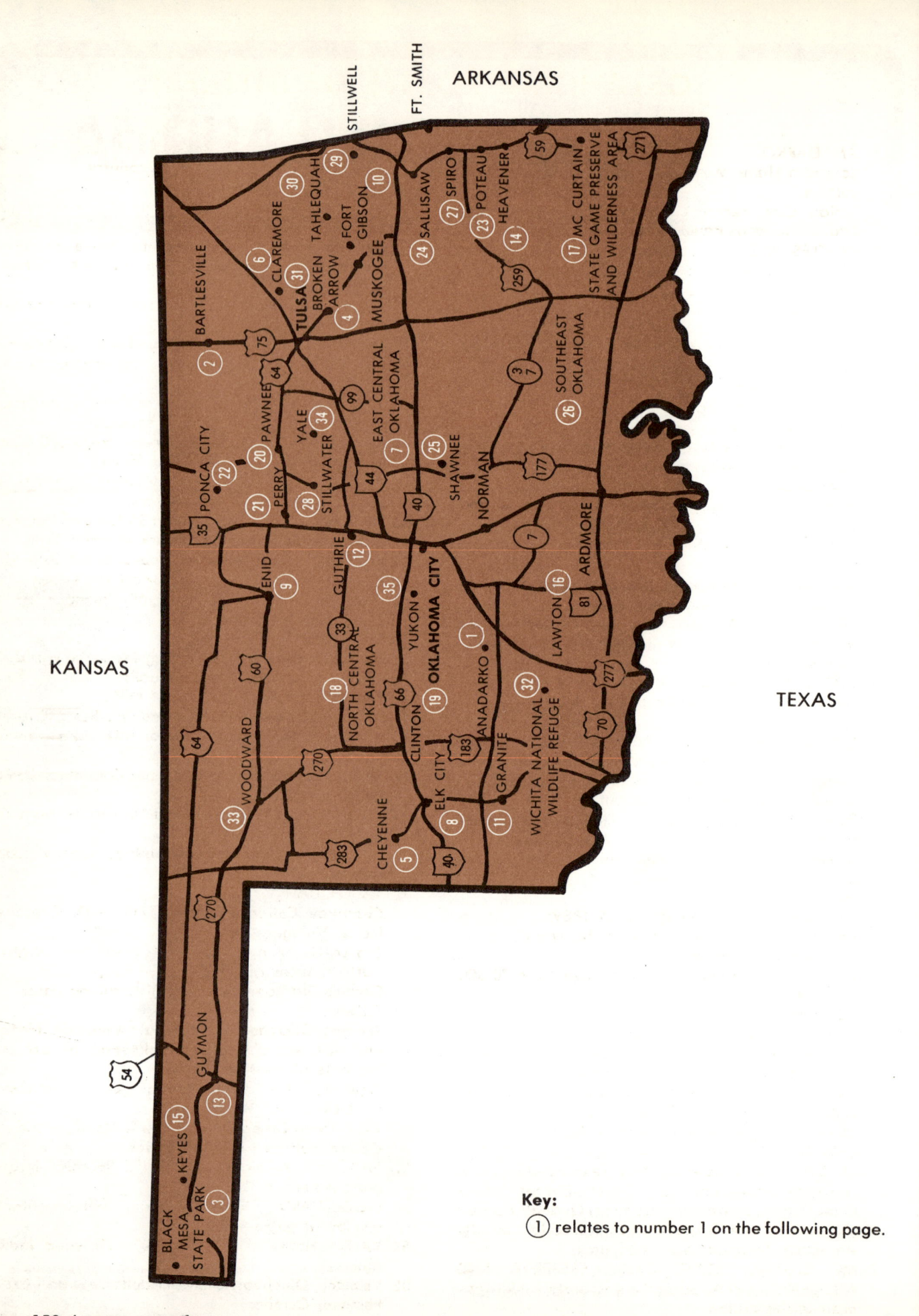

OKLAHOMA POINTS OF INTEREST

1. ANADARKO
   Southern Plains Museum, displays of Plains Indian culture;
   Indian City, reconstructed villages of Apache, Caddo, Navaho, Pawnee, Pueblo, etc.
2. BARTLESVILLE
   Woolaroc Museum, $5 million museum tells the story of man in America;
   The Price Tower Building, designed by Frank Lloyd Wright, famous architect
3. BLACK MESA STATE PARK - lava formations, dinosaur pits, and Indian artifacts
4. BROKEN ARROW
   "Quarter Horse Capital";
   Site of large pecan groves
5. CHEYENNE Black Kettle Museum, Indian relics, and early pioneer articles
6. CLAREMORE
   Home of Will Rogers, world-known humorist and statesman;
   The Will Rogers Memorial, sunken, landscaped gardens;
   J.M. Davis Gun Museum, world's largest privately owned gun collection, 20,000 guns
7. EAST CENTRAL OKLAHOMA - Five Civilized Tribes Museum, established 1874, art, literature, photographs
8. ELK CITY - Elk City Museum and Old Town, restored school, 1900 home and documents
9. ENID
   Cherokee Strip Historical Museum, Indian artifacts, materials pertaining to settlement of Cherokee Strip;
   World's largest wheat elevator
10. FORT GIBSON - Old Ft. Gibson, chief military center for Indian Territory
11. GRANITE - Granite Works, one of the largest quarries in the world
12. GUTHRIE
    First Capitol of Oklahoma, built 1889;
    Largest Scottish Rite Temple in the world;
    Oklahoma Territorial Museum
13. GUYMON - 14 feeder lots, each have 10 to 20,000 head of cattle
14. HEAVENER
    Clem Hamilton Heavener Runestone State Park, shows evidence that Norsemen explored Oklahoma 500 years before Columbus;
    Peter Conser Home, memorial to the Lighthorsemen, Tribal Police Force
15. KEYES - Largest helium plant in the U.S.
16. LAWTON
    Ft. Sill, 95,000 acre military reservation, 1869, contains museum, old Post Corral, Post Guardhouse, graves of Geronimo, Quanah Parker;
    Museum of the Great Plains, accredited by the American Association of Museums
17. MC CURTAIN STATE GAME PRESERVE AND WILDERNESS AREA - Second oldest state wilderness area in the nation
18. NORTH CENTRAL OKLAHOMA - Great Salt Plains, only salt lake in this part of the country
19. OKLAHOMA CITY
    State Capitol Building, sits on top of a producing oil well;
    Oklahoma Historical Society Museum, from prehistoric archeological to present, nation's largest Indian collections;
    National Cowboy Hall of Fame and Western Heritage Center;
    Oklahoma Science & Art Foundation, Kirkpatrick Planetarium, Milligan ivory collection, Focault pendulum;
    Oklahoma Art Center, sales and rental gallery;
    Lincoln Park Zoo, huge bird sanctuary
20. PAWNEE - Pawnee Bill Museum, $100,000 home built in 1910, had Wild West Show
21. PERRY - Cherokee Strip Museum, artifacts of pioneers and early day settlers
22. PONCA CITY - Pioneer Woman Statue and Museum, bronz statue, symbol of Ozark Frontier Trail
23. POTEAU - Kerr Museum, mansion of late U.S. Senator Robert S. Kerr, historical materials
24. SALLISAW - Home of Sequoyah, inventor of the Cherokee alphabet
25. SHAWNEE
    Fort Cobb, largest crow nesting site in the world, 10 million crows stop there annually;
    Peanut capital, large peanut mill
26. SOUTHEAST OKLAHOMA - Beavers Bend, Cypress trees and Spanish moss cover this state's lowest point
27. SPIRO - Spiro Indian Mounds, pre-Columbian Indian burial grounds
28. STILLWATER - Oklahoma State University, begun in 1891
29. STILLWELL - Strawberry country, festival each season
30. TAHLEQUAH
    Cherokee Cultural Center, 1700 A.D. Cherokee Indian Village;
    Tsa-La-Gi Amphitheatre, presents nightly performances of "The Trail of Tears";
    Golda's Old Stone Mill, grist mills, run by water
31. TULSA
    Thomas Gilcrease Institute of American History and Art, world's largest collection of art and artifacts of western history;
    Ogilbrook Art Center, formal gardens, mansion built by oilman Waite Philips;
    T.L. Osborn Green Country World Museum and Art Center, culture from 100 nations
32. WHICHITA NATIONAL WILDLIFE REFUGE, largest buffalo herd in the U.S.
33. WOODWARD - Pioneer Museum, Indian artifacts, display of pioneer life
34. YALE - Home of Jim Thorpe, renowned Indian athlete
35. YUKON - Oklahoma's Czech Capital, colorful Czech Festival, October

treasure trails / page 151

Here is a scene in Oklahoma's "Red Carpet Country" with a view of the Glass Mountains on the horizon.
Photographs furnished by Oklahoma Tourism & Recreation Department.

Reminiscent of the old West days is this buffalo herd grazing on plains of Oklahoma.

At the National Cowboy Hall of Fame and Western Heritage Center in Oklahoma City, exhibits include Art Gallery of the American West, Western Memorabilia, and the sculpture "End of the Trail" [above].

page 152 / treasure trails

STATE MOTTO: The Union
STATE BIRD: Western Meadowlark
STATE FLOWER: Oregon Grape

OREGON
Admitted to the Union in 1859

FOR FURTHER INFORMATION WRITE:

- Regional Office
  U.S. Forest Service
  P.O. Box 3623
  Portland, Oregon 97208

- National Park Service
  920 S.E. 7th Avenue
  Portland, Oregon 97208

- Oregon State Game Commission
  P.O. Box 3503
  Portland, Oregon 97208

- Travel Information Section
  State Highway Building
  Salem, Oregon 97310

The history of Oregon, as recorded by the white man, began with sea explorations, most notably the discovery and naming of the Columbia River by Captain Robert Gray in 1792. The Lewis and Clark Expedition opened the way for the fur traders and trappers who followed to establish the first permanent settlements in the early 1800's. Missionaries to the Indians left their chapter in Oregon history, but it was the pioneers looking for good farm land and mild weather who settled Oregon. Granted statehood in 1859, Oregon became our 33rd state.

The Coast Range, the rugged volcanic Cascade Range and the Blue Mountains dominated Oregon's terrain with the many tributaries of the Columbia River winding through much of the state. Temperatures are moderate west of the Cascades with some of the heaviest rainfall amounts in the United States falling on the Coast Range. East of the Cascades the high arid desert provides a startling contrast to the verdant green western portion of the state.

Only 23 of the 400 miles of the Oregon Coast are privately owned and many of the state's 232 state parks are located along the coast, offering fishing, hunting, camping and boating.

The economy of Oregon is based foremost on the wood products industry. Agriculture and the food processing industry are second in importance. High quality fruits and vegetables are also grown.

A strong dairy industry markets excellent cheeses. Oregon turkey is featured also. Also ranking in importance is the harvesting and processing of products of the sea.

Oregon has led the nation in pollution control, requiring its industry to control air and water pollution.

Oregon's Multnomah Falls is located 30 miles east of Portland. It was discovered by Lewis & Clark in 1805.

treasure trails / page 153

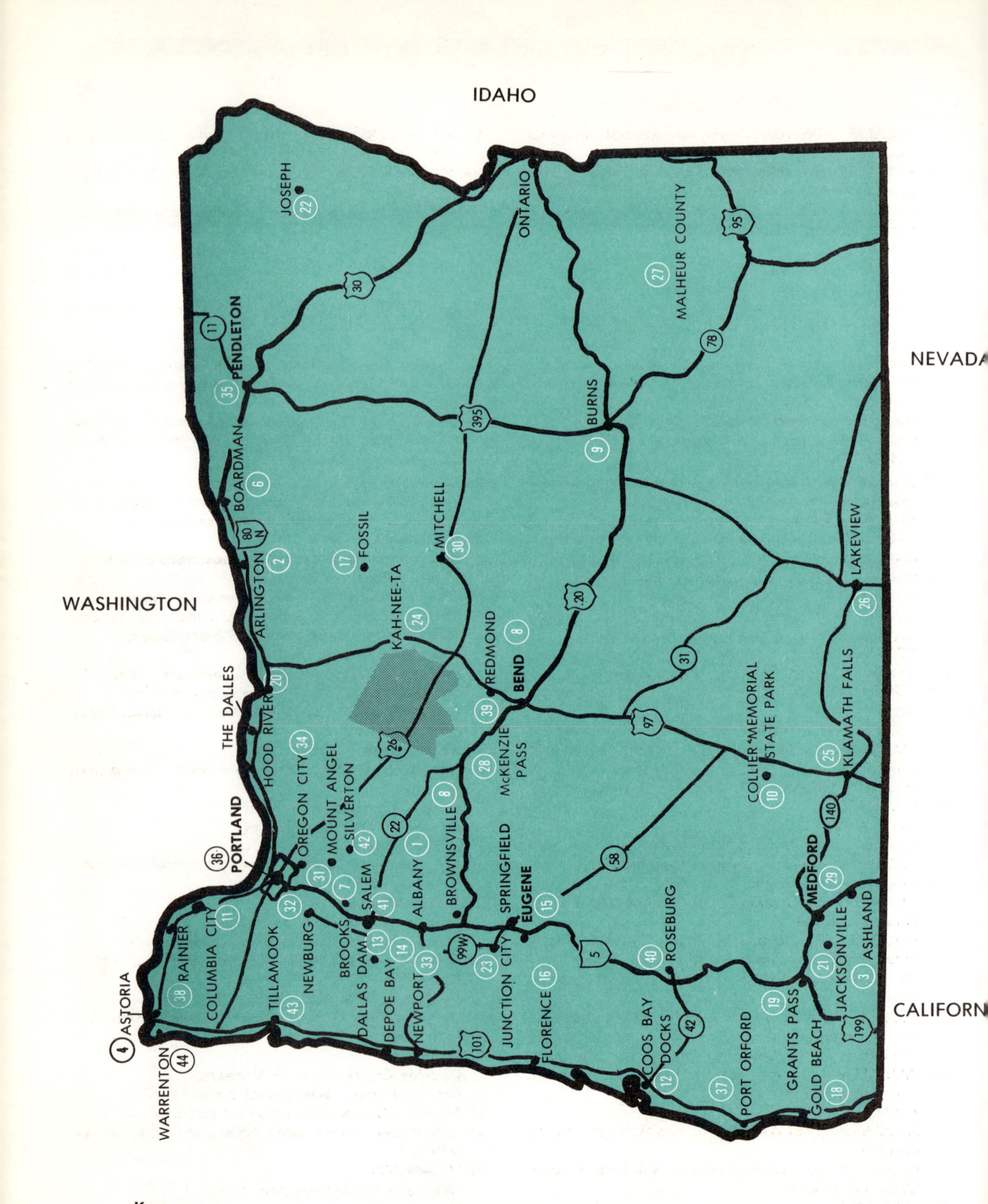

Key:

① relates to number 1 on the following page.

page 154 / treasure trails

OREGON POINTS OF INTEREST

1. ALBANY - World's Champion Timber Carnival, August
2. ARLINGTON - John Day Dam, greatest power producing dam in the world
3. ASHLAND - Shakespearean Theater, replica of Globe Theater, plays in summer
4. ASTORIA
   Columbia River Maritime Museum;
   Bumblebee Cannery, tours during fish canning season;
   Astor Column, history of the area in murals
5. BEND
   Deschutes Lava Lands, lava river caves, ice caves;
   Newberry Crater, volcanic crater lakes in crater;
   Fort Rock, rock formations;
   Glass Buttes, black volcanic glass on slopes;
   Hole in the Ground, cavity one mile in diameter and 300 feet deep
6. BOARDMAN - Circle farming, desert turned to farm land by irrigation
7. BROOKS - Scanton Mill, lumber mill, tours
8. BROWNSVILLE - Look-Meyer House and museum, restored, 1890's
9. BURNS - Malheur National Wildlife Refuge, bird sanctuary
10. COLLIER MEMORIAL STATE PARK - display of early day locomotives and logging equipment
11. COLUMBIA CITY - Caples House Museum, house and outbuildings, built 1870, great view
12. COOS BAY DOCKS - world's largest lumber exporting port
13. DALLAS DAM - navigation locks, fish ladders
14. DEPOE BAY - headquarters for Pacific salmon fishing
15. EUGENE - Oriental Art Museum (U. of Oregon)
16. FLORENCE
    Sand Dunes;
    Sea Lion Caves, trip down to caves to see sea lions
17. FOSSIL - area rich in fossils, free diggings
18. GOLD BEACH - Rogue River Boat Trip
19. GRANTS PASS - Oregon Caves National Monument, limestone caves
20. HOOD RIVER - Diamond Fruit Growers Plant, noted for apples grown, Hood River Valley
21. JACKSONVILLE - Historical Museum, historic homes open
22. JOSEPH - Hells Canyon Viewpoint, deepest canyon on the continent, rugged driving
23. JUNCTION CITY - Scandinavian Festival, August
24. KAH-NEE-TA - Warms Springs Indian Reservation, hot springs resort
25. KLAMATH FALLS
    Favell Museum of Western Art and Artifacts, Indian artifacts;
    Upper Klamath Lake National Wildlife Refuge, birds and wildlife
26. LAKEVIEW
    Hunters Hot Springs, 60 foot geyser, 200 degree water;
    Hart Mountain National Antelope Refuge
27. MALHEUR COUNTY - Lake Owyhee, 53 mile long lake rimmed by geological formations
28. McKENZIE PASS - Highway drive through lava beds used to test moon equipment
29. MEDFORD - Crater Lake National Park, blue lake filling volcanic crater
30. MITCHELL - Painted Hills State Park, geology fossils
31. MOUNT ANGEL - Oktoberfest, festival featuring German heritage
32. NEWBURG - Champoeg State Park, museum, pioneer log cabin, 1843
33. NEWPORT
    Yaquina Bay State Park, old lighthouse, built 1871;
    Newport Marine Science Center, marine science exhibits
34. OREGON CITY - McLaughlin House National Historic Site, built in 1845, by John McLaughlin, of Hudson Bay Company
35. PENDLETON
    Home of world's top ranking rodeos, September;
    Pendleton Woolen Mill, wool yardage
36. PORTLAND
    Multnemah Falls, second highest falls in U.S.;
    Western Forestry Center;
    Oregon Historical Museum, western history;
    Oregon Museum of Science and Industry, natural science, physical science and planetarium;
    Japanese Gardens;
    Timberline Lodge, created by artisans, 1935;
    Portland Zoological Gardens, children's zoo;
    Bybee-Howell House and Howell Territorial Farm, historic home;
    Art Museum;
    International Rose Test Gardens, landscaped gardens;
    Pioneer Courthouse, still in use;
    Bonneville Dam, fish ladder;
    Blitz-Weinhard Brewery, tours;
    Rhododendron Test Gardens, 2500 rhododendrons bloom in May
37. PORT ORFORD
    Cape Blanco Lighthouse, tours;
    Prehistoric Gardens, replicas of dinosours
38. RAINIER - Trojan Nuclear Plant, newest plant
39. REDMOND
    Petersen's Rock Gardens;
    Crooked River Gorge, straight walled canyon 304 feet deep
40. ROSEBURG
    Douglas County Pioneer Museum;
    Diamond Lake, recreational center
41. SALEM - Oregon State Capitol Building
42. SILVERTON - Silver Creek Falls State Park, eleven falls
43. TILLAMOOK
    Tillamook Cheese Kitchen, tours;
    Tillamook Pioneer Museum, wildlife displays
44. WARRENTON - Fort Clatsop National Historical Monument, replica of quarters used by Lewis and Clark 1805-1806

treasure trails / page 155

Horseback riders have a beautiful view overlooking Wallowa Lake. Horseback riding is popular in the Wallowa Mountain area.

The Bandon Ocean Wayside is about one-half mile south of Bandon. Many of the rocks resemble animals and humans.

Smith Rocks is one of Oregon's newest state park areas. The rocks form a deep gorge sliced by the Crooked River.

Crater Lake, near Collier State Park, is set in the crater of the extinct volcano Mt. Mazama. Later volcanic action built Wizard Island.

page 156 / treasure trails

STATE MOTTO: Virtue, Liberty And Independence
STATE BIRD: Ruffed Grouse
STATE FLOWER: Mountain Laurel

PENNSYLVANIA
Admitted to the Union in 1787

FOR FURTHER INFORMATION WRITE:

- Pennsylvania Department of Commerce
  Bureau of Travel Development
  South Office Building
  Harrisburg, Pennsylvania 17120

- Pennsylvania Chamber of Commerce
  222 North 3rd
  Harrisburg, Pennsylvania 17101

Often spoken of as a "state", the official designation of Pennsylvania is "commonwealth". Both the English and Dutch traded in this area, but the Swedish people made the first permanent settlement. The British won claim in 1664, but it was in 1681 that William Penn, a Quaker, received it as a grant from Charles II. Penn's philosophy led him to make a treaty with the Indians that ensured a long period of peace. Those who followed Penn did not use the same method of dealing with people, the result was in proportion to their differences in method. The commonwealth lay in the center of activity during the Revolutionary War, the Battle of Brandywine, and in the Civil War. Men like Andrew Carnegie and Gifford Pinchot are among the great of Pennsylvania.

The borders extend from the coastal plain to the Appalachians, giving 5 distinct physiographic divisions. The highest point, Mount Davis, is located in the northwest. Flooding has been a problem but recent developments have assured a lessening of this type of disaster.

Industry leads economically but agriculture remains important. The nearness to densely populated centers and the background of the residents have kept farming in the near forefront. Manufacturing ranks second only to New York in monetary value. Coal, petroleum, iron and natural gas resources are extensive. Trade and finance, transportation and communication employ many people.

Woodlands of oak, maple, pine, and hemlock occupy more than half the state. The Pocono Mountains are a beautiful resort area that draws thousands of people each year. Rivers, waterfalls, lakes, and streams abundant with fish accent the beauty of the highlands and the rolling hills of the Pocono Mountains. The southeastern area of the state is a rich farming area.

The formal gardens with the Great house and Church steeple in the background at Old Economy, Pennsylvania.

treasure trails / page 157

Key:
① relates to number 1 on the following page.

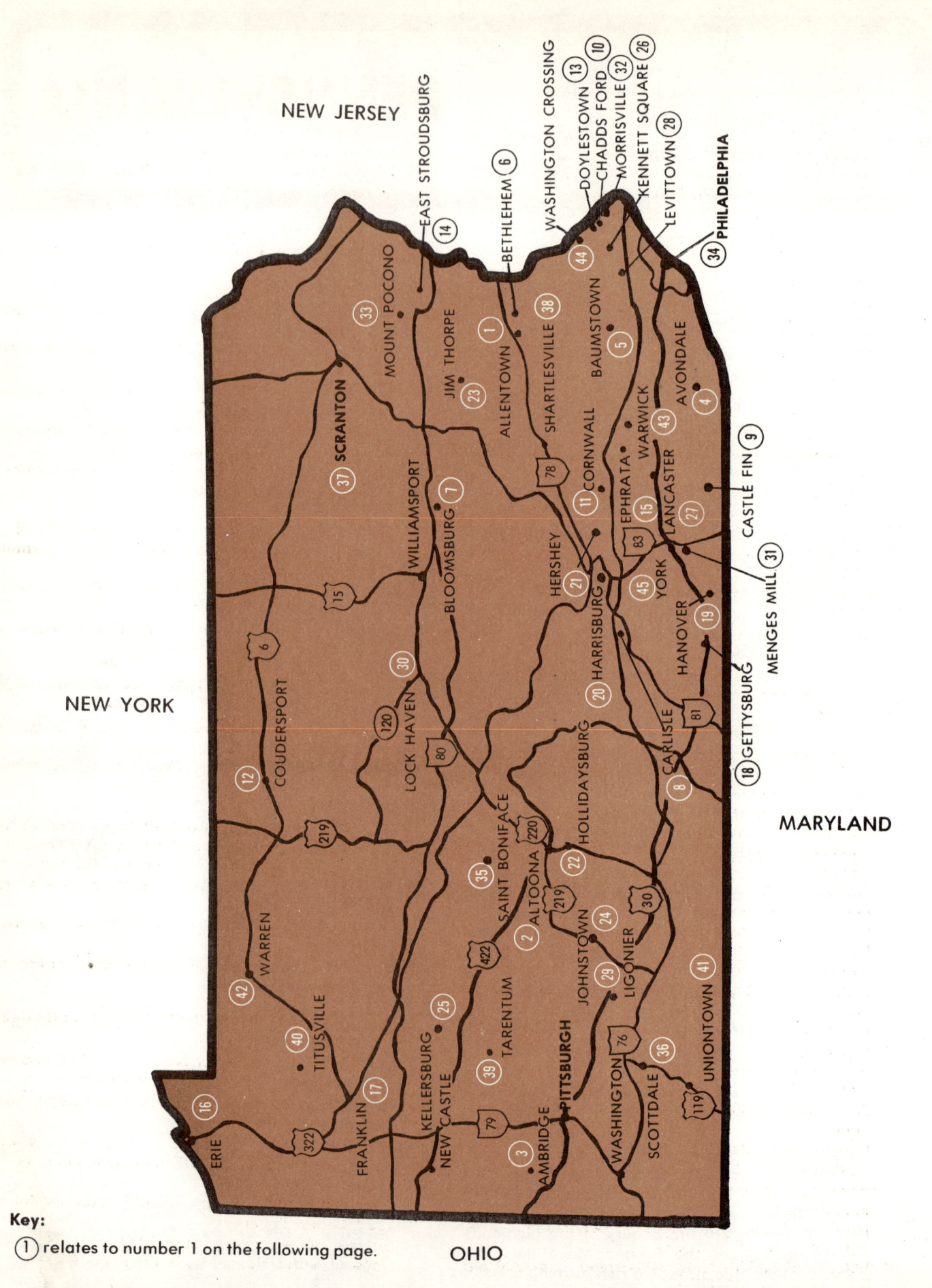

page 158 / treasure trails

PENNSYLVANIA POINTS OF INTEREST

1. ALLENTOWN - Liberty Bell Shrine, commemorates hiding of bell under church
2. ALTOONA - Horseshoe Curve, Penn Central Railroad makes 2,376 foot sweep
3. AMBRIDGE - Harmony Society, Old Economy, restored home of religious group
4. AVONDALE - Mushroom Farms, growing, canning
5. BAUMSTOWN - Daniel Boone Homestead, site of pioneer's birthplace
6. BETHLEHEM - Moravian Museum, oldest building still standing in Bethlehem
7. BLOOMSBURG - Carroll Park & Western Railroad, four-foot gauge steam train
8. CARLISLE - Carlisle Barracks, once military post, then Indian school
9. CASTLE FIN - Atomic Power Station, exhibits deal with practical uses
10. CHADDS FORD - Brandywine River Museum, paintings by Howard Pyle and Wyeths
11. CORNWALL - Cornwall Furnace, oldest coal-blast furnace in U.S.
12. COUDERSPORT - The Ice Mine, natural phenomenon, heavy ice forms in spring
13. DOYLESTOWN - Mercer Museum, tools and machines used by early Americans
14. EAST STROUDSBURG - Air Tours
15. EPHRATA - Ephrata Cloister, Seventh-Day Baptist monastic house
16. ERIE
    Brig Niagara, flagship of Commodore Perry;
    Perry Monument, commemorates the building of the victorious fleet;
    Wayne Blockhouse, replica of place where "Mad Anthony" Wayne died;
17. FRANKLIN - Venango County Museum, models of English and French forts
18. GETTYSBURG
    Gettysburg National Military Park, 1863 memorial;
    Gettysburg Cyclorama;
    Dobbin House and Museum, electric map of battle;
    Lincoln Room Museum, where Lincoln wrote the Gettysburg Address;
    National Civil War Wax Museum, tableaux of Civil War period;
    Hall of Presidents, life-size figures of all Presidents
19. HANOVER - Hanover Shoe Farms, large harness horse breeding farm
20. HARRISBURG
    State Capitol Building, built in Italian Renaissance Style;
    William Penn Memorial Museum
21. HERSHEY
    Hershey Chocolate Plant, world's largest manufacturer;
    Hershey Rose Garden and Arboretum, over 120,000 roses;
22. HOLLIDAYSBURG - Automobilorama, over 200 old cars dating to 1898
23. JIM THORPE - Asa Parker Mansion, home of founder of Lehigh University
24. JOHNSTOWN - The Incline Plane, built as a "lifesaver" after 1889 flood
25. KELLERSBURG - Quiet Valley Farm Museum, 1765 log house and hand-pegged barn
26. KENNETT SQUARE - Longwood Gardens, extensive gardens
27. LANCASTER
    Wheatland, restored home of President James Buchanan;
    Pennsylvania Farm Museum of Landis Valley
28. LEVITTOWN - Pennsbury Manor, re-created country home of William Penn
29. LIGONIER - Fort Ligonier, built 1758-83, outpost of the French and Indian War
30. LOCK HAVEN - Piper Aircraft Corporation, manufacturer of airplanes
31. MENGES MILL
    Colonial Valley, features 225 year old sawmill;
    Laucks Museum, water-powered stone gristmill and old tools
32. MORRISVILLE - Fallsington, colonial village where William Penn worshipped
33. MOUNT POCONO - Pocono International Raceway stock, sports cars and motorcycles
34. PHILADELPHIA
    Independence Hall, Liberty Bell and ink stand used by signers;
    Old City Hall and Congress Hall, where Congress met, 1790;
35. SAINT BONIFACE - Seldom Seen Valley Coal Mine, electric train trips
36. SCOTTDALE
    Historical House, special period rooms, built 1838;
    Stone Cottage, birthplace of Henry Clay Frick
37. SCRANTON - Everhart Museum, natural history
38. SHARTLESVILLE - Roadside America, miniature cities
39. TARENTUM - Tour-Ed Mine, demonstrations of coal mining
40. TITUSVILLE - Drake Well Memorial Park, replica of world's first oil well
41. UNIONTOWN - Fort Necessity National Battlefield, Washington's first battle
42. WARREN - Allegheny National Forest, 74,000 acres Tionesta Scenic Area, primitive forest
43. WARWICK - Hopewell Village National Historic Site, iron-making
44. WASHINGTON CROSSING - Thompson-Neely House, where attack on Trenton was planned
45. YORK
    Historical Society of York County, scale model of 1830 Center Square;
    Golden Plough Tavern, built 1741, restored;
    General Gates House, built 1751, restored;

treasure trails / page 159

Seminary Ridge, General Lee watched charge of July 3. The store wall is line of Confederate batteries.

Like palace guards, the stalks of corn stand watch over the golden fields at harvest time in Lancaster County.

Three River Stadium, new home of Pittsburgh Pirates and Steelers, [left] on Monongahela River. Pennsylvania's Golden Triangle [right].

page 160 / treasure trails

Photographs furnished by The Gettysburg Travel Council, Inc.

STATE MOTTO: Joannes Est Nomen Ejvs
STATE BIRD: No Official State Bird
STATE FLOWER: No Official State Flower

PUERTO RICO
Congress established civil government in 1900

FOR FURTHER INFORMATION WRITE:

- Director, Institute of Tropical Forestry
  Box AQ
  Rio Piedras, Puerto Rico 00928

- Puerto Rico Tourism Information Center
  8 West 51 Street
  New York, New York 10022

The smallest of the Greater Antilles Island group in the Caribbean, Puerto Rico is a rectangle about 100 miles long and 35 miles wide, or nearly the size of Connecticut. It is home for 2,700,000 people. The mountainous center portion which constitutes three quarters of the islands terrain is boundered by a broad coastal plain, trimmed with palm-lined beaches meeting the turquoise waters of the Caribbean Sea, on the south and the Atlantic Ocean on the north.

On his second voyage to the New World in 1493, Columbus discovered the island, claimed it for Spain, and christened it San Juan Bautista (St. John the Baptist). In 1506 Juan Ponce de Leon, who had been a seaman with Columbus on his voyage of discovery, returned to the island with a small group of Spaniards and founded the first settlement.

For half a century, the island served as a stepping stone between Spain and its more distant New World outposts. On July 25, 1898 during the Spanish-American War, United States Army troops landed on the southern coast at Guanica and occupied Puerto Rico. Five months later, by the Treaty of Paris ending the war, Spain ceded autonomy over Puerto Rico to the United States.

Puerto Rico's unique status as a "Commonwealth" has no direct parallel in the American system. Puerto Rico is not a state, nor is it a territory. Instead it is a special status created by the 81st Congress in 1950, and ratified the following year by the Puerto Rican people. Puerto Ricans are citizens of the United States, and have most of the rights, privileges and obligations of any other citizen.

In the early 1940's the Puerto Rican Government went on a campaign to promote their economy. Before this time the country was mainly agricultural. Per capita income increased from $269 in 1950 to $1,250 in 1969, while in the same period gross national product more than quintupled.

Typical quiet street in old San Juan.

treasure trails / page 161

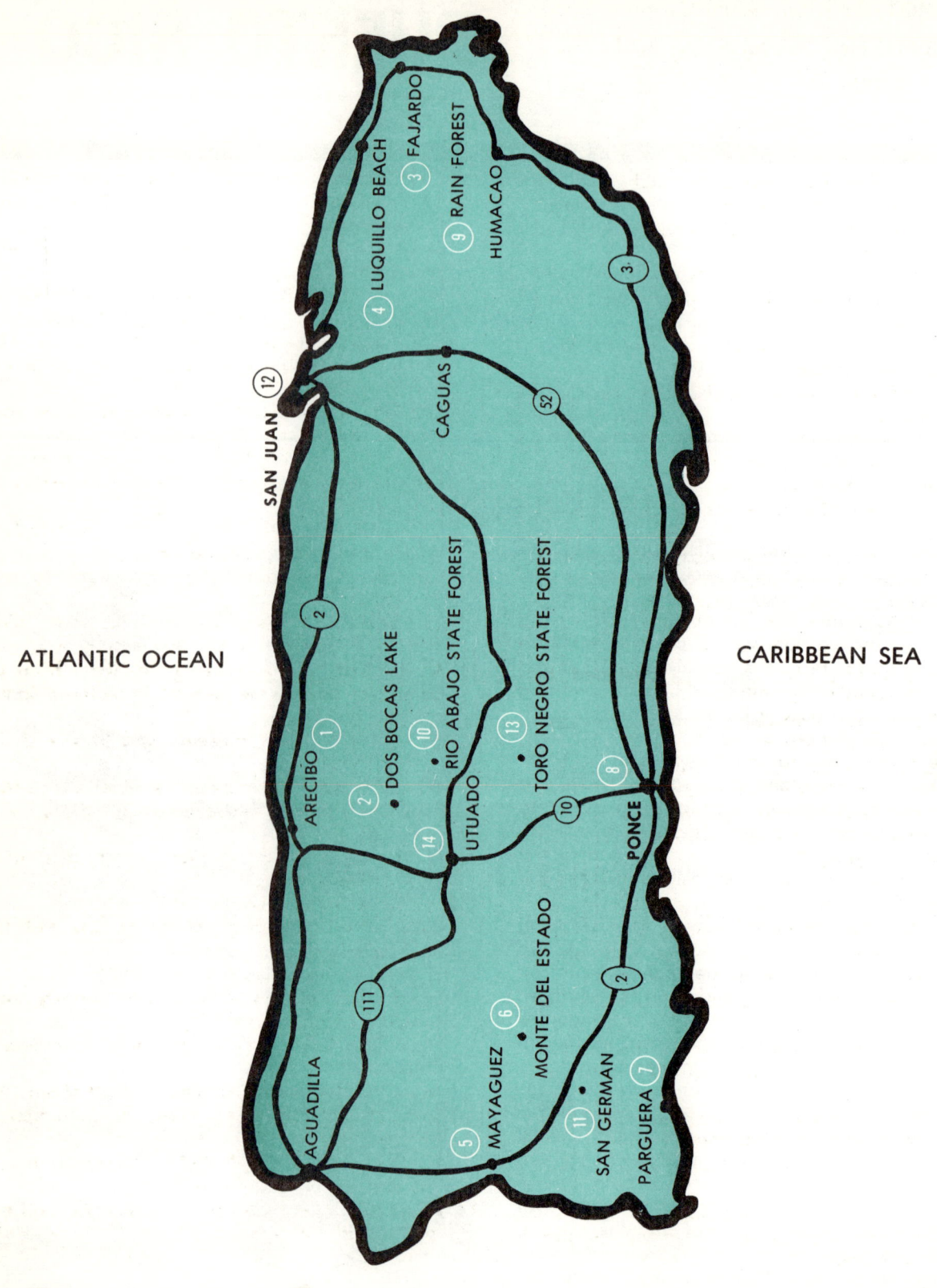

Key:

① relates to number 1 on the following page.

page 162 / treasure trails

PUERTO RICO POINTS OF INTEREST

1. **ARECIBO** - Arecibo Ionospheric Observatory, largest radar radio telescope in the world, operated by Cornell University for the National Science Foundation
2. **DOS BOCAS LAKE** - wharf for launches, lovely man-made lake, reservoir used for producing hydro-electric power
3. **FAJARDO** - Historic Railroad of Puerto Rico, narrow-gauge railroad
4. **LUQUILLO BEACH** - recreational center, near vast coconut grove
5. **MAYAGUEZ** - Experimental Station, Puerto Rico's largest city and island's capital for nature lovers, exotic gardens, bird sanctuary
6. **MONTE DEL ESTADO** - Maricao State Forest, recreational area
7. **PARGUERA** - Phosphorescent Bay, large population of luminescent dinoflagellates, a tiny form of marine life that produces sparks of chemical light when disturbed
8. **PONCE**
   Ponce Museum of Art, building designed by architect, Edward Durell Stone;
   Parque De Bombas, Main Plaza, fantastic structure - firehouse, built in 1883
9. **RAIN FOREST** - Luquillo Experimental Forest, tropical forest, 240 different tree species
10. **RIO ABAJO STATE FOREST** - recreational area
11. **SAN GERMAN** - Porta Coeli, 17th century chapel, Spanish architecture
12. **SAN JUAN**
    El Morro, fort built in 1595, protection against invasion, San Juan National Historic Site;
    San Juan Cemetery, circular chapel, built about 1865, prominent Puerto Ricans buried there;
    City Wall, built 1630 of solid sandstone blocks, 40 feet tall;
    Dominican Convent, Headquarters of the Institute of Puerto Rican Culture, started in 1523, now used for cultural activities;
    San Jose Church, one of the most beautiful in the hemisphere, voulted ceilings, built in 1532;
    Plaza De San Jose, statue of Juan Ponce de Leon, made in 1797;
    Casa De Los Contrafuertes, oldest house still remaining in the city, houses Pharmacy Museum, and Santos Museum;
    Casa Blanca, Juan Ponce de Leon home, rebuilt in 1523, decendants occupied it for 250 years, closed for restoration;
    Step Streets, only two streets built with steps remain in the city;
    Plazuela De La Rogativa, statue of a Bishop and three women, in specially designed plaza;
    San Juan Cathedral, cathedral built in 1540, remarkable circular staircase, Juan Ponce de Leon buried here;
    City Hall, constructed from 1604 to 1789, tower clock installed in 1889;
    Plaza De Armas, city built in 1521, plaza built at the same time, four statues preside over the plaza, 100 years old;
    La Intendencia, beautiful building with neoclassic facade, built from 1851 to 1898;
    San Juan Gate, gate first constructed to greet dignitaries;
    La Fortaleza, original fort built in 1540, oldest executive mansion in the hemisphere still used;
    Museum of Puerto Rican Art, exhibits from pre-Columbian days to the present, in restored Spanish colonial building;
    La Casa Del Libro, museum and library in 18th century house;
    Cristo Chapel, houses beautiful silver alter said to have been made from exvotos put there by the faithful;
    Parque De Las Palomas, park, offers magnificent view of the harbor;
    La Princesa Jail, built in 1837;
    Bastion De Las Palmas, bastion on City Wall built for emplacement of guns;
    El Arsenal, naval station, built 1800;
    La Casa Del Callejon, restored 18th century house, contains two museums;
    Plaza De Colon, plaza, contains a statue of Columbus;
    Tapia Theater, municipal theater, built about 1832;
    San Cristobal, fort built in 1766, San Juan National Historic Site;
13. **TORO NEGRO STATE FOREST** - recreational area, flowers and brook with pathways
14. **UTUADO** - Indian Ceremonial Ball Park, ball park constructed 700 years ago

treasure trails / page 163

Mountains and valley of Puerto Rico's central mountain range.

Condado Lagoon, with view of elegant condominiums and fashionable hotels in the background.

El Morro fortress protects the entrance to San Juan Bay.

One of the many very beautiful palm beaches of Puerto Rico.

page 164 / treasure trails

Photographs furnished by Puerto Rico Information Center.

STATE MOTTO: Hope
STATE BIRD: Rhode Island Red Hen
STATE FLOWER: Violet

RHODE ISLAND
Admitted to the Union in 1790

FOR FURTHER INFORMATION WRITE:

- Rhode Island Development Council
  Roger Williams Building
  Hayes Street
  Providence, Rhode Island 02908

Rhode Island, one of the New England States of the United States, ranks as the 48th state in the Union in area, the 36th in population and 13th in order of admission to the Union. The smallest state in the Union, Rhode Island possesses an extreme length from north to south of 48 miles, and an extreme width from east to west of 37 miles.

Roger Williams, who had been banished from the Massachusetts Bay Colony, established the first settlement in Rhode Island at Providence in June, 1636, on land purchased from the Narragansett Indians.

The surface of the state is hilly, though the general elevation is not great. The average elevation of Rhode Island is about 200 feet above sea level. Most of the shore is bordered by marshes and lagoons.

Though the rivers of Rhode Island are small, they are swift and important as a source of hydroelectric power.

The climate of the state is mild compared to that of most of New England. The most important industry of Rhode Island is manufacturing. The state possesses the largest per capita industrial output in the U.S. The manufacture of textiles accounts for almost 50% of the total value of products per year, and other important products are jewelry, woolen goods, silverware, fine tools, and machinery.

The state ranks low agriculturally, because of its small area and the sterility of the soil. Livestock is of greater value than the crops. Fisheries are important to the state's economy. Rhode Island is known for their oysters, lobsters, scallops and quahaughs.

Providence, the capital of Rhode Island and New England's second largest city, was founded in 1636 by Roger Williams.

Rhode Island is a very photogenic state.

Beavertail Point, on Conanicut Island, is one of the most popular visitor attractions of Rhode Island.

treasure trails / page 165

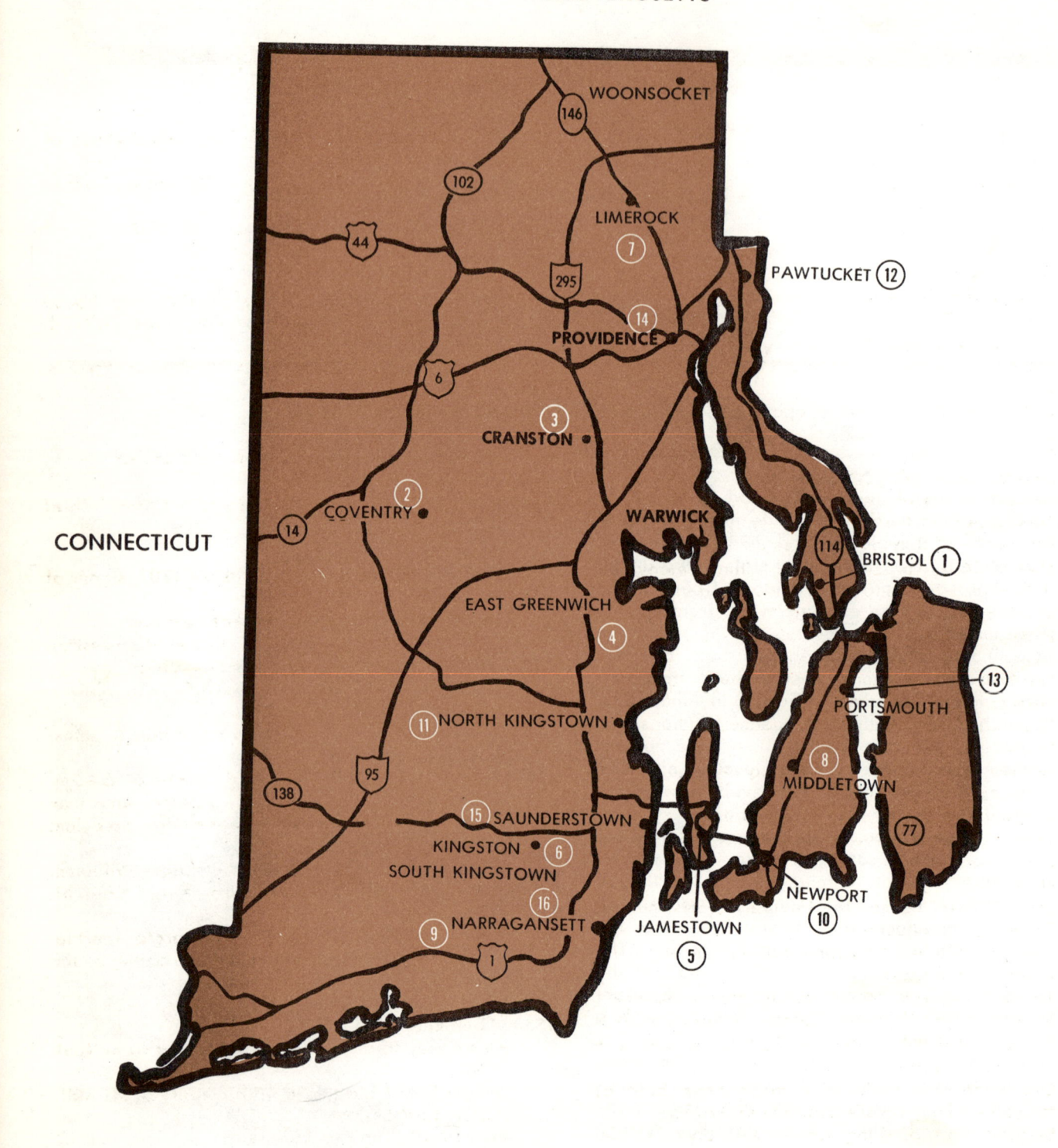

Key:
① relates to number 1 on the following page.

page 166 / treasure trails

RHODE ISLAND POINTS OF INTEREST

1. BRISTOL
   Haffenreffer Museum of Anthropology, American Indian artifacts and relics;
   Colt State Park, 3 mile drive around shoreline of former Colt Family Estate
2. COVENTRY - General Nathanael Green Homestead, patriotic shrine
3. CRANSTON - Governor Sprague Mansion, 28 rooms built in 1790
4. EAST GREENWICH - Kent County Courthouse, built 1750
5. JAMESTOWN
   Old Windmill, restored to operating condition as built in 1787;
   Beavertail Lighthouse, early colonial stonework;
   Fire Museum, antique firefighting equipment
6. KINGSTON - 18th century main street
   Fayerweather House;
   University of Rhode Island, established 1892;
7. LIMEROCK - rural area containing many old dwellings. Limestone quarries, worked since 1643
8. MIDDLETOWN
   Purgatory Chasm, narrow cleft in rock ledges, formed by eroding of sea water;
   Norman Bird Sanctuary and Museum, 300 acre wildlife preserve;
   Green End Fort, built by British in 1777
9. NARRAGANSETT
   Galilee, Jerusalem noted fishing villages;
   Point Judith Lighthouse;
   Octagonal stone building erected in 1816;
   Coast Guard and tower beacon used during the Revolution
10. NEWPORT
    Brick Market, houses the Newport Crafts, historic Newport reproductions;
    Newport Artillery Company, nation's oldest active military organization;
    Touro Synagogue, oldest synagogue in America;
    St. Mary's Church, oldest Roman Catholic parish in Rhode Island, where Jacqueline Bouvier was wed to John Fitzgerald Kennedy;
    Old Stone Mill, believed to have been built by Norsemen long before Columbus's voyage;
    Belcourt Castle, King Louis XIII style castle, treasures from 32 countries
    Ocean Drive and Cliff Walk, unparalled views of coastline;
    The Breakers, 70-room Vanderbilt mansion built in 1895;
    Hunter House — Georgian mansion, 1748;
    Newport furniture, silver and art
11. NORTH KINGSTOWN
    Smith's Castle, believed to be the only house standing in which Roger Williams preached, 18th century garden;
    Old Narragansett Church, oldest Episcopal Church, built 1707
12. PAWTUCKET
    Slater Park and Zoo;
    Old Slater Mill Museum, birthplace of the textile industry in America
13. PORTSMOUTH - Benedictine Abbey and Preparatory School
14. PROVIDENCE
    Stephen Hopkins House, built about 1707, signer of Declaration of Independence;
    John Brown House, magnificent mansion;
    Annmary Brown Memorial (Brown University), exhibits of early paintings and printing;
    Brown University, John D. Rockfeller, Jr. Library, John Hay Library;
    First Baptist Church in America, nation's oldest Baptist congregation;
    Musuem of Art, Rhode Island School of Design, Greco-Roman sculpture, 18th century American furniture, French Impressionist paintings, porcelain collection;
    Prospect Terrace, burial place of Roger Williams;
    Cathedral of St. John (originally King's Church), 1722;
    State Capitol, built of white Georgia marble, second largest unsupported marble dome in the world;
    Betsy Williams Cottage, 1773
15. SAUNDERSTOWN
    Silas Casey farm, typical New England farm, built 1750;
    Gilbert Stuart birthplace 18th century Snuff Mill
16. SOUTH KINGSTOWN
    Museum of Primitive Cultures

treasure trails / page 167

Mohegan Bluffs rise 200 feet above the Atlantic Ocean and stretch for five miles along the Atlantic coastline. Southeast Point Lighthouse (above), built in 1875, is one of the strongest and most important lights on the New England coast, Block Island. Photographs furnished by Rhode Island Development Council

The Gilbert Stuart Birthplace and Snuff Mill, near Saunderstown, built in 1751, was the home of America's foremost painter of portraits of George Washington.

Shown here is the interior of Touro Synagogue, the oldest in America (1763) located in Newport, Rhode Island.

One of the five classes crosses the starting line in the biennial Newport to Bermuda Yacht Race, a 689 mile blue water trophy contest.

page 168 / treasure trails

STATE MOTTO: Prepared In Mind And Resources
STATE BIRD: Carolina Wren
STATE FLOWER: Carolina Yellow Jessamine

SOUTH CAROLINA
Admitted to the Union in 1788

FOR FURTHER INFORMATION WRITE:

- I & E Division
  P.O. Box 167
  Columbia, South Carolina 29202

- Wildlife Resources Dept.
  Box 167
  Columbia, South Carolina 29202

- Travel Division Parks, Recreation and Tourism
  P.O. Box 1358
  Columbia, South Carolina 29202

It's a traveler's delight from its 281 miles of sandy beaches and sparkling blue Atlantic to the waterfalls and trout streams of the Upcountry. Three hundred years of history, unexcelled natural beauty and fabled southern hospitality blend to make the Sandlapper State one of the greatest of the fifty for the vacationer.

Charleston's old section with its shaded porticos is undergoing extensive restoration. Along with international culinary greats, one may find local specialties such as Hopping John, corn fritters, she-crab soup and the like.

South Carolina is horse country and the rolling hills abound with show and race breeds. The Camden Steeplechase is an annual spring event in the locale of a famous Revolutionary War battlefield.

The Upcountry is crammed with eye-staggering sights. A large percentage of the state's 12,000,000 acres of forested land is found here, creating a boon for hunters, fishermen and camping enthusiasts. Spectacular rivers and craggy mountains combine in the fall of the year to present an unequalled show of color.

Clemson University, the state's land grant college, is located on the John C. Calhoun plantation in the center of the Pendleton Historical District. A hotbed of history awaits the visitor so inclined. Famous houses and recreational facilities are everywhere and tours are available through the Pendleton District Historical and Recreational Commission located in the picturesque village of Pendleton.

Golfer's vacations are available statewide all year and are increasingly appealing to Northerners coming South to thaw.

Cultivated land and livestock farms are plentiful, with great fields of corn, tobacco and cotton. Dairy herds roam the pasture lands and poultry farms are big business.

Sumter, South Carolina, site of the first Home Demonstration Club, established in March, 1915.

treasure trails / page 169

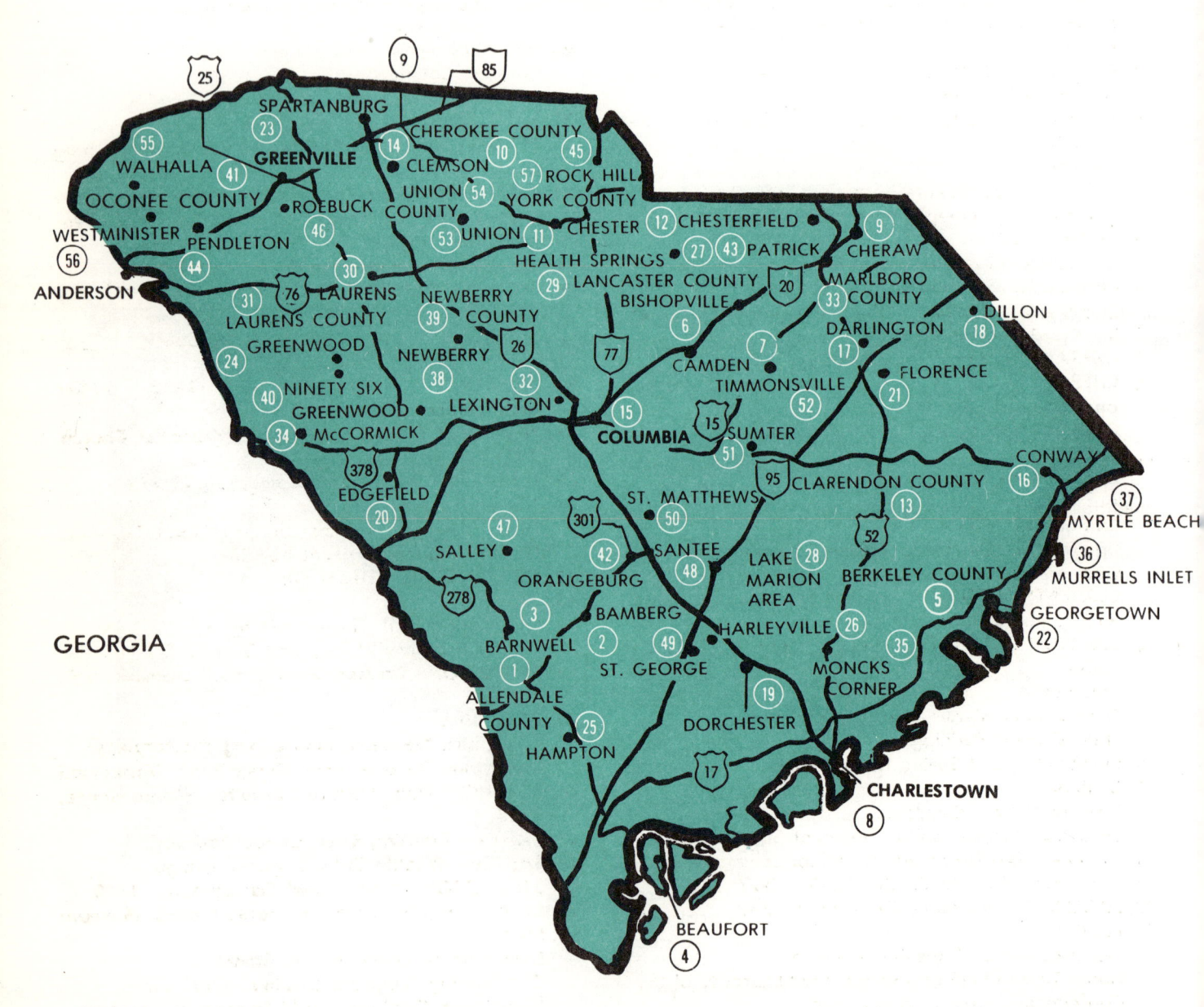

Key:

① relates to number 1 on the following page.

page 170 / treasure trails

SOUTH CAROLINA POINTS OF INTEREST

1. ALLENDALE COUNTY - Home of Dora D. Walker, 1st Home Demonstration Agent
2. BAMBERG - Voohees College, established 1897 by Negro woman
3. BARNWELL - one of two vertical sundials ever made, still works
4. BEAUFORT
   Beaufort Museum, relics date from 1711;
   National Cemetery, 12,000 Union soldiers buried there
5. BERKELEY COUNTY - Fishing Derby, world's championship contest
6. BISHOPVILLE - Site of the Cash-Shannon Duel, July 5, 1880
7. CAMDEN
   Carolina Cup, steeplechase race, March;
   Colonial Cup, steeplechase race, November
8. CHARLESTON
   Charleston Museum, oldest in U.S.;
   Charles Towne Landing, unusual park;
   Charleston Dock Street Theatre, original costumes for Porgie and Bess designed here
9. CHERAW - Bomar Water Gardens, 22 acres
10. CHEROKEE COUNTY - Possum Trot School, restored one-room school, 1880;
    Cowpens Battlefield, National monument
11. CHESTER
    Chester Hall, Old Opera House;
    Aaron Burr Rock;
    Confederate Monument
12. CHESTERFIELD - Craig House, headquarters for General Sherman
13. CLARENDON COUNTY - Fort Watson, battleground during Revolutionary War
14. CLEMSON - Clemson University, John C. Calhoun house
15. COLUMBIA
    Robert Mills Historical House and Park;
    State Capitol Building
16. CONWAY - Old Spring Home, 1870
17. DARLINGTON
    Natural Kalmia Gardens;
    Stock car racing capital, home of Southern 500
18. DILLON - The Dillon House, historical museum
19. DORCHESTER - Old Ft. Dorchester, built 1757
20. EDGEFIELD - Magnolia Dale, built 1839
21. FLORENCE
    Florence Air and Missile Museum;
    Henry Timrod Park and Shrine, Poet Laureate of the Confederacy taught school here
22. GEORGETOWN - Rice Museum, 1842
23. GREENVILLE
    Bob Jones Biblical Museum, Sacred and Biblical Art;
    Poinsette Rock Bridge, oldest rock bridge still in use, 1820
24. GREENWOOD - Festival of Flowers, 3rd largest in United States, July
25. HAMPTON - Watermelon Festival, June
26. HARLEYVILLE - St. Paul's Campground, **established** 1881
27. HEALTH SPRINGS - Mineral Spring
28. LAKE MARION AREA - recreational center
29. LANCASTER COUNTY
    Birthplace of Andrew Jackson, 7th President of the United States;
    Hanging Rock, natural wonder;
    Forty Acre Rock
30. LAURENS
    Laurens County Courthouse, 1785;
    Laurens Glass Works, oldest in U.S., 1910
31. LAURENS COUNTY - Hickory Tavern, 1864
32. LEXINGTON - John Fox House, unique threshing house
33. MARLBORO COUNTY - Pegues House, document signed for exchange of Revolutionary War prisoners
34. McCORMICK - Gold Mines, in use
35. MONCKS CORNER - The Confederate States ship "David"
36. MURRELLS INLET - Brookgreen Gardens
37. MYRTLE BEACH - Sun Fun Festival, June
38. NEWBERRY - Opera House, 1882, Gothic architecture
39. NEWBERRY COUNTY - Bush River Baptist Church, 1771
40. NINETY SIX - Star Fort Museum, built 1780
41. OCONEE COUNTY
    Duke Power Nuclear Station, 1st in South Carolina;
    Oconee Station, unusual building
42. ORANGEBURG - Edisto Gardens
43. PATRICK
    Old Market Hall, slaves sold here;
    Tenner Brothers Winery and Vineyards
44. PENDLETON - Farmers Society Hall, oldest in U.S., 1815
45. ROCK HILL
    Glenclairn Gardens, landscaping masterpiece;
    Carowinds, 73 acre park, styled after Disneyland
46. ROEBUCK - Walnut Grove Plantation, Manor House, 1765
47. SALLEY - Chittling Strut, annual festival
48. SANTEE - Wildlife Rufuge, geese refuge
49. ST. GEORGE - Indian Field Campground, 1800
50. ST. MATTHEWS - Calhoun County Library Museum
51. SUMTER
    Bethel Home Demonstration marker;
    Outstanding Sculpture Display, totem poles;
    Swan Lake Gardens, world famous iris gardens
52. TIMMONSVILLE - Tobacco Markets
53. UNION - Musgrove Mill Monument Site, 1861
54. UNION COUNTY - Monument Site to Balloonist Professor T. S. C. Lowe, April 20, 1861
55. WALHALLA - Walhalla Fish Hatchery
56. WESTMINISTER - Prather's Covered Bridge
57. YORK COUNTY - Kings Mountain National Park and York

treasure trails / page 171

South Carolina State House, completed 1907, overlooks capital city, Columbia. Bronze stars mark cannon hits from General Sherman's army during Civil War.

Defenders Monument, Charleston, stands tribute to Confederates of Civil War.

The architecture of Old Charleston dates back to pre-1776

Fort Sumter, in the harbor of Charleston, South Carolina, was the site of the first shot of the Civil War.

page 172 / treasure trails

STATE MOTTO: Under God The People Rule
STATE BIRD: Chinese Ringneck Pheasant
STATE FLOWER: Pasque

SOUTH DAKOTA
Admitted to the Union in 1889

FOR FURTHER INFORMATION WRITE:

- State Highway Publicity Office
  Pierre, South Dakota 57501

- State Game, Fish and Parks
  Pierre, South Dakota 57501

South Dakota is a large land area, 75,955 square miles, with a sparse population. Flat prairie land, much of which is Indian Reservation, and wheat fields are the scene until the great Missouri River which divides the state at about midpoint. Harnessed by four man-made dams forming lakes, this river region provides good fishing and other recreational opportunities. Quite different from the ranch and prairie country of the west is the rolling and fertile farmland east of the Missouri River. For the most part this land is under cultivation and divided into smaller farms and dairies.

The weather is as varied as the land, from the severe cold in the winter to very warm in the summer with golden days in October.

Indians and buffalo roamed this land for hundreds of years. The Verendrye Brothers who claimed the land for France in 1743 were the first known white men. French fur traders coming up the Missouri River settled here before the explorations of Lewis and Clark in 1804 and 1805. It was not until 1861 that the Dakota Territory was created. Gold discovered in the Black Hills in 1875 brought a rush of adventurers. Homestake Mine, the largest gold mine operating in the Western Hemisphere, is located at Lead.

The economy of the state is based upon a diversified agriculture with livestock production, crop production, and dairying as the number one industry. The Morrell meat-packing plant located in Sioux Falls is the largest agriculturally oriented industrial plant in the state. EROS, or Earth Resources Observation System, is just north of Sioux Falls, the state's largest city. The only center of its kind, it dispenses throughout the entire world information learned from satellite filming. The second largest industry is tourism. Mount Rushmore National Monument, chosen as a focal point for the nation's 1976 bicentennial celebration, attracts over a million tourists annually.

Mount Rushmore, near Keystone, chosen as a focal point for the nation's 1976 bicentennial celebration, attracts over a million tourists annually.

treasure trails / page 173

MINNESOTA

NORTH DAKOTA

NEBRASKA

WYOMING

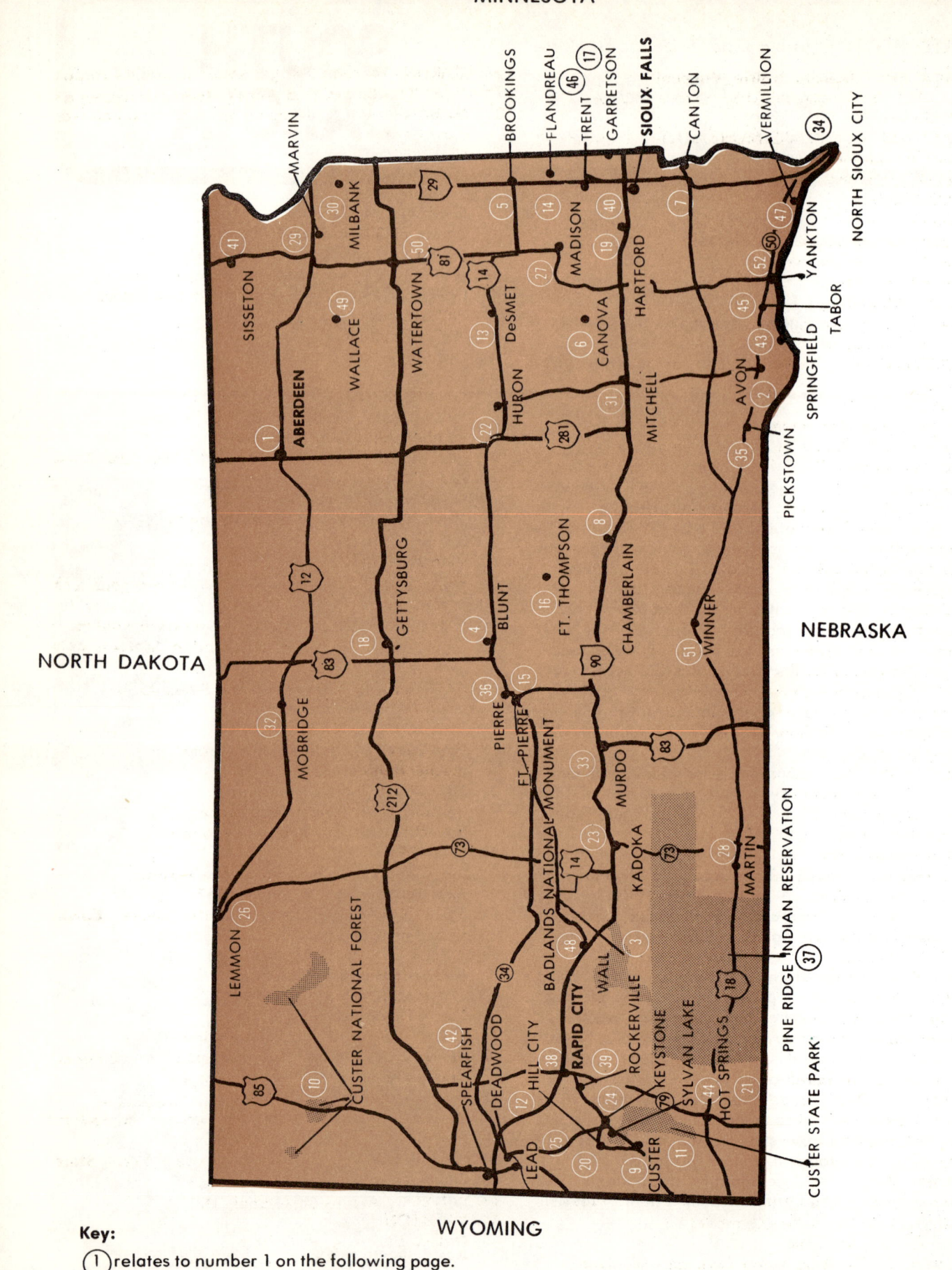

Key:
① relates to number 1 on the following page.

page 174 / treasure trails

SOUTH DAKOTA POINTS OF INTEREST

1. ABERDEEN - Dakota Prairie Museum
2. AVON - Birthplace of U.S. Senator, George S. McGovern
3. BADLANDS NATIONAL MONUMENT - Prehistoric Rock Formation
4. BLUNT - Mentor House, teacher of Abe Lincoln
5. BROOKINGS
   Memorial Art Center, Harvey Dunn Paintings;
   Coughlin Campanile, (South Dakota State Univ.);
   Ron-Lin Mushroom Farm
6. CANOVA - Angus Broadview Farm, International Grand Champion
7. CANTON - Newton Hills, legends of buried gold, Indian massacres and horse-thief hangout
8. CHAMBERLAIN - Excursion Boat, on the Missouri River
9. CUSTER
   Crazy Horse Monument;
   Badger Hole, home of 1st poet Laureate;
   Harney Peak, 7242 ft. highest point east of "Rockies";
   Black Hills Play House, summer theatre
10. CUSTER NATIONAL FOREST
    Slim Buttes;
    Custer Battlefield
11. CUSTER STATE PARK - Buffalo herd
12. DEADWOOD
    "Days of 76", August;
    Mount Moriah Cemetery, graves of Calamity Jane, Wild Bill Hickok and Preacher Smith
13. DeSMET - Laura Ingalls Wilder Home and Pageant, pioneer writer "Little House Books"
14. FLANDREAU - Indian Boarding School, world's largest
15. FT. PIERRE - Verendrye Monument and Museum, early French explorers
16. FT. THOMPSON
    Big Bend Dam;
    Several old forts
17. GARRETSON - Palisades, unusual rock formations along Sioux River
18. GETTYSBURG - Houck Ranch, largest privately owned buffalo herd in South Dakota
19. HARTFORD - Buffalo Ridge Horse Ranch
20. HILL CITY - 1880 Train Ride, narrow gauge
21. HOT SPRINGS
    Evans Plunge, natural indoor swimming pool;
    Wind Cave National Monument, unusual wind movement
22. HURON - State fairgrounds
23. KADOKA - Red Cloud Indian Musuem
24. KEYSTONE
    Mt. Rushmore, nature tours;
    Shrine of Democracy
25. LEAD
    Homestake Gold Mine, largest in western hemisphere, tours May-October;
    Terry Peak, ski area
26. LEMMON - Petrified Wood Park and Museum
27. MADISON
    Karl Mundt Library, Dakota State College campus;
28. MARTIN - LaCreek Refuge, national wildlife refuge
29. MARVIN - Blue Cloud Abbey, Indian information
30. MILBANK - American Legion Baseball, baseball was born here
31. MITCHELL
    Corn Palace;
32. MOBRIDGE
    Sioux Indian Museum;
    Grave of Sitting Bull;
    Sitting Bull Stampede, Rodeo, July 4th
33. MURDO - Pioneer Museum, antique autos
34. NORTH SIOUX CITY - Greyhound Dog Races
35. PICKSTOWN
    Ft. Randall Dam;
    Old Fort Chapel
36. PIERRE
    Oahe Dam, large recreational area;
    State Capitol, Inaugural Doll Collection;
    Paddlefishing, Missouri River
37. PINE RIDGE INDIAN RESERVATION - Wounded Knee
38. RAPID CITY
    Ellsworth Air Force Base;
    Stave Kirk Church (Chapel in the Hills);
    Reptile Gardens;
    Dinosaur Park, life size dinosaurs;
39. ROCKERVILLE - ghost town revived from gold rush
40. SIOUX FALLS
    Augustana College, center for western studies;
    EROS, Earth Resource Observation System, only one in world;
    "The Falls," waterfalls on Big Sioux River;
    Husett's Stock Car Races
41. SISSETON
    Fort Sisseton, restored Army Fort;
    Sieche Hollow, nature area;
42. SPEARFISH — Indian Art Center
    Passion Play, June to September;
    Spearfish Canyon, beautiful scenery
43. SPRINGFIELD
    Ferry Boat, only ferry in South Dakota;
    First Schoolhouse in State, 1859
44. SYLVAN LAKE - Summer White House, Calvin Coolidge lived there
45. TABOR
    Rockport Hutterite Colonies;
    Old Water Mill attraction;
    Czeck Days, March
46. TRENT - Chuck Wagon Feed, June
47. VERMILLION - Collection of Musical Instruments, University of South Dakota Campus
48. WALL - Wall Drug, world famous drugstore
49. WALLACE - Birthplace of U.S. Senator, Hubert H. Humphrey
50. WATERTOWN - Mellette House, first State Governor's Mansion
51. WINNER - Ascension Chapel, 1897
52. YANKTON
    Oldest city in South Dakota;
    Gavins Point Dam, recreation area

treasure trails / page 175

South Dakota is a cattle and farming state. In small grain production it ranks among the top states in the nation.

When frost settles and colors brighten, Spearfish Canyon, Roughlock Falls and Iron Creek are of special beauty to photographers.

Sportsmen enjoy the abundant fishing and hunting found in the state.

A drive on Needles Highway in the Black Hills provides a breath-taking view of the unique granite structure.

Cattle and beef production is a large part of South Dakota's economy.

All types of outdoor recreation are offered to visitors in the Black Hills area of South Dakota.

Photographs furnished by South Dakota Department of Highways.

page 176 / treasure trails

STATE MOTTO: It Just Comes Natural
STATE BIRD: Mockingbird
STATE FLOWER: Iris

TENNESSEE
Admitted to the Union in 1796

FOR FURTHER INFORMATION WRITE:

- Tennessee Conservation Dept.
  Forestry Division
  2611 West End Avenue
  Nashville, Tennessee 37209

- Tennessee Game & Fish Commission
  Ellington Agricultural Center
  Nashville, Tennessee 37211

- Frank McGuire
  1028 Andrew Jackson Bldg.
  Nashville, Tennessee 37211

The Cherokee, Chickasaw, Muskhogan and other Indian tribes knew Tennessee long before Davy Crockett or Daniel Boone found the tranquil beauty and peace of the state.

While the settlers were searching for a place to establish settlements on the seaboard, Tennessee remained an unsettled, untamed land. In 1757, Tennessee was the "West", America's first frontier.

During the American Revolution Tennessee saw its first town. In 1796 it became the 16th state in the union. Elected that year as one of our first senators was Andrew Jackson.

Bravery at the Battle of New Orleans made Andrew Jackson a national hero overnight, and 13 years later he was elected to the highest office in the land. Tennessee has also sent two other distinguished statesmen to Washington. James K. Polk was elected in 1844 and when Abraham Lincoln was assassinated in 1865, Andrew Johnson became the nation's 17th president.

The Civil War brought both fame and destruction to this beautiful natural land. More battles were fought here than in any other state with the exception of Virginia.

After the war ended Tennesseans laid down their arms and began to restore their homes, farm lands and commercial businesses. New settlements sprang up near the Mississippi River.

In 1933 the Tennessee Valley Authority was established to harness the great power of the rivers for cheaper electricity for Tennessee and six of her sister states. Some of the best fishing, boating and camping facilities in the nation are on the lakes created by the T.V.A.

Tennessee's heart beats to music. The folk music that came over the mountains with the first settlers has led to one of Tennessee's biggest economic industries. Nashville has earned the name of Music City, U.S.A.

On May 26, 1972, Opryland U.S.A. was opened on 110 acres by the Cumberland River near the city of Nashville.

View of the Smokies and Gatlinburg from Mt. LeConte.

page 178 / treasure trails

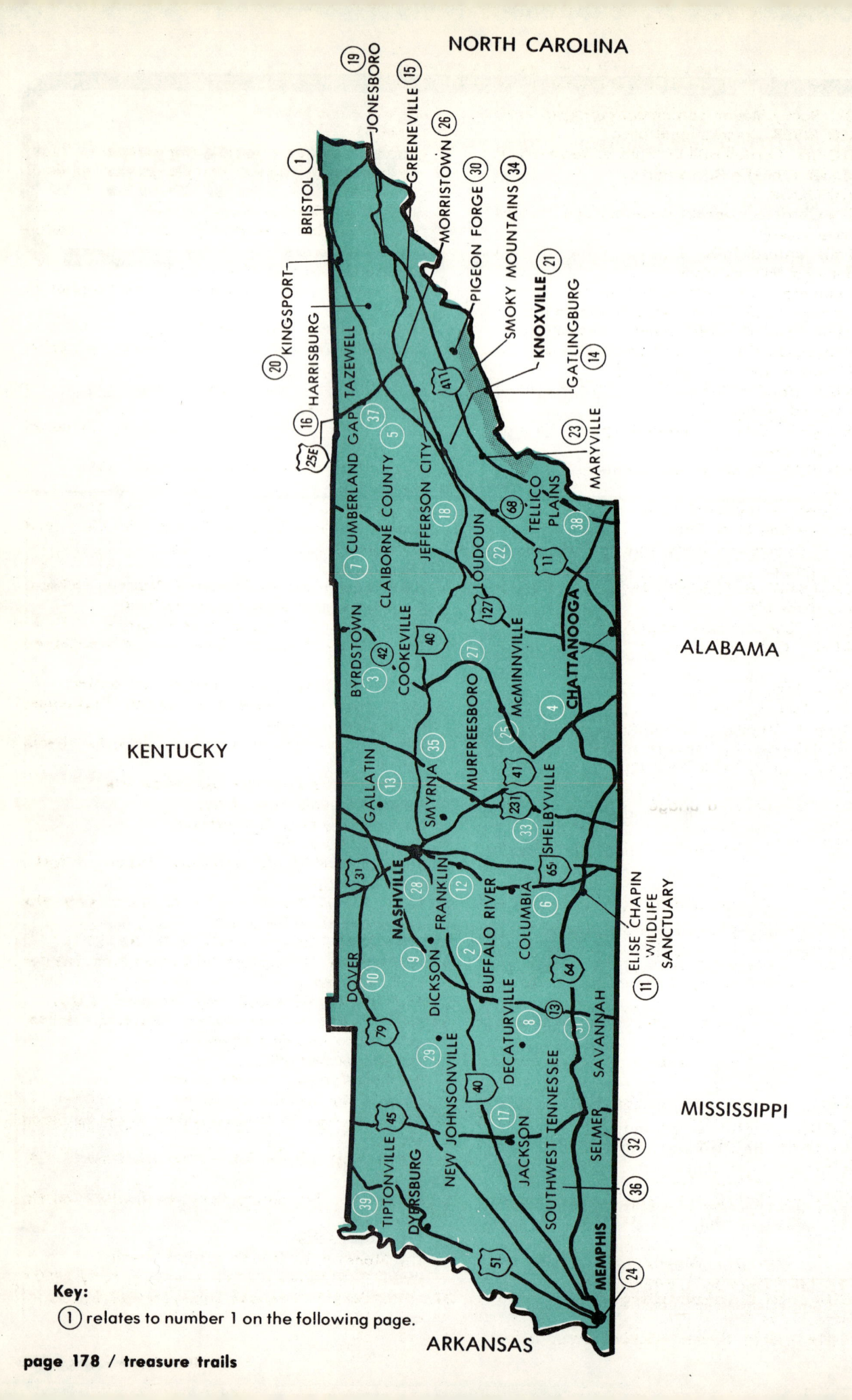

TENNESSEE POINTS OF INTEREST

1. BRISTOL - Rocky Mount, settlement dating to 1770
2. BUFFALO RIVER - recreational area
3. BYRDSTOWN - Cordell Hull Birthplace, Secretary of State under Franklin Roosevelt
4. CHATTANOOGA
   Rock City Gardens, Lookout Mountain, see 7 states from Lovers Leap;
   Ruby Falls, natural falls;
   Chickamauga Military Park;
   Signal Mountain, Civil War battle site;
   Chickamauga Lake, T.V.A. recreational center;
   Fuller Gun Museum, world's most complete display
5. CLAIBORNE COUNTY - Lincoln Memorial University, over 16,000 memorabilia of Lincoln
6. COLUMBIA - Home of James K. Polk, 11th President of the United States
7. CUMBERLAND GAP - natural pass through Cumberland Mountains
8. DECATURVILLE - Redd House, haunted, 1805
9. DICKSON
   Ruskin Cave, recreational center;
   Montgomery Bell State Park
10. DOVER - Ft. Donelson Military National Park, site of Civil War battles
11. ELISE CHAPIN WILDLIFE SANCTUARY - preserve for bird and plant life
12. FRANKLIN - Carter House, restored house
13. GALLATIN - Cragfont, home of General James Winchester
14. GATLINGBURG
    Craftsman Fair, October;
    Wildflower Pilgrimage—Springtime
15. GREENEVILLE - Home of Andrew Johnson, 17th U.S. President, original Tailor Shop and furnishings on grounds
16. HARRISBURG - Covered Bridge
17. JACKSON - Casey Jones Home, museum
18. JEFFERSON CITY - Glenmore, Victorian mansion, built 1868
19. JONESBORO - Tennessee's oldest town, 1779
20. KINGSPORT - Cumberland Gap, where Daniel Boone blazed trail
21. KNOXVILLE
    Gatlingburg, mountain resort;
    Great Smoky Mountains, half million acres of forest;
    Blount Mansion, home of William Blount, Constitution signer, built 1792;
    Marble Springs, home of first governor, John Sevier;
    Oak Ridge, museum of nuclear energy;
    Norris Lake;
    Ramsey House, founder of the University of Tennessee;
    Dogwood Arts Festival, April;
    Craighead-Jackson House, houses famous antiques and silver service, built 1818 Knox County first stone house;
    Frank H. McClung Museum, exhibits on anthropology and natural history
22. LOUDOUN - Fort Loudoun, 1st English built fort in Tennessee, 1756
23. MARYVILLE - Sam Houston Schoolhouse, oldest original schoolhouse
24. MEMPHIS
    Chucalissa Indian Village, restored Indian village;
    The Pink Palace, museum and planetarium made of pink stone;
    Handy Park, Sear of Black Culture;
    Front Street Cotton Market, handles 1/3 of cotton market in world;
    Graceland, home of Elvis Presley;
    St. Judes Hospital, largest children's hospital in world;
    Cotton Carnival, 2nd week in May
25. McMINNVILLE - Fall Creek Falls, highest waterfall east of Mississippi
26. MORRISTOWN - Davy Crockett Tavern
27. MURFREESBORO
    Stones River National Battlefield, oldest memorial of Civil War;
    Oakland, three houses in one, built 1815
28. NASHVILLE
    Opryland U.S.A., 110 acre amusement park;
    Ryman Auditorium, First Grand Ole Opry and Opryland, U.S.A.;
    State capital;
    Hermitage, home of President Andrew Jackson;
    Tulip Grove, home of Rachel Jackson;
    Travellers Rest, home of John Overton;
    Belle Meade Mansion, famous as thoroughbred nursery;
    Center Hill Lake, T.V.A. recreational center;
    Parthenon, exact replica of Greek Parthenon, houses art museum;
    Ellington Agriculture Center, arena for horse shows;
    Natchez Trace Parkway, old Indian trail;
    Iroquois Steeplechase, May;
    Pro-Celebrity Golf Tournament;
    Fort Nashborough;
    Thurston Collection, prehistoric Indian artifacts, Vanderbilt University
29. NEW JOHNSONVILLE - T.V.A. harnessing the Tennessee river for power
30. PIGEON FORGE - grist mill, built 1830
31. SAVANNAH - Shiloh National Military Park, famous Civil War site
32. SELMER - Marive Fossil Beds, exposed in U.S.
33. SHELBYVILLE - Tennessee Walking Horse, celebration to select champion
34. SMOKY MOUNTAINS
    Foothills Parkway, scenic drive;
    Cades Cove, wildlife sanctuary
35. SMYRNA - Sam Davis Home, killed as spy by Union soldiers
36. SOUTHWEST TENNESSEE - Pickwich Dam, T.V.A. structure
37. TAZEWELL - Big Spring Primitive Baptist Church, built 1795
38. TELLICO PLAINS
    The Mansion, built with escape tunnel;
    Placer Gold Mines, gold discovered in early 1800's
39. TIPTONVILLE - Reelfoot Lake, formed by earthquake, 1811

treasure trails / page 179

Chucalissa in Memphis, Tennessee.

A bird's eye view of the Cumberland Mountains in Tennessee.

Bloody Pond at Shiloh near Savanna, Tennessee.

Parthenon, Nashville, Tennessee.

page 180 / treasure trails

STATE MOTTO: Friendship
STATE BIRD: Mockingbird
STATE FLOWER: Bluebonnet

TEXAS
Admitted to the Union in 1845

FOR FURTHER INFORMATION WRITE:

- Texas Highway Department
  Travel and Information Division
  P.O. Box 5084
  Austin, Texas 78763

Texas with its 296,000 square miles in land area, makes up 7 1/2% of the United States. It has 624 miles of coast line along the Gulf of Mexico. Over 26 million acres of woodland. The climate in Texas is generally hot in summer, cool falls, reasonable winters, and balmy springs.

There are 70 state parks with scenic and recreational facilities. Texas has over 6,000 square miles of inland hunting and fishing, plus the 624 miles of shoreland. Hunters will find white-tail deer, javalins, wild boars, squirrels, mule deer, pronghorn antelope and game birds which include migratory waterfowl, white-wing doves, pheasants, prairie chickens, sandhill cranes.

Industries and manufacturing ranks eighth in the United States. These include manufacturing of machinery, transportation equipment, electrical equipment, medical and communication equipment. Other industries are apparel and textile plants, chemical and petroleum refining, dairy products, canned, cured, and frozen foods, lumber and wood products, iron and steel foundries and fabricated metal products.

Farming is big business in Texas. Main crops include sorghum, cotton, cottonseed, rice, wheat, rye, barley, oats, corn, peanuts, soybeans, and truck crops of vegetables, fruits, and nuts.

Ranching, another big business, with the raising of cattle makes Texas rank first in farming and cattle.

Some flowers of Texas, with 5,000 varieties, are the beautiful bluebonnet, pitcher plants, cacti, morning glorys, buttercups, Indian paint brush **bougainvillea**, roses, dogwood and poinsettias, and many others.

Texas has several very interesting caverns and caves. The Longhorn Cavern, Wonder Cave, The Natural Bridge Cavern, also Devils Sinkhole, Palace, Dagoal, Kickapoo and Green Caves, make some very enjoyable trips under the earth.

Thrilling Log Flume at Six Flags over Texas, in Arlington, Texas.

treasure trails / page 181

Key:
① relates to number 1 on the following page.

page 182 / treasure trails

TEXAS POINTS OF INTEREST

1. ABILENE - Old Abilene Town, western city restored
2. ALAMO - Live Steam Museum
3. ARLINGTON
   Six Flags over Texas, amusement park;
   Seven Seas Marine Park, Home of the American League Baseball Team for Texas;
   Western Wax Museum;
   Lion Country Safari
4. AUSTIN
   State Capitol Building;
   Lyndon B. Johnson Library
5. BALMORHEA - Largest swimming pool, fed by natural springs
6. BEAUMONT - Birthplace of First Oil Boom, spindletop monument
7. BIG BEND NATIONAL PARK - 707,221 acres
8. BONHAM - Sam Rayburn Library
9. BURNET - Longhorns Caverns
10. CLARENDON - Pete Borden's Gun Collection
11. CLIFTON - Norwegian Settlement
12. CRESSON
    Pate Museum of Transportation;
    H.B. Smith Museum, steam tractors and threshing machines
13. CROCKETT - Davy Crockett National Forest
14. DALHART - XIT Ranch, 110,721 head of cattle
15. DALLAS
    State Fair of Texas, October;
    John F. Kennedy Memorial
16. DEL RIO - Val Verde Winery, founded in 1880
17. DENISON
    Birthplace of Dwight D. Eisenhower, home and park;
    Lake Texamo Recreational Area
18. DENTON - Pilot Know, hide-out of Sam Bass, 19th century outlaw
19. EL PASO
    Tramway, aerial view of Texas, New Mexico, and Mexico;
    Astez Colorado Store, missions, museums, and monuments
20. FALFURRIAS - Texas Rangers Museum
21. FORT DAVIS
    Davis Mountain, recreational area;
    McDonald Observatory;
    Neill Museum, toys made in Texas
22. FORT STOCKTON - Dinosaur Park
23. FORT WORTH
    Amon Carter Western Art Museum;
    Botanic Gardens
24. GALVESTON
    Sea Arama Marine World;
    Free ferry ride across to Port Bolivar Lighthouse
25. GLEN ROSE - Dinosaur Prints and State Park
26. HARLINGEN - Marine Military Academy
27. HENDERSON - Great Texas Oil Well Tour
28. HOUSTON
    Astrodome, domed baseball and football stadium;
    National Aeronautics (NASA) Space Administration Manned Space Center, now the Johnson Space Center;
    Battleship Texas and Houston Monument
29. JACKSONVILLE - Hamlins Gardens, azaleas, dogwood, and redbud tours
30. JEFFERSON - historical restored town
31. JOHNSON CITY - Home and birthplace of Lyndon B. Johnson, buried here
32. KARNACK - birthplace of Mrs. Lyndon B. Johnson
33. KINGSVILLE - Kings Ranch, largest in the U.S.
34. LAREDO - Cactus Gardens, fossils and Indian artifacts
35. LONGVIEW - Franks Museum, 800 antique and rare dolls
36. MIDLAND - Midland Museum, history of early man
37. MISSION - Poinsettia Gardens
38. ODESSA - Meteor Crater, formed over 20,000 years ago, second largest in United States
39. OLNEY - Buffalo, a private herd
40. PALACIOS - Marine Fishery Research Station
41. PANNA MARIA - oldest Polish settlement
42. PARIS
    Flying Tigers Air Museum;
    Canada Goose Refuge
43. PERRYTON - Buried City, 1,000 rooms 70 opened
44. PHARR - Old Clock Museum
45. PORT ARANSAS - University of Texas Marine Life Institute
46. RIO GRANDE CITY - Our Lady of Lourdes Grotto, replica of the one in France
47. ROCKPORT - winter home of the near extinct whooping cranes
48. ROUNDROCK - El Milagro Museum, American and Oriental antiques
49. SAINT JO - Milners Mill, operating grist mill
50. SALT FLAT - Salt Flats
51. SAN ANTONIO
    Alamo, historical mission;
    River Walk and Hemis Fair Plaza, site of 1968 World's Fair;
    Museum of Fiesta Dress, antique cars, parks
52. SAN AUGUSTINE - Old Town Restored
53. SAN JUAN - Shrine of Our Lady of the Valley
54. SAN MARCOS
    Aquarene show;
    Wonder Cave
55. SIERRA BLANCA - Dogie Wright Collection of Firearms and Relics of Frontier Lawmen and Desperadoes
56. STINETT - Battle of the Adobe Walls, historical battleground between Kit Carson and Indians
57. SULPHUR SPRINGS
    Mineral Springs;
    Music Box Gallery, over 300 music boxes
58. TERLINGUA - Old Waldron Mine, rock hounds paradise, inactive cinnabar mine
59. TYLER
    Goodmans Museum and Hudnall Planetarium, replicas of planes;
    Municipal Rose Gardens, 35,000 bushes of roses, "Rose Capital of the World"
60. VERNON - Bird Egg Collection, 10,000 eggs of 750 varieties

treasure trails / page 183

Houston Astrodome

Photographs furnished by Houston Chamber Commerce.

The Alamo, Shrine of Texas Liberty. Present building is old chapel of Mission San Antonio de Valero, founded 1718 by Franciscan padres, in San Antonio.

Photographs furnished by San Antonio Convention & Visitors Bureau.

Big Bend National Park, Green Gulch from road leading to Basin.

Photographs furnished by National Park Concessions

page 184 / treasure trails

STATE MOTTO: Industry
STATE BIRD: California Gull
STATE FLOWER: Sego Lily

UTAH
Admitted to the Union in 1896

FOR FURTHER INFORMATION WRITE:

- Utah Tourist & Publicity Council
  State Capitol
  Salt Lake City, Utah 84114

- State Chamber of Commerce
  19 East 2nd South
  Salt Lake City, Utah 84114

- Utah Travel Council
  Council Hall, Capital Hill
  Salt Lake City, Utah 84114

The Spanish were the first to explore Utah around 1776. At that time Utah was occupied by Shoshonean, Plute, Navaho, and the Ute Indians. It was known as the Spanish Trail. Fur trappers in search of beaver pelts passed into Utah between 1811 and 1840. The trappers were the first white men to settle in Utah.

The westward moving Mormons under the direction of Brigham Young reached Salt Lake in July of 1847 and established a commonwealth. Utah came under United States sovereignty in 1848. In 1850 Congress created the territory of Utah. There was much friction between United States officials and Brigham Young. The Utah War of 1857-58 followed.

Utah gained statehood in 1896 and became the 45th state.

Salt Lake City is the seat of the Church of Jesus Christ of Latter Day Saints (Mormon Church), and its hub is the Mormon Temple, a Gothic edifice of native gray granite that was 40 years under construction (1853-1893).

Utah, a great basin state, is the 10th largest state in the union. The surface of Utah is irregular, high mountain ranges, altitude ranges from 13,528 in the Uintas to 3,000 in the southwest corner which comprise the eastern rim of the Great Basin. East of that divide lies a fantastically eroded country which makes Utah a scenic marvel. There are deep canyons, natural bridges, towers. The western half of the state is without drainage to the sea; its streams flow into alkali flats or saline lakes of which Great Salt Lake is the largest.

There are three basic industries in Utah; manufacturing, mining and agriculture. Food processing is the number one manufacturing activity in Utah. The production of nonelectrical machinery and the production of petroleum and coal products are the second and third sources.

Temple Square, Salt Lake City

treasure trails / page 185

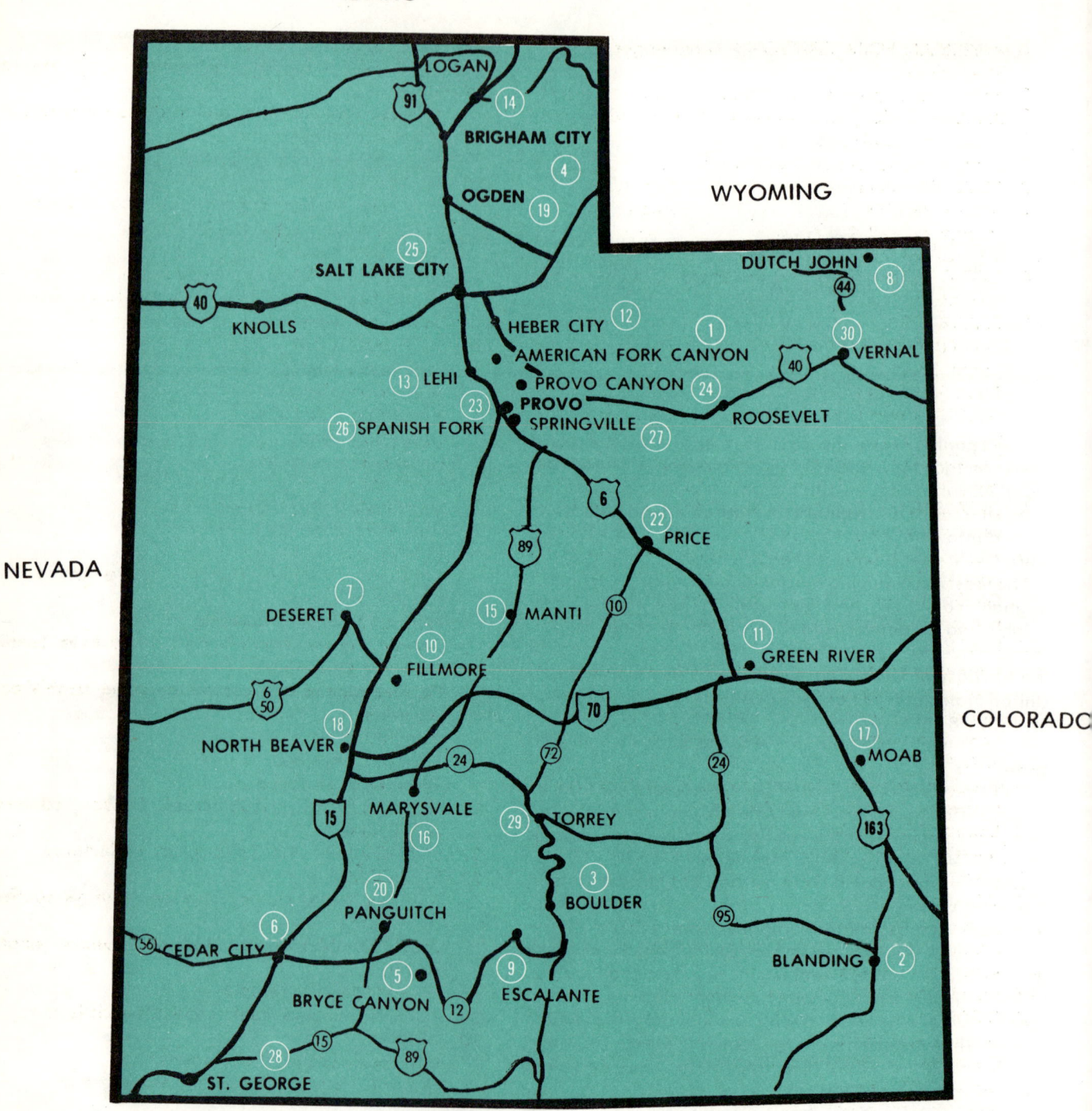

Key:

① relates to number 1 on the following page.

page 186 / treasure trails

UTAH POINTS OF INTEREST

1. AMERICAN FORK CANYON - Timpanogos Cave
2. BLANDING
   Hovenweep, prehistoric Indian towers;
   Rainbow Bridge, salmon colored arch over gorge;
   Four Corners Area;
   Bluff, Navaho Indian Reservation
3. BOULDER - Anasazi State Park, Indian village
4. BRIGHAM CITY   Refuge;
   Migratory Bird Refuge;
   Intermountain Indian School
6. BRYCE CANYON - Paria State Park, unique formations
5. CEDAR CITY
   Zion National Park, interesting eroded landscapes;
   Cedar Breaks, pink cliffs, lava beds;
   Brian Head, ski area
7. DESERET - Fort Deseret State Park, remains of fort built in 1865
8. DUTCH JOHN - Flamingo Gorge Dam, recreation area
9. ESCALANTE - Escalante State Park, deposits of petrified wood
10. FILLMORE - Old Capital, Utah's first territorial capital, 1855
11. GREEN RIVER - Green River State Park, main tributary of Colorado, "white water" float trips
12. HEBER CITY
    Wasatch Mountain, mountain slopes, canyons, golf course, and campground;
    Homestead, hotpots, golf course, campsites
13. LEHI - Fort Douglas, military base
14. LOGAN
    Historic agriculture Intermountain Heborium, Museum (Utah State University);
    Logan LDS temple
15. MANTI - Manti Temple, Mormon temple
16. MARYSVALE - Big Rock Candy Mountain
17. MOAB
    Arches Monument, eroded giant arches;
    Natural Bridges, carved from sandstone, wildlife sanctuary, Indian ruins
18. NORTH BEAVER - Historic Cove Fort
19. OGDEN
    Willard Bay State Park, huge reservoir;
    Collection of Browning firearms;
    Ogden LDS Temple;
    Solitude, ski area;
    Hill Air Force Base
    Weber State College
20. PANGUITCH - Bryce Canyon
21. PARK CITY - mining, recreation area, ski resort
22. PRICE
    Dinosaur Prehistoric Museum, dinosaur bones and geologic displays;
    Geological & Prehistoric Museum
23. PROVO
    Utah Lake, largest fresh-water lake in Utah;
    Geneva Steel, large steel mill;
    Provo LDS Temple
2   PROVO CANYON
    Alpine Scenic Loop, beautiful mountain drive;
    Bridal Veil Falls
25. SALT LAKE CITY
    Antelope Island;
    Beehive House;
    Bonneville Salt Flats;
    Great Salt Lake;
    Hansen Planetarium;
    Hogle Zoo;
    Kennecott Copper Mine;
    Liberty Park;
    Lion House;
    Museum of Natural History—University of Utah;
    Pioneer Museum;
    Pioneer Memorial Building;
    Temple Square, Organ Recital, Tabernacle, Temple;
    Utah State Capital;
    Pioneer Monument, commemorating Utah's early pioneers;
    Alta, ski area;
    Brighton, ski area;
    Snow Bird, ski area
26. SPANISH FORK - Hobblecreek Canyon, campsite, golf course
27. SPRINGVILLE - Art Gallery, art collection
28. ST. GEORGE
    Brigham Young Home, Brigham Young's southern Utah home;
    Jocob Hamblin Home, Mormon Leaders, summer home;
    St. George LDS Temple
29. TORREY - Capitol Reef, sandstone cliffs
30. VERNAL
    Dinosaur, fossils of dinosaurs;
    Natural History, life-size dinosaur group

treasure trails / page 187

Bryce Canyon National Park, near Escalante, Utah.

Utah State Capitol Building in Salt Lake City.

Skiing in Utah

Photographs furnished by Utah tourist and Publicity Council (Hal Rumel).

page 188 / treasure trails

STATE MOTTO: Freedom And Unity
STATE BIRD: Hermit Thrush
STATE FLOWER: Red Clover

VERMONT
Admitted to the Union in 1791

FOR FURTHER INFORMATION WRITE:

- State of Vermont
  Department of Forests and Parks
  Montpelier, Vermont 05602

- State of Vermont
  Department of Fish and Game
  Montpelier, Vermont 05602

- Agency of Development and Community Affairs
  Information/Travel Division
  Montpelier, Vermont 05602

On March 4, 1791 Vermont was admitted to the Union as the 14th State. Vermont's Green Mountain range forms a virtually unbroken chain from Canada to the North and the Massachusetts border to the South. Softened by wooded hills and rolling farmlands, Vermont nestles serenely between the Connecticut River to the east and Lake Champlain to the west. Her nature's changing seasons arrive with great enthusiasm, each in its turn offering a whirl of weather and activities, with something for everyone.

Perhaps no other state in the nation is more economically dependent on the caprices of nature than Vermont. The people are very aware of the importance of Vermont's natural beauty, not only as a major asset to the tourist industry, but as a supportive foundation to the "Good Life". Vermont has led the country in forward-thinking environmental protection legislation. There is much to be protected here. The countryside comes alive in spring with pale greens, there is white-water canoeing, fishing, late spring skiing, and early planting. Summer is green and lush, cool nights and warm days are conducive to many kinds of outdoor activities. Scenic wonders invite the visitor to "stop and tarry awhile." The Fall foliage season is a riot of color, a photographers paradise, with hunting season, game suppers, country fairs and bazaars, pick-your-own apples, and cold fresh cider. Snow often greets Thanksgiving and winter offers snowshoeing, snowmobiling, ice fishing, and of course skiing.

Vermont industries make use of what is available while protecting the environment for future generations. The many craftsmen preserve the best of the old while making use of the new. In Vermont the old and the new co-exist preserving the best of two worlds. Those who have the opportunity to travel the length and breadth of Vermont can't help but observe the Yankee Pride that citizens of Vermont take in the "Green Mountain State" they call home.

A changing autumn landscape in South Woodbury.

treasure trails / page 189

Vermont Treasure Trails Map

Key:
① relates to number 1 on the following page.

Locations shown on map:

- ㉚ Jay Peak Area
- 56 St. Albans
- Newport ㊶
- ⑰ Coventry
- Brownington ⑪
- ⑭ North Fairfield ㊷
- 32 Lowell
- Barton ④
- 105 Westmore 66
- 39 Newark
- East Craftsbury ㉒
- East Haven ㉓
- Milton 36
- Mount Mansfield 38
- ⑬ Caledonia County
- Victory 62
- ㉗ Guildhall
- ㉖ Grand Isle
- 15 Williston 71
- Stowe 58
- Calais ⑫
- ㉙ Isle La Motte
- Burlington
- 54 Shelburne
- 15 Charlotte
- ㉕ Ferrisburg
- Champlain Valley ⑭
- 68 Weybridge
- 16 Chimney Point
- Duxbury 20
- 34 McCullough Turnpike
- ⑨
- Bristol ⑰
- Lincoln 31
- Montpelier 37
- Barre ③
- ⑩ Brookfield
- ㊵ Newbury
- 35 Middlebury
- Ripton 50
- Randolph 49
- Tunbridge 61
- Strafford 59
- ㉔ Fairlee
- ⑦ Brandon
- ㉘ Hubbardton
- Proctor 47
- ② Barnard
- ⑧
- ⑦⓪ White River Junction
- Woodstock 72
- 53 Rutland Region
- Rutland
- 52 Bridgewater
- Plymouth Notch 45
- 64 Wells
- Danby ⑲
- Cuttingsville 18
- Springfield 55
- 100
- Weston 65
- 11
- 103
- Rockingham 51
- Stratton Mountain 60
- Bellows Falls 5
- 63 Wardsboro
- 48 Putney
- West Townsend 67
- ⑥ Bennington
- Old Bennington ㊸
- ㉑ Dover
- ㉚ Marlboro
- ㊻ Pownal
- Whitingham 69
- 33
- Brattleboro
- ㊹ Old Ft. Dummer
- St. Johnsbury 57

New York / **New Hampshire** / **Massachusetts**

page 190 / treasure trails / Vermont

VERMONT POINTS OF INTEREST

1. ADDISON COUNTY - Green Mountain National Forest
2. BARNARD - Silver Lake State Park
3. BARRE - Granite Center of the World
4. BARTON - Orleans, Ethan Allen Furniture is manufactured
5. BELLOWS FALLS - Steam Town U.S.A., Steam Engine Museum
6. BENNINGTON
   Bennington Museum, major collection of Grandma Moses, paintings
7. BRANDON - Stephen A. Douglas birthplace
8. BRIDGEWATER - Woolen Mills, tours
9. BRISTOL - The Lords Prayer Rock, boulder
10. BROOKFIELD - Brookfield Historical Society Museum, 100-year-old floating bridge
11. BROWNINGTON - Orleans County Historical Society Museum, outstanding museum
12. CALAIS - Kent Museum, period furnishings
13. CALEDONIA COUNTY - Danville, annual Dowsing convention, October
14. CHAMPLAIN VALLEY - Panton, where Benedict Arnold ran his fleet aground, rather than surrender, 1778
15. CHARLOTTE - Fisher Landing, Champlain Ferry
16. CHIMNEY POINT - 18th century tavern, being restored
17. COVENTRY - Christmas tree center
18. CUTTINGSVILLE - Mount Holly, remains of prehistoric elephant found, 1848
19. DANBY - Home of Pearl S. Buck, restored village
20. DUXBURY - Camels Hump, natural landmark
21. DOVER - Mt. Snow, resort area
22. EAST CRAFTSBURY - Simpson Memorial Library and Museum
23. EAST HAVEN - one of New England's last virgin woodland communities
24. FAIRLEE - Lake Morey, Samuel Morey launched the world's first steamship
25. FERRISBURG - Collection of Vermont history
26. GRAND ISLE - Hyde Log Cabin, museum, 1783
27. GUILDHALL - North burying grounds, whimsical epitaphs, 1795
28. HUBBARDTON - Battlefield and monument, only Revolutionary War in Vermont
29. ISLE LA MOTTE - Shrine of St. Anne, site of French fortress built in 1666
30. JAY PEAK AREA - Hazens Notch Mountain Pass, four season area
31. LINCOLN - Lincoln Gap, scenic home of wildlife chronicler Ronald Rood
32. LOWELL - largest asbestos producer
33. MARLBORO - Marlboro Music Festival
34. McCULLOUGH TURNPIKE - magnificent mountain pass
35. MIDDLEBURY
   Sheldon Museum, filled with Americana; Middlebury College, Egbert Starr Library
36. MILTON - Sand Bar, State park and waterfowl area
37. MONTPELIER - State capitol
38. MOUNT MANSFIELD - Smugglers Notch, Vermont's highest mountain
39. NEWARK - State Fish Hatchery
40. NEWBURY - Hazen Military Road, historic invasion route to Canada
41. NEWPORT - Lake Memphremagog, second largest body of water
42. NORTH FAIRFIELD - Chester A. Arthur birthplace, America's 21st president
43. OLD BENNINGTON - Bennington Battle Monument, 1777
44. OLD FORT DUMMER - 1724
45. PLYMOUTH NOTCH - Calvin Coolidge State Forest, birthplace of President Coolidge, burial place
46. POWNAL - Green Mountain Park, thoroughbred race track
47. PROCTOR
   Vermont Marble Company exhibit, marble museum;
   Wilson Castle, 19th century
48. PUTNEY
   Wild Flower Nurseries
49. RANDOLPH - Grave of Justin Morgan Horse, sire of the Morgan House
50. RIPTON - Robert Frost Memorial Drive, where Vermont's poet Laurete spent last years of life
51. ROCKINGHAM - Meetinghouse and churchyard
52. RUTLAND
   State fair, after Labor Day;
53. RUTLAND REGION - Otter Creek, canoeists route
54. SHELBURNE - Shelburne Museum, complex on forty-five acres
55. SPRINGFIELD
   Precision tool capital of the world, tours; Eureka School house, oldest school
56. ST. ALBANS - Franklin County Museum
57. ST. JOHNSBURY - Maple Grove Maple Museum, Maple sugar making
58. STOWE - "Ski Capital of the East"
59. STRAFFORD - Justin Morrill Homestead
60. STRATTON MOUNTAIN - Daniel Webster Monument
61. TUNBRIDGE - century old world's fair held in September
62. VICTORY - Holiday in the Hills, autumn foliage celebration, September
63. WARDSBORO - settled by Samuel Hammond, member of Boston Tea Party, buried here
64. WELLS - Lake St. Catherine State Park
65. WESTON - Farrar Mansur House, 1797 tavern, maintained as museum
66. WESTMORE - Lake Willoughby, wild alpine scenery
67. WEST TOWNSEND - Scott covered bridge
68. WEYBRIDGE - University of Vermont Morgan House farm, Morgan Horses are raised
69. WHITINGHAM - Harriman Dam, birthplace of the Mormon leader Brigham Young
70. WHITE RIVER JUNCTION - The Joseph Smith Memorial, birthplace of the Morman prophet
71. WILLISTON - The Old Williston Graveyard, Vermont's first governor's grave, Thomas Chittenden
72. WOODSTOCK
   Old colonial town, bells cast by Paul Revere;

treasure trails / page 191

Covered bridges and waterfalls are one of the many attractions to the Warren area.

Constitution House, Headquarters for Bicentennial in Windsor.

Weston band concert and barbecue. Fun and games are summer activities in many Vermont communities.

Vermont's maples give up their sap under March and April sunshine.

page 192 / treasure trails

Photographs furnished by Vermont Development Department.

STATE MOTTO: Sic Semper Tyrannis
(Thus Ever To Tyrants)
STATE BIRD: Cardinal
STATE FLOWER: Dogwood

VIRGINIA
Admitted to the Union in 1788

FOR FURTHER INFORMATION WRITE:

- Virginia State Travel Service
  906-17th Street N.W.
  Washington, D.C. 20006

- Virginia State Travel Service
  Dept. of Conservation and Economic Development
  6 North 6th Street
  Richmond, Virginia 23219

- Virginia State Travel Service
  11 Rockefeller Plaza
  New York, New York 10020

Virginia is a state of history and fun, mountains and beaches, campgrounds and hoedowns. Northern Virginia is the "Gateway to Virginia" and the South. You will find a green quiet land of thoroughbred horses and magnificent plantations and an exciting land with bustling skyscrapers, superhighways and fashionable shops.

Virginia's tidewater is the timeless adventure of Jamestown, where America began; Williamsburg, where patriots plotted the course of history; and Yorktown, where a nation was born. There's future history here, at NASA's Langley Research Center, where astronauts trained for a walk on the moon. And there's mouth-watering seafood and a great outdoors. Here we find one of the seven engineering wonders of the world, the Chesapeake Bay Bridge Tunnel, a 17.6 mile link over and under the Bay between the Virginia Beach-Norfolk area and Virginia's next exciting world: The Eastern Shore. This is a magic world apart, a world of enchantment, rich tradition and a serene, yet exciting, present. The first settlers came in 1619.

In the Central-South side of the state we find Richmond; Virginia's capital city since 1770.

Virginia's manufacturing and processing products have more than doubled in recent years. The James River, with its many plants and manufacturing centers produce synthetic fibers, chemical products, textiles and tobacco products. Two of the nation's most important shipyards are found at Newport News and Portsmouth. Virginia leads the states in oyster production and ranks high in coal production.

If you're looking for a pioneer country, then drive into the state's magnificent Southwest. There's nature a-plenty. Many of Virginia's 450 public fishing streams, rivers and lakes are here in this Southwest area. The Blue Ridge, Allegheny, and Cumberland Mountains are filled with nature trails, bridle paths, parks, picnic areas and campgrounds.

George Wythe House, Williamsburg. Wythe, the first professor of law in America, taught Thomas Jefferson, John Marshall, James Monroe and Henry Clay and was the first signer of the Declaration of Independence.

treasure trails / page 193

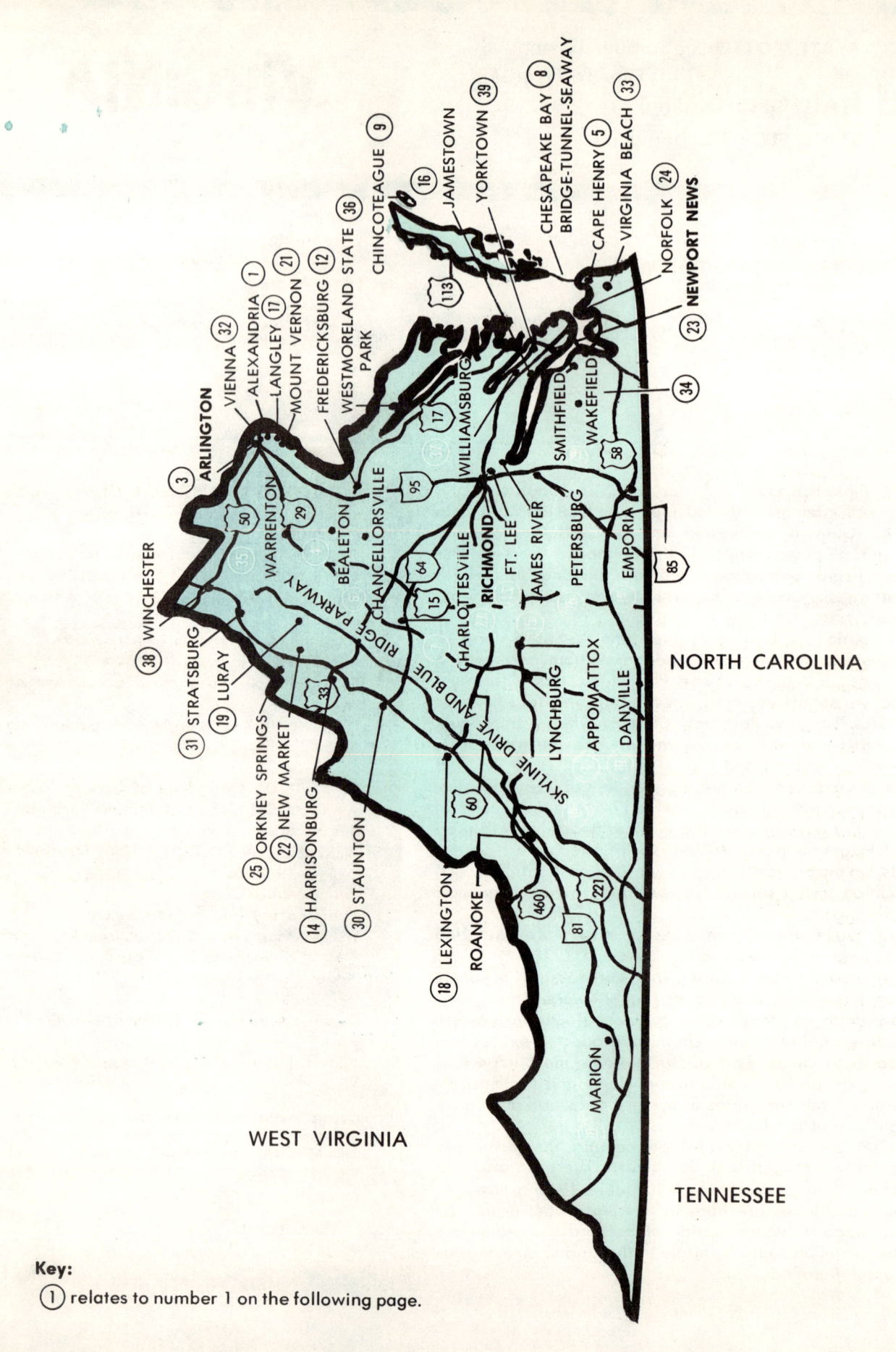

Key:

① relates to number 1 on the following page.

page 194 / treasure trails / Virginia

VIRGINIA POINTS OF INTEREST

1. ALEXANDRIA
   Gunston Hall, house of George Mason, wrote Virginia Declaration of Rights;
   George Washington National Masonic Memorial
2. APPOMATTOX
   Appomattox Court House, National Historical Park;
   McLean House, where Lee surrendered in 1865
3. ARLINGTON
   Custis-Lee Mansion, home of Robert E. Lee;
   Site of John F. Kennedy's grave;
   Tomb of the Unknown Soldiers
4. BEALETON - Flying circus earodrome, colorful re-enactment of dogfights
5. CAPE HENRY - first permanent English settlers landed
6. CHANCELLORSVILLE - Fredericksburg & Spotsylvania National Military Park
7. CHARLOTTESVILLE
   Monticello, home of statesman Thomas Jefferson;
   University of Virginia, founded by Jefferson;
   Ashlawn, home of James Monroe
8. CHESAPEAKE BAY BRIDGE-TUNNEL-SEAWAY - wonder of the world
9. CHINCOTEAGUE - where wild ponies are rounded up on Assateague Island and driven to the sea to swim to Chincoteague
10. DANVILLE - Tobacco auctions
11. EMPORIA - area of peanut crops and annual festival
12. FREDERICKSBURG
    James Monroe Museum and Library, law office;
    home of Mary Washington
13. FT. LEE - U.S. Army Post
14. HARRISONBURG - home of annual Virginia Poultry Festival
15. JAMES RIVER - birthplace of R.E. Lee's mother, Anne Hill Carter
16. JAMESTOWN - where the nation began
17. LANGLEY - N.A.S.A. Research Center
18. LEXINGTON - National Bridge, one of 7 wonders of the world
19. LURAY - Luray Caverns, underground caverns
20. MARION - Old Time Fiddlers and Bluegrass Convention
21. MOUNT VERNON - estate of George Washington
22. NEW MARKET
    Shenandoah Valley Caverns, geologic wonders;
    Hall of Valor, museum of civil war
23. NEWPORT NEWS - Mariner's Museum, world's largest nautical collection
24. NORFOLK
    Gen. MacArthur Memorial, burial site;
    place of International Azalea festival
25. ORKNEY SPRINGS - site of annual Shenandoah Valley Music Festival
26. PETERSBURG - Blandford Church, only British general to be buried in America
27. RICHMOND
    Capital, designed by Thomas Jefferson;
    Museum of Fine Arts, South's largest art museum
28. SKYLINE DRIVE AND BLUE RIDGE PARKWAY - scenic drive
29. SMITHFIELD - home of famous hams
30. STAUNTON - Woodrow Wilson's birthplace
31. STRATSBURG - American Oberammergan Passion Play
32. VIENNA - Wolf Trap Farm Park, performing arts site
33. VIRGINIA BEACH - Shoreline along first permanent colonists
34. WAKEFIELD - birthplace of George Washington
35. WARRENTON - home of famous Virginia Gold Cup horse races
36. WESTMORELAND STATE PARK - Stratford Hall, R.E. Lee's birthplace
37. WILLIAMSBURG
    18th century homes, shops, etc.;
    William and Mary College, founded 1693;
    "The Common Glory", outdoor drama of the American Revolution
38. WINCHESTER
    Stonewall Jackson's Headquarters, Civil War battle sites;
    Home of annual Apple Blossom Festival
39. YORKTOWN - where Independence was won

treasure trails / page 195

The Susan Constant, Godspeed, and the Discovery arrived 13 years before the Mayflower. Reproductions in Jamestown.

Virginia is noted for the beautiful mountains including the Blueridge Parkway and Skyline Drive.

Mount Vernon, home and final resting place of George Washington. Overlooks the Potomac River, near Alexandria.

James Fort, Jamestown, full-scale reconstruction of triangular palisade built by settlers in 1607.

Photographs furnished by Virginia State travel service.

STATE MOTTO: ALKI (Bye And Bye)
STATE BIRD: Willow Goldfinch
STATE FLOWER: Coast Rhododendron

WASHINGTON
Admitted to the Union in 1889

FOR FURTHER INFORMATION WRITE:

- U.S. Forest Service, Federal Building
  1st and Marion
  Seattle, Washington 98100

- State Travel Director, Al Hunter
  Department of Commerce & Economic Development
  Olympia, Washington 98501

- Hunting & Fishing, State Parks & Recreational Commission
  P.O. Box 1128
  Olympia, Washington 98504

Washington is the only state named for a President. It was named in honor of George Washington.

The state lies on the Pacific Coast in the northwestern part of the United States.

To live in Washington and love it, you must become a Rain Worshipper. All of Washington is not evergreen. East of the Cascade Mountains there are hot and dry summers.

In 1775 Brune Hecota and Juan Francisco de la Bodega y Quadra of Spain made the first landing on Washington soil. In 1792 Robert Gray discovered the Columbia River, and George Vancouver surveyed the coast of Washington and Puget Sound. In 1805 Lewis and Clark reached Washington and the Pacific Ocean.

During the early 1800's, British and American fur traders both operated in the region.

A bill creating the Oregon Territory, of which Washington was a part, passed Congress in 1848. President Benjamin Harrison proclaimed the territory as the 42nd state on Nov. 11, 1889. Elisha P. Ferry was the state's first governor. Olympia is the state capital.

The Cascade Mountains divide Washington into two major economic regions. The region east of the Cascades is important for agriculture. Farmers in eastern Washington raise large wheat and fruit crops, beef cattle, and many vegetables. Spokane is eastern Washington's chief financial and marketing center.

Most of Washington's industrial centers are in the western lowlands. Seattle, Tacoma, and other port cities are centers for trade, fishing, and shipbuilding. Western Washington is also a dairy farming and bulb-producing region. Lumbering and the processing of wood products are important in many parts of the state.

To learn more about the Washington people, come and visit with us and find out for yourself why we love Washington the Evergreen State.

The Peace Arch near the U.S.-Canadian border at Blaine symbolizes the largest unfortified border between two powers.

treasure trails / page 197

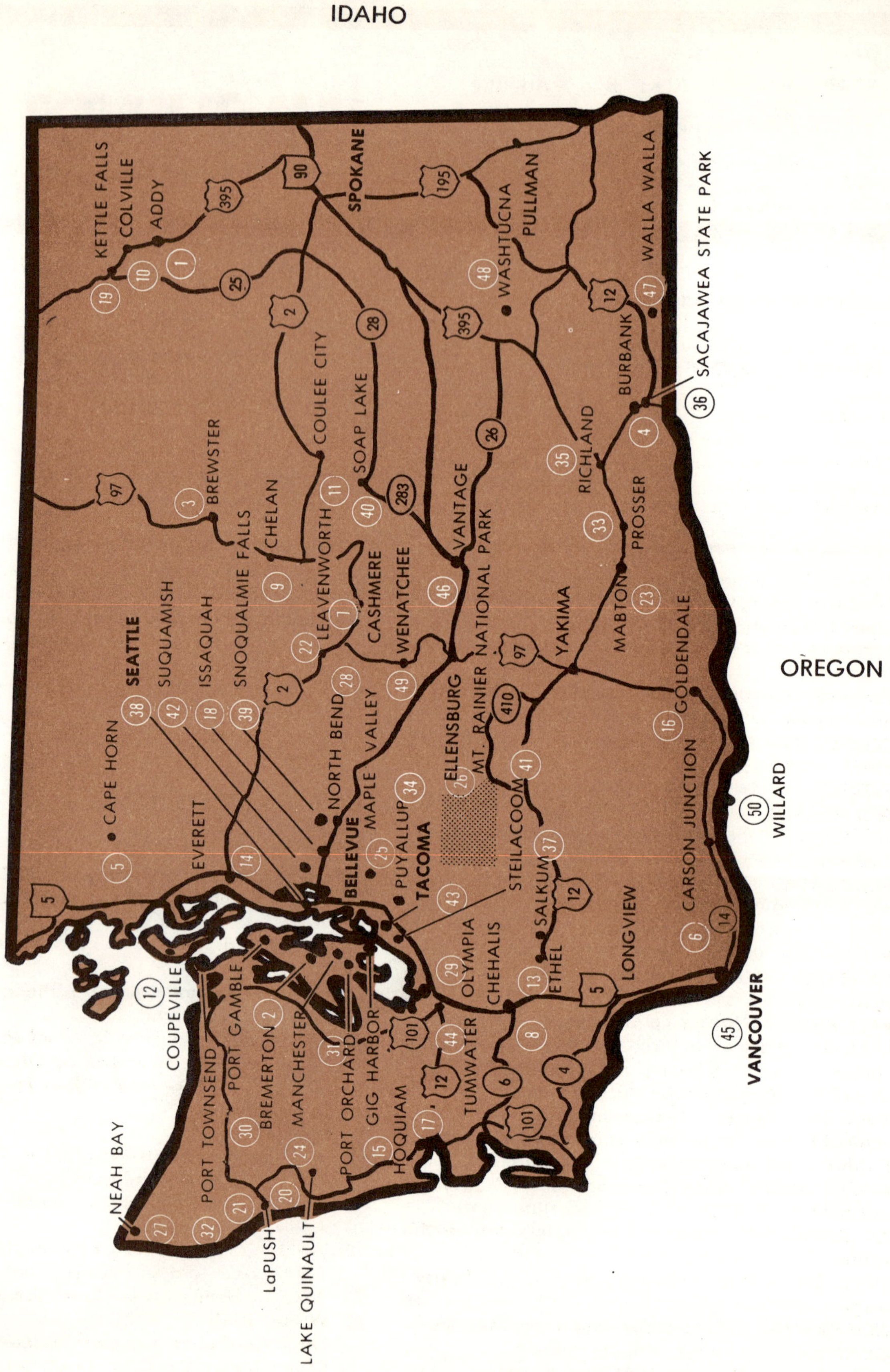

Key:

(1) relates to number 1 on the following page.

WASHINGTON POINTS OF INTEREST

1. ADDY
   Northwest Alloys, Inc.;
   Fossil beds
2. BREMERTON
   Battleship Missouri, where in 1945 General Douglas MacArthur accepted the surrender of Japan;
   Naval Shipyard Museum, maritime history
3. BREWSTER - "Big Ear", communications satellite, tours
4. BURBANK - McNary National Wildlife Refuge, migrating waterfowl and songbirds
5. CAPE HORN - Mt. Pleasant Grange, oldest grange in the state, 1890
6. CARSON JUNCTION - Hemlock Nursery, largest confier government nursery, 1909
7. CASHMERE - Pioneer Village
8. CHEHALIS - Claquato Church, built in 1850
9. CHELAN - Lake Chelan, largest inland bodies of fresh water
10. COLVILLE - Ft. Colville, established 1859
11. COULEE CITY
    Dry Falls, cataract;
    once power of 100 Niagaras
12. COUPEVILLE - Historic Methodist Church, 1853
13. ETHEL - Trout Hatchery, among world's largest
14. EVERETT - 80-foot totem pole
15. GIG HARBOR
    Old fishing town, White Whale Museum;
    Scandia Gaard, museum, Scandinavian cultures
16. GOLDENDALE - Maryhill Mansion, formal Flemish architectural, now Maryhill Museum of Fine Arts, 1914
17. HOQUIAM - Lytle Mansion, Victorian elegance
18. ISSAQUAH - Issaquah Fish Hatchery, supplies millions of baby salmon
19. KETTLE FALLS - St. Paul's Mission, built 1845
20. LAKE QUINAULT - rain forest, elk herds, waterfalls
21. LaPUSH - center for sports and commercial fishing
22. LEAVENWORTH - Bavarian Alpine Village, ski area
23. MABTON - Gannon Museum of Wagons
24. MANCHESTER - Shell Fish Lab, National Marine Fisheries, salmon hatcheries
25. MAPLE VALLEY - Black Diamond Bakery, 100 year old bakery
26. MT. RAINER NATIONAL PARK - recreational center center
27. NEAH BAY - Makah Days, celebration of feasts, August
28. NORTH BEND - Snoqualmie Falls Train Museum
29. OLYMPIA
    State Capitol Museum, Washington history;
    The Olympia Oyster Company, tours
30. PORT GAMBLE - Hood Canal Bridge, longest salt-water floating bridge in the world
31. PORT ORCHARD - Old Sidney Hotel, built 1893
32. PORT TOWNSEND - Chinese Tree of Heaven, presented by Emperor of China, 100 years old
33. PROSSER - Prosser Falls, Indian fishing area
34. PUYALLUP - Ezra Meeker Mansion, built 1890, architectural features
35. RICHLAND - Science exhibit in Federal Building
36. SACAJAWEA STATE PARK - statue of Sacajawea, museum
37. SALKUM - Salmon hatchery, largest in the world
38. SEATTLE
    Space Needle Restaurant, rotates;
    Monorail;
    Pacific Science Center;
    Funland;
    Arboretum, Japanese garden;
    Ferryboats, scenic salt water trips;
    Underground Seattle, historic Pioneer Square;
    Woodland Park Zoo, largest in northwest;
    The Wharf, fisherman's terminal, seafood
39. SNOQUALMIE FALLS - waterfalls
40. SOAP LAKE - Indian encampment area, summer
41. STEILACOOM
    Glenn Orr House, built 1857;
    Philip Keach residence, known as "Rolling Hill", built 1858
42. SUQUAMISH - Old Man House, site of Chief Seattle's home
43. TACOMA
    Point Defiance Park, Aquarium, Children's Farm;
    Fort Nisqually, oldest standing building in Washington, 1843;
    Wright Park, orchids, tropical plants
44. TUMWATER
    Olympia Brewing Company, tours;
    Tumwater Falls Park
45. VANCOUVER - Ulysses S. Grant Museum, antique glassware, furniture used by Grant
46. VANTAGE - Ginkgo Petrified Forest State Park, fossil forests
47. WALLA WALLA
    Whitman Mission, established in 1836;
    Fort Walla Walla, museum;
    Walla Walla Game Farm, game bird hatchings, April
48. WASHTUCNA - Marmes Rock Shelter, remains of a 10,000 year old prehistoric man—oldest in the Western Hemisphere—were discovered in 1968
49. WENATCHEE
    North Central Washington Museum, local history;
    Ohme Alpine Gardens, seven acres
50. WILLARD - Willard Flume, operating flume, built 1922

The Seattle Skyline.

The Pacific Science Center, one of the buildings constructed for the 1962 World's Fair in Seattle.

Lake Cle Elum, north of Cle Elum, off Highway 90.

page 200 / treasure trails

STATE MOTTO: Montani Semper Liberi (Mountaineers Are Always Free)
STATE BIRD: Cardinal
STATE FLOWER: Rhododendron Maximum or "Big Laurel"

WEST VIRGINIA
Admitted to the Union in 1863

FOR FURTHER INFORMATION WRITE:

- Supervisor
  Monongahela National Forest
  USDA Building
  Elkins, West Virginia 25241

- Department of Natural Resources
  Charleston, West Virginia 25305

- Travel Development Division
  West Virginia Department of Commerce
  Charleston, West Virginia 25305

Wild, wonderful, West Virginia is located in the eastern part of the United States. Boundary lines of West Virginia total 1,170 miles which for the most part follow the course of rivers or the line of mountain ranges. The state encloses a total area of only 24,282.45 square miles of which 120 are water surface. The easternmost tip has the same longitude as Rochester, N. Y., and the most westerly as Port Huron, Michigan. The northwest panhandle pushes into a latitude well north of Pittsburgh, Penn., while in the opposite direction the state dips further south than Richmond, Virginia.

June 20, 1863 is the day West Virginia became the 35th State in the Union, the only state born out of the cauldron of the Civil War. On April 20, 1863 President Abraham Lincoln issued a proclamation under which 60 days later West Virginia would become a State. On that day Arthur I. Boreman, the first governor and other officers were inaugurated. Wheeling became the first capital. April 1, 1870 the capital was moved to Charleston. In 1875 the capital returned to Wheeling. On August 7, 1877 the citizens of West Virginia voted to make Charleston the site of its capital. The State Capitol stands on the banks of the Kanawha River. The Governor's Mansion at Kanawha Boulevard and Duffy Street is just west of the Capitol.

West Virginia has been endowed with exceptional scenery. Its extremes in elevations and pattern of precipitation have produced a wide variety of plants and animals. Its forests, soil and water mineral resources have generated important agricultural and industrial developments. The course of time and the kinds of people who settled here have influenced the historical events and cultural aspects of the Mountain State.

The Allegheny Mountains are at their scenic best in West Virginia. Numerous state parks and forests, natural wonders, fine resorts and many historic sites are interesting highlights to be found in the Mountain State.

New River Gorge, near Hinton, West Virginia.

treasure trails / page 201

Key:

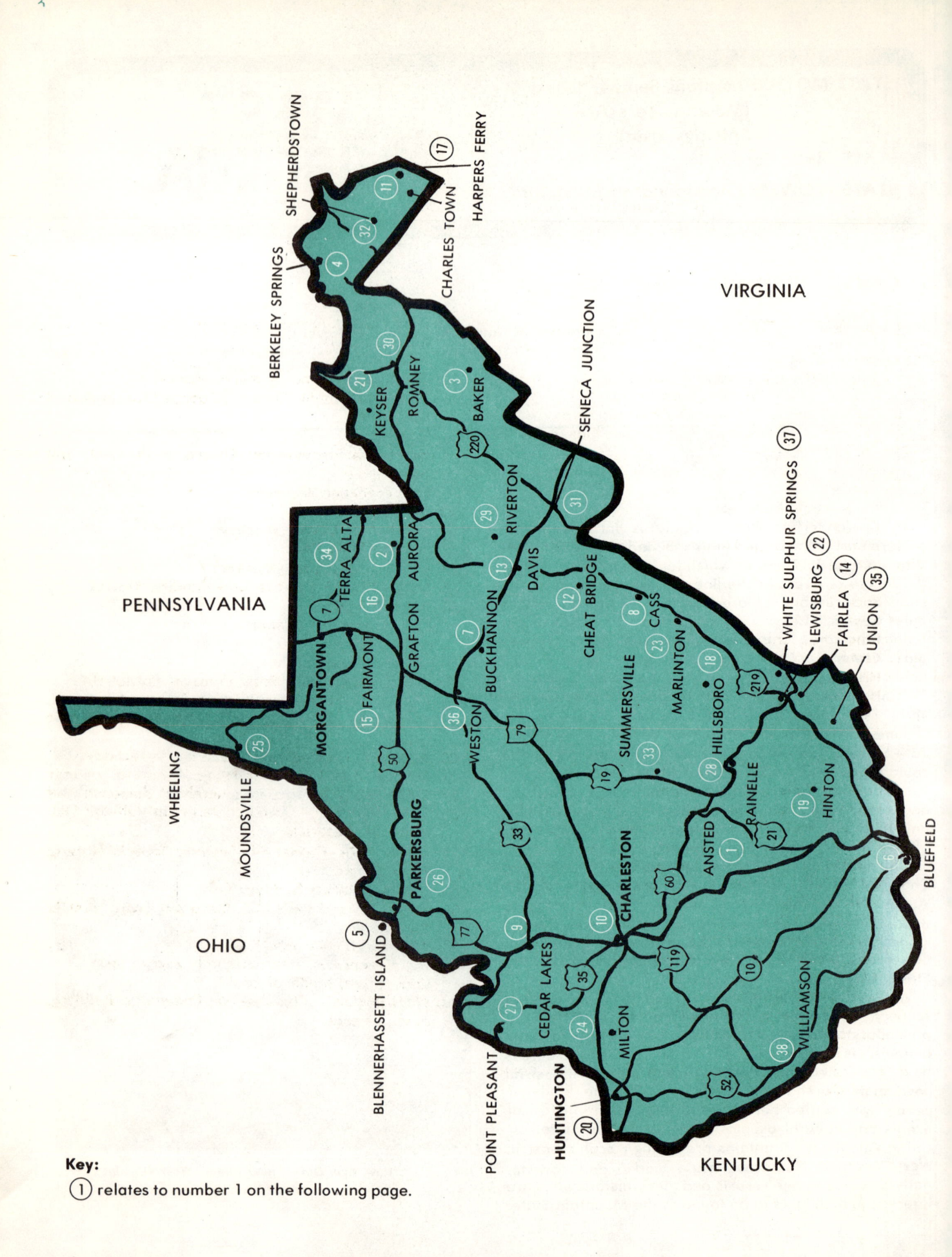

① relates to number 1 on the following page.

page 202 / treasure trails / West Virginia

WEST VIRGINIA POINTS OF INTEREST

1. ANSTED - Hawk's Nest, canyon
2. AURORA - Cathedral, virgin timber
3. BAKER - Lost River, river disappears
4. BERKELEY SPRINGS
   The Castle, Washington's home;
   Colonel Lewis Washington's home
5. BLENNERHASSETT ISLAND - historic area
6. BLUEFIELD - Pinnacle Rock, resembles ruins of ancient castle
7. BUCKHANNON - French Creek Game Farm
8. CASS
   Cass Scenic Railroad;
   Civil War Museum
9. CEDAR LAKES - Mountain State Arts & Crafts Fair, July
10. CHARLESTON
    State Capitol and Museum;
    Sunrise, culture center;
    Kanawha State Forest, migratory birds, wildflowers
11. CHARLES TOWN
    Historic homes;
    Harewood, Dolly Payne Todd and James Madison were married
12. CHEAT BRIDGE - Gaudineer Knob, scenic area
13. DAVIS
    Blackwater Falls, popular attraction;
    Canaan Valley, upland valley;
    Mountain State Museum;
    Canaan Valley, winter sports center
14. FAIRLEA - State Fair, August
15. FAIRMONT - Prickett's Fort, built 1774
16. GRAFTON - Mother's Day Shrine site of first Mother's Day
17. HARPERS FERRY
    National Historical Park;
    John Brown's Fort, site of capture
18. HILLSBORO
    Pearl Buck birthplace;
    Droop Mountain Battlefield, Civil War site;
    Beartown, rock formations
19. HINTON
    Bluestone Gorge, canyon with aerial Bluestone State Park, water sports
20. HUNTINGTON
    Huntington Galleries, museum;
    Rose Gardens
21. KEYSER
    The Saddle, home of Nancy Hanks;
    Fort Ashby, built 1775 by George Washington
22. LEWISBURG
    Caverns;
    Old Stone Presbyterian Church, built 1792, still used;
    Fort Savannah Museum
23. MARLINTON
    Pocahontas County Museum;
    Watoga State Park;
24. MILTON - Morgan's Museum
25. MOUNDSVILLE - Grave Creek Indian Mound
26. PARKERSBURG
    Parkersburg Art Center;
    Art Gallery;
    Historical homes
27. POINT PLEASANT - Point Pleasant Battlefield
28. RAINELLE - Ponderosa Wildlife Preserve
29. RIVERTON - Germany Valley, outstanding scenic area
30. ROMNEY - Ice Mountain, ice on the hottest days
31. SENECA JUNCTION - Seneca Falls, natural wonder
32. SHEPHERDSTOWN - first steamboat demonstrated
33. SUMMERSVILLE - Carnifex Ferry Battlefield, Civil War site, historical
34. TERRA ALTA - Cranesville Swamp, National Natural History Landmark
35. UNION - Rehoboth Church
36. WESTON - Jackson's Mill, State 4-H Camp, first in the nation
37. WHITE SULPHUR SPRINGS
    The Greenbrier, internationally known spa;
    Coal House, made of coal
38. WILLIAMSON - Chamber of Commerce Building, made of coal

treasure trails / page 203

Blackwater Falls State Park, near Thomas, West Virginia.

Harpers Ferry

Photographs furnished by Gerald S. Ratliff.

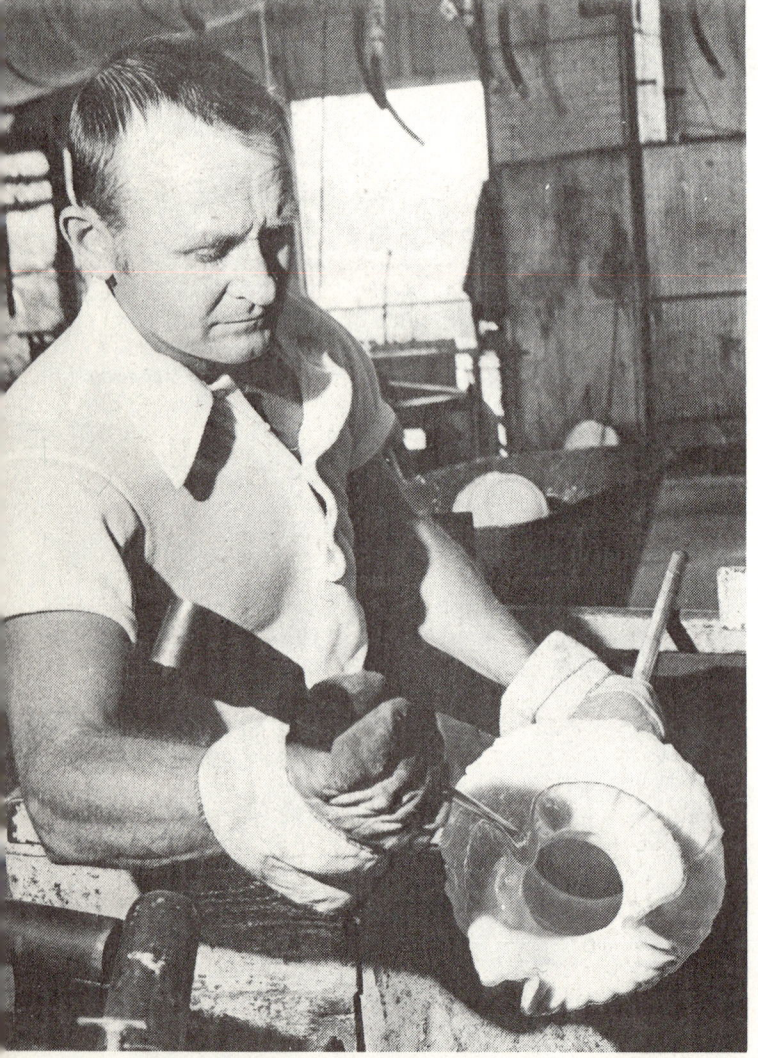

Fenton Glass

Mansion House Museum, Oglebay Park, in Charleston.

page 204 / treasure trails

STATE MOTTO: Forward
STATE BIRD: Robin
STATE FLOWER: Wood Violet

WISCONSIN
Admitted to the Union in 1848

FOR FURTHER INFORMATION WRITE:

- Vacation and Travel Service of Wisconsin
  Dept. of Natural Resources
  Box 450
  Madison, Wisconsin 53701

- Fishing and Hunting Regulations
  Department of Natural Resources
  Box 450
  Madison, Wisconsin 53701

- The State Historical Society of Wisconsin
  816 State Street
  Madison, Wisconsin 53706

In 1634, Jean Nicolet, French explorer, landed in Green Bay, the first white man in the state to cement relations between the Indians and the French. The state is rich in Indian history. The word Wisconsin is of Indian origin, meaning "the place of the gathering of the waters". Tribes found in the state are Chippewa, Menominee, Oneida, Winnebago, Stockbridge-Munsee and Potowatomi.

The first territorial legislature met on October 25, 1836, in Belmont. Wisconsin became a state on May 29, 1848; the state capitol is Madison.

In the early days, mining, fur trapping and logging were important. Gradually farming increased in importance to gain the state title, "America's Dairyland". Now manufacturing and touristry vie with agriculture in making Wisconsin a prosperous state.

Wisconsin, located at the headwaters of the Mississippi and the St. Lawrence river system, has some of the best scenery in our nation. Thousands of lakes dot the state adding to the beauty and pleasure of resident and tourist. In addition, the state has 10,000 miles of trout streams, 3,000 miles of navigable rivers, 500 miles of Great Lakes Shores and 242 miles of Mississippi River Shores.

The state boasts major league athletics in all three major sports—football with the Green Bay Packers, basketball with the Milwaukee Bucks, and the Milwaukee Brewers Wisconsin's baseball team. Other sports include hunting, fishing, skiing, bicycling, snowmobiling, hockey, curling, swimming, boating, tennis and golf. Milwaukee has the nation's only Olympic-sized skating rink.

Wisconsin has an excellent system of toll-free highways making driving a pleasure. More than 100 historical markers along the highways tell a fascinating saga of the long-vanished Indian tribe. The markers also pay tribute to outstanding citizens making substantial contributions in literature, politics, architecture, education, medicine and conservation.

Little Norway in Dane Country, near Mt. Horeb.

treasure trails / page 205

Key:

① relates to number 1 on the following page.

WISCONSIN POINTS OF INTEREST

1. APPLETON - Dard Hunter Paper Museum, traces paper making from 105 A.D. until the machine age
2. ARLINGTON - University of Wisconsin Experimental Farm
3. BALSAM LAKE - historical museum
4. BARABOO - World Circus Museum, winter quarters of Ringling Brothers
5. BELMONT - First State Capitol
6. BOULDER JUNCTION - Trout Lake State Forestry Nursery
7. BRULE RIVER - famous trout stream
8. BURLINGTON - Nestle Co., tours
9. CASSVILLE - Stonefield, farm museum
10. EAST TROY - Cobblestone Hotel, example of cobblestone architecture
11. EAU CLAIRE - Paul Bunyan Logging Museum
12. ELKHART LAKE - Road America Sportscar Races
13. ELKHORN - Webster House, 19th century home of Joseph Webster
14. FOND DU LAC - Galloway House Museum
15. FRIENDSHIP - Friendship Mound, 385 feet above plain
16. GREEN BAY
    Packer Hall of Fame;
    National Museum of Railroading
17. GREENBUSH
    Old Wade House, former Stage Coach Inn;
    Carriage Museum, one of America's finest carriage collections
18. HARTFORD - Holy Hill Shrine & Monastery, Castle-like Church
19. HAYWARD - Historyland Lumberjack Bowl, Lumberjack World Championships
20. HORICON - Horicon Marsh, wildlife area, geese
21. HUDSON - Octagon House, doll collection
22. HURLEY - National Finnish-American Center
23. LAC DU FLAMBEAU - Indian Ceremonials, held in summer months
24. LAKE MILLS - Aztalan State Park, foremost archeological site
25. LAONA - World's largest hardwood sawmill
26. MADISON
    State Capitol, Frank Lloyd Wright architecture;
    University of Wisconsin, planetarium, arboretum and observatory;
    State Historical Society Museum;
    U.S. Forest Products Laboratory;
    Oscar Mayer, 2 hour tour
27. MANITOWOC - Manitowoc Maritime Museum
28. MILTON - Milton House, oldest cement building in U.S., slave tunnels
29. MILWAUKEE
    Milwaukee Zoo;
    Mitchell Park Conservatory, sunken gardens, botanical conservatory;
    Annunciation Greek Orthodox Church, last major work of Frank Lloyd Wright;
    Joan of Arc Chapel, rebuilt French chapel;
    Port of Milwaukee;
    Milwaukee Art Center;
    Brewery tours, Pabst, Schlitz, Blatz, Miller
30. MONROE - Swiss Cheese Center of the U.S., tours
31. MONTREAL - Abandoned Iron Mines
32. NEW GLARUS - Swiss Lace factory, museum
33. NEW LONDON - Carr Museum, natural history
34. OCONTO
    Copper Culture Indian Burial Grounds, exhibits from 5556 B.C.;
    Beyer Home, Civil War Museum
35. OSHKOSH - Paine Art Center & Aboretum, period rooms
36. PORTAGE - Indian Agency House, 1832
37. PRAIRIE DU CHIEN
    Villa Louis, Victorian home of Hercules Dousman;
    Medical Museum, history of medicine in Wisconsin
38. RACINE - Johnson Wax Administration and Research Center, designed by Frank Lloyd Wright
39. RHINELANDER - Logging Museum
40. RIPON - Birthplace of Republican Party
41. SARONA - Audubon Camp
42. SHULLSBURG - Badger Mine and Museum, tours
43. SOLON SPRINGS - Upland Bird Sanctuary
44. SPOONER
    State Fish Hatchery, hatchery for muskellunge;
    Wood Carving Museum, biblical scenes
45. SPRING GREEN - The House on the Rock, home atop a chimney-like rock
46. STEPHENSON ISLAND - Marinette Historical Museum
47. SUPERIOR - Largest Iron Ore Docks in the world
48. WATERTOWN - Octagon House and First Kindergarten
49. WAUZEKA - Phetteplace Museum, mosaics
50. WILLIAMS BAY - Yerkes Observatory
51. WISCONSIN DELLS
    Water show;
    Ceremonial dances;
    Biblical gardens

Tallman House, Janesville

Chalet of the Golden Fleece, New Glarus

Covered Bridge, near Cedarburg

Railway at North Freedom

page 208 / treasure trails

Photographs furnished by Wisconsin Natural Resources Department, Madison.

STATE MOTTO: Equal Rights
STATE BIRD: Meadow Lark
STATE FLOWER: Indian Paint Brush

WYOMING
Admitted to the Union in 1890

FOR FURTHER INFORMATION WRITE:

- Wyoming Game & Fish Department
  Cheyenne, Wyoming 82001

- William Crump, District Director
  Wyoming Game & Fish Department
  Lander, Wyoming 82520

- Wyoming Travel Commission
  2320 Capitol Avenue
  Capitol Building
  Cheyenne, Wyoming 82001

The largest part of the state of Wyoming was acquired by the Government in the Louisiana purchase in 1803. The area that is now the state of Wyoming became a territory by the passing of the Ashley Bill in Congress, July 25, 1868. The territorial government was set up a year later, and 21 years later July 10, 1890 the territory became the forty-fourth state to be admitted to the Union.

John Colter is the first white man known to enter present Wyoming and also discovered the phenomenon we know now as Yellowstone Park. Every mile conjures recollections of the mountain men, the explorers, the missionaries and the soldiers.

The great plains meet the Rocky Mountains in Wyoming, the state being a great plateau broken by a number of mountain ranges. The Continental Divide cuts through Wyoming from the northwest to the south central border. The climate of Wyoming is generally arid, precipitation averaging about 15" annually.

Wyoming's industry is diversified. Primarily the state produces food products such as cheese, flour and beet sugar. Other products include lumber, petroleum, coal products, iron ore and uranium.

Wyoming is world famous for its bountiful game. Elk, deer, antelope, moose and bear are abundant. The fisherman's reel seldom returns empty for the wily trout and other Rocky Mountain species prove the state to be the sportsmen's choice.

Wyoming is primarily a livestock state, cattle and sheep far out number the populace and accounts for Wyoming's second largest industry.

Dude ranches are a growing industry, thousands from across the nation and foreign countries spend their vacations on these ranches.

Devils Tower National Monument, northwest of Sundance, approximately 50 million years old, 1,280 feet high, valley of Belle Fourche River.

treasure trails / page 209

page 210 / treasure trails

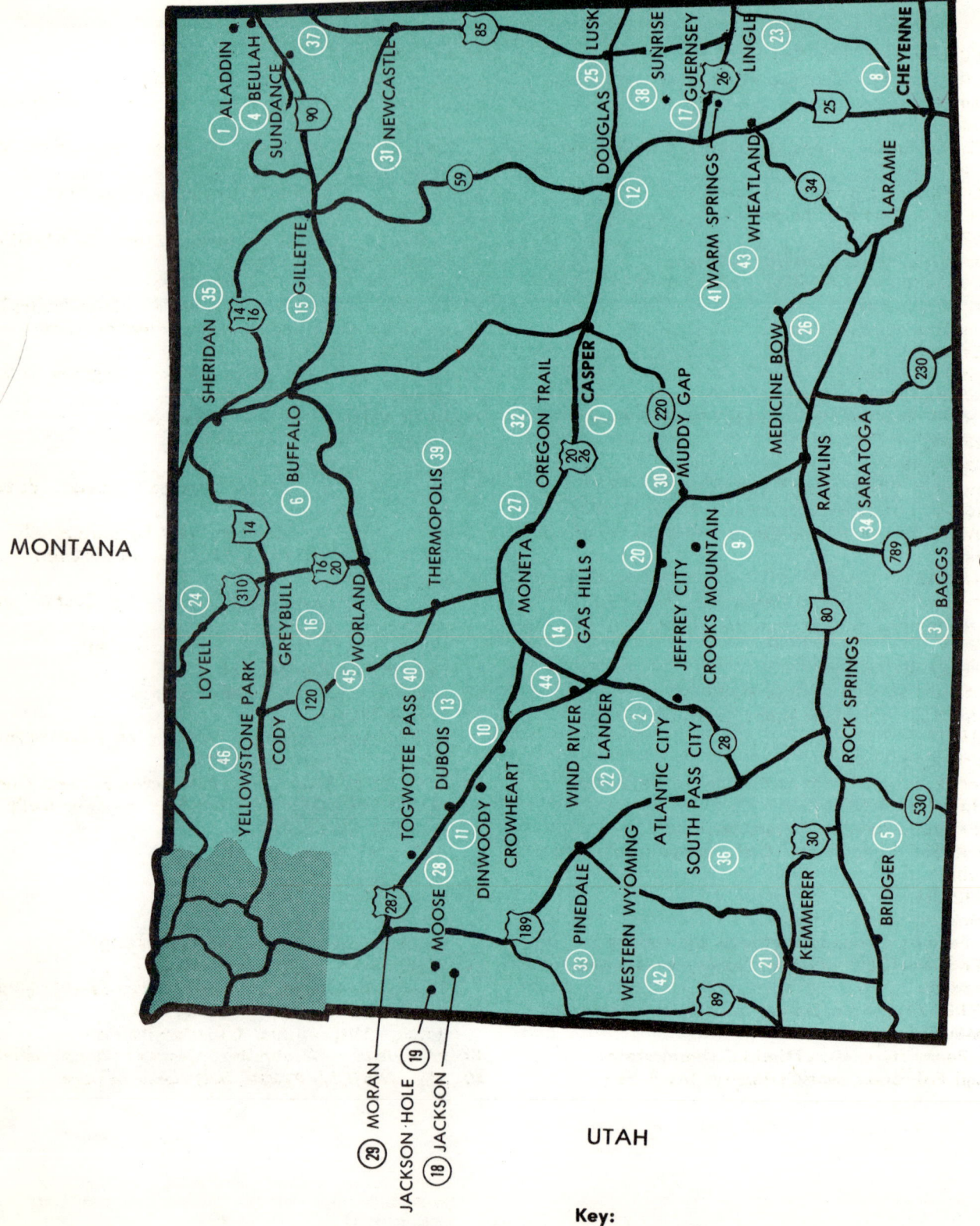

WYOMING POINTS OF INTEREST

1. ALADDIN - Old-Time Country Store
2. ATLANTIC CITY - Caraissa Mine, best and largest preserved
3. BAGGS - Rendezvous of bad men
4. BEULAH - Buffalo Jumps, excavating buffalo bones, Indian artifacts
5. BRIDGER - Fort Bridger, restored fort
6. BUFFALO - Fort Phil Kearney, historical fort
7. CASPER
   Hole-in-Wall, Butch Cassidy hide-away;
   Bessemer Bend, site of first cabin built by white men in Wyoming;
   Hell's Half Acre, badlands
8. CHEYENNE
   Capitol Building;
   Cheyenne Frontier Days
9. CROOKS MOUNTAIN - Jade Fields, finest in Wyoming
10. CROWHEART
    Crowheart Butte, site of Indian battle;
    Dinwoody Glaciers, year-round glacier field
11. DINWOODY - Dinwoody Caves, Indian writings on cliffs
12. DOUGLAS
    Fort Fetterman, site of Fetterman Massacre;
    Ayre's Natural Bridge, natural wonder
13. DUBOIS
    Tie Hack Memorial;
    Petrified Forest, complete stone forest
14. GAS HILLS - Uranium Mines, open-pit mining
15. GILLETTE
    Prairie Dog Town;
    Wyodak, largest strip coal mine in the world;
    Buffalo Ranch
16. GREYBULL - Devil's Kitchen, badlands
17. GUERNSEY - Register Cliff, grave of Lucinda Rawlins
18. JACKSON
    Alpine Village, ski resort;
    Elk Feeding Grounds, National Elk Refuge
19. JACKSON HOLE - Grand Tetons, Swiss Alps of America
20. JEFFREY CITY - Ice Slough, pioneer's refrigerator
21. KEMMERER
    J.C. Penny Store, site of first J.C. Penny store;
    Fossil Fish Beds, world's largest fossil bed
22. LANDER
    South Pass, restored gold mining town;
    Sinks, Popo Agie River sinks under mountains to rise again;
    One Shot Hunt, world famous, one bullet for antelope
23. LINGLE - Fort Laramie, restored Army Post
24. LOVELL - Fish Hatchery
25. LUSK - Running Water Station, Cheyenne Deadwood Stage Station
26. MEDICINE BOW - Virginian Hotel
27. MONETA - Castle Gardens, prehistoric petroglyphs
28. MOOSE - Gros Ventre, rock formation slide
29. MORAN - Teton Park
30. MUDDY GAP - Independence Rock, Register of the Desert
31. NEWCASTLE - Cambria, ghost town
32. OREGON TRAIL - ruts visible
33. PINEDALE - Chariot Races
34. SARATOGA - Snowy Range, scenic drive, recreational area
35. SHERIDAN - Sheridan Inn, built by Buffalo Bill
36. SOUTH PASS CITY - Gold Mines, abandoned
37. SUNDANCE
    Custer Monument, trail made by Custer and Soldiers;
    Devil's Tower, first National Monument;
    Federal Fish Genetic Lab
38. SUNRISE - Sunrise Mines, iron ore
39. THERMOPOLIS
    Gift of Water Pageant, Wedding of the Waters;
    Mineral Hot Springs Park
40. TOGWOTEE PASS - Snowmobile Races, oval track
41. WARM SPRINGS - Emigrant Ruts, pioneer trails
42. WESTERN WYOMING
    Antelope Herds;
    Dude Ranches
43. WHEATLAND
    Spanish Diggings;
    Basin Engineering, marble processing
44. WIND RIVER
    Sacajawea Cemetery, grave of Sacajawea, guide for the Lewis and Clark expedition;
    Roberts Mission, first Christian mission
45. WORLAND - Oktoberfest, German dance festival
46. YELLOWSTONE PARK - first national park

Hot Springs State Park, world's largest mineral hot springs, 18,600,000 gallons of water flows over milti-colored terraces every 24 hours. In Thermopolis on Big Horn River.

Photographs furnished by Wyoming Travel Commis...

Ft. Caspar, replica of fort named for Caspar Collins, lieutenant killed rescuing wagon train in 1865.

Rodeos, West at its most rugged. Plenty of Wild West thrills chills.

Gannett Peak-Dinwoody Glacier, in Wind River Mountains, Gannett is tallest Wyoming mountain.

page 212 / treasure trails

NATIONAL EXTENSION HOMEMAKERS COUNCIL

The National Extension Homemakers Council is associated with the Home Economics Program of the Cooperative Extension Service at each of the Landgrant Universities in the United States. They receive off-campus training in Home Economics and related areas under the sponsorship or guidance of the County and State Home Economists, (or Agents), of the Cooperative Extension.

They are closely associated with 4-H and call themselves the 'Mother' of 4-H since most of the Homemakers serve as volunteer leaders of 4-H Clubs and their children have been, or are 4-H members themselves.

The NEHC is a volunteer, non-profit organization that functions solely for the purpose of improving the knowledge and skills of the housewife in making her a better homemaker, not only for her family but her community, state and nation. There are 35,000 clubs in forty-two states and they have a membership of 600,000.

STATE NICKNAMES AND MEANINGS

ALABAMA
Meaning of name: from Indian tribe named Alibamu, meaning I open (or clear) the thicket
Nickname: Heart of Dixie

ALASKA
Meaning of name: great land (from the Aleut people)
Nickname: The Last Frontier

ARIZONA
Meaning of name: Indian meaning small springs
Nickname: Grand Canyon State

ARKANSAS
Meaning of name: Indian meaning downstream people
Nickname: Land of Opportunity

CALIFORNIA
Meaning of name: from name of treasure island in Spanish tale of 1500's. Spanish word cala—a little cove of the sea, Latin term fornix—vault of a building
Nickname: The Golden State

COLORADO
Meaning of name: Spanish verb meaning to color
Nickname: The Centennial State

CONNECTICUT
Meaning of name: Indian meaning the long river
Nickname: The Constitution State

DELAWARE
Meaning of name: from Lord De La War, early governor of Virginia
Nicknames: The First State
The Blue Hen State
The Diamond State

FLORIDA
Meaning of name: Spanish meaning flowery
Nicknames: Sunshine State
The Peninsula State
The Everglade State

GEORGIA
Meaning of name: Greek noun meaning tillage
Nicknames: The Empire of the South
The Peach State

HAWAII
Meaning unknown
Nicknames: The Aloha State
The Crossroads of the Pacific

IDAHO
Meaning of name: Indian meaning sun comes down th[e] mountains
Nickname: Gem of the Mountains

ILLINOIS
Meaning of name: Indian meaning men perfect an[d] accomplished
Nickname: Land of Lincoln

INDIANA
Meaning of name: land of the Indians
Nicknames: The Hoosier State
The Mother of Vice Presidents

IOWA
Meaning of name: Indian meaning this is the place
Nicknames: The Hawkeye State
The Corn State

KANSAS
Meaning of name: from the Kansa or Kaw Indians. Kans[a] means people of the south wind
Nicknames: The Sunflower State
The Wheat State
The Bread Basket of America
The Central State

KENTUCKY
Meaning of name: Indian meaning great meadow
Nickname: The Bluegrass State

LOUISIANA
Meaning of name: from name Louis, plus suffix "iana["] meaning of or belonging to
Nicknames: The Pelican State
The Bayou State
The Creole State

MAINE
Meaning of name: from French province name meaning great, large, rich, powerful
Nickname: The Pine Tree State

MARYLAND
Meaning of name: named for Queen Henrietta Maria
Nickname: The Old Line State

MASSACHUSETTS
Meaning of name: Indian meaning masa (great) and wachesett (a mountain place) the place of the great hil[l]
Nickname: The Bay State

MICHIGAN
Meaning of name: Indian word michiguma meaning big water
Nickname: The Water Wonderland

MINNESOTA
Meaning of name: Dakota Indian name Minne meaning water, and sota meaning appearance of the sky (sky-tinted water)
Nickname: The Gopher State

MISSISSIPPI
Meaning of name: Indian words meeche or mescha meaning great, and cebe meaning river (The Father of Waters)
Nickname: The Magnolia State

MISSOURI
Meaning of name: Indian meaning muddy water
Nickname: The Show Me State

MONTANA
Meaning of name: Spanish form of Latin word meaning mountainous regions
Nickname: The Treasure State

NEBRASKA
Meaning of name: Indian meaning flat water
Nickname: The Cornhusker State

NEVADA
Meaning of name: Indian meaning snow fall
Nickname: The Silver State

NEW HAMPSHIRE
Meaning of name: Old Anglo-Saxon word Hāmtūn scīr meaning a permanent dwelling place
Nickname: The Granite State

NEW JERSEY
Meaning of name: from island of Jersey in the English Channel
Nickname: The Granite State

NEW MEXICO
Meaning of name: Mexico the land of the Aztec god Mexitle
Nickname: The Land of Enchantment

NEW YORK
Meaning of name: in honor of the Duke of York
Nickname: The Empire State

NORTH CAROLINA
Meaning of name: Carolina is Latin form of Charles meaning white thistle
Nickname: The Tarheel State

NORTH DAKOTA
Meaning of name: Dakota means joined together in friendly compact
Nickname: The Flickertail State

OHIO
Meaning of name: Iroquois Indian word meaning something big
Nickname: Buckeye State

OKLAHOMA
Meaning of name: Choctaw words Okla meaning people and home meaning red
Nickname: The Sooner State

OREGON
Meaning of name: comes from ouragon meaning hurricane
Nickname: The Beaver State

PENNSYLVANIA
Meaning of name: Old Celtic term, penn, meaning a head and sylvanus derived from name meaning wood forest
Nickname: Keystone State

RHODE ISLAND
Meaning of name: from Greek island Rhodos meaning Island of Roses
Nickname: Little Rhody

SOUTH CAROLINA
Meaning of name: same as North Carolina
Nickname: the Palmetto State

SOUTH DAKOTA
Meaning of name: same as North Dakota
Nickname: The Coyote State

TENNESSEE
Meaning of name: Indian meaning unknown
Nickname: The Volunteer State

TEXAS
Meaning of name: Indian name Texia or Spanish form, Tejas meaning allies, friends
Nickname: The Lone Star State

UTAH
Meaning of name: Indian meaning upper people or hill dwellers
Nickname: The Beehive State

VERMONT
Meaning of name: French: vert mont meaning green mountains
Nickname: The Green Mountain State

VIRGINIA
Meaning of name: Named for Queen Elizabeth I of England, "The Virgin Queen"
Nickname: The Old Dominion

WASHINGTON
Meaning of name: named for President Washington meaning farm or settlement of the people of Wassa
Nickname: The Evergreen State

WEST VIRGINIA
Meaning of name: named for Virginia from which it broke away
Nickname: The Mountain State

WISCONSIN
Meaning of name: Chippewa Indian word meskousing meaning gathering of waters
Nickname: The Badger State

WYOMING
Meaning of name: Indian meaning upon the great plain
Nickname: The Equality State

MAJOR BICENTENNIAL FESTIVITIES

MOUNT RUSHMORE NATIONAL MEMORIAL
In the Black Hills of South Dakota

The carved faces of Washington, Jefferson, Roosevelt and Lincoln were created by sculptor Gutzon Borglum. "The Shrine of Democracy" has been chosen as the focal point for the bicentennial celebration. At an elevation of 6,200 feet, the faces are approximately sixty feet high.

SEATTLE
Festival of entertainment, art and technology. Ethnic displays and celebrations. Children's exhibits. Freedom train display days.

SALT LAKE CITY
Musical presentations by the Mormon Tabernacle Choir. Art center opening. Freedom train display days.

SAN FRANCISCO
Pedestrian trail following historic sites. Exhibits, conferences. Historic buildings restored.

CLARK COUNTY, NEVADA
Parades, festival of nations for ethnic groups, rodeos, square dance meeting, restoration of historic buildings.

DENVER
Sports activities, concerts, festivals, in the new performing arts and sports arena. Ethnic displays, and park dedications. Freedom train display days.

DALLAS, FORT WORTH AREA
Museum built in Old City Park, Dallas. Freedom train display days, Dallas. Fort Worth, exhibits, dramas, restored areas.

page 216 / treasure trails

DES MOINES
Displays, museum exhibits, botanical garden and historic farms with exhibits. Freedom train display days.

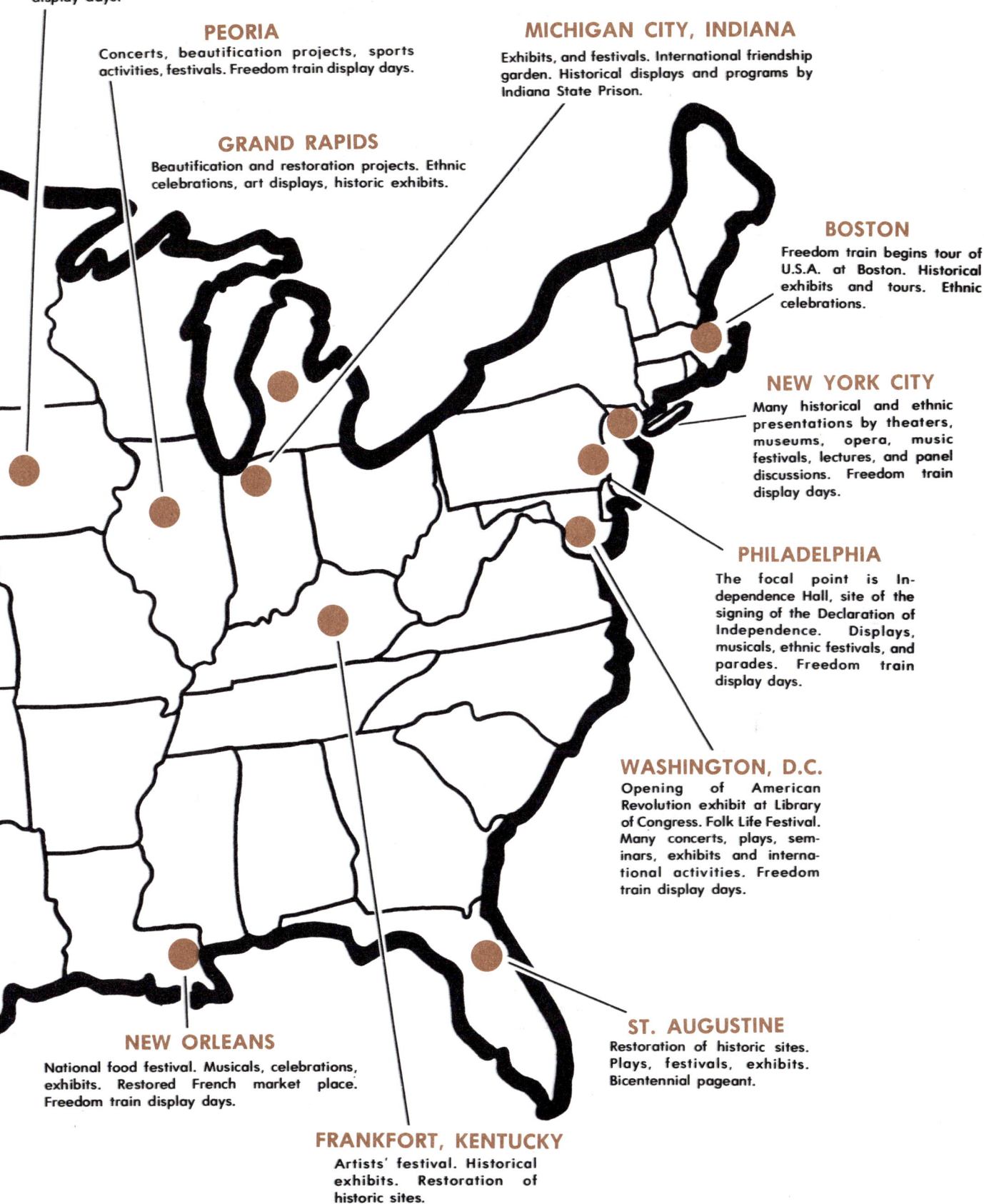

PEORIA
Concerts, beautification projects, sports activities, festivals. Freedom train display days.

MICHIGAN CITY, INDIANA
Exhibits, and festivals. International friendship garden. Historical displays and programs by Indiana State Prison.

GRAND RAPIDS
Beautification and restoration projects. Ethnic celebrations, art displays, historic exhibits.

BOSTON
Freedom train begins tour of U.S.A. at Boston. Historical exhibits and tours. Ethnic celebrations.

NEW YORK CITY
Many historical and ethnic presentations by theaters, museums, opera, music festivals, lectures, and panel discussions. Freedom train display days.

PHILADELPHIA
The focal point is Independence Hall, site of the signing of the Declaration of Independence. Displays, musicals, ethnic festivals, and parades. Freedom train display days.

WASHINGTON, D.C.
Opening of American Revolution exhibit at Library of Congress. Folk Life Festival. Many concerts, plays, seminars, exhibits and international activities. Freedom train display days.

NEW ORLEANS
National food festival. Musicals, celebrations, exhibits. Restored French market place. Freedom train display days.

ST. AUGUSTINE
Restoration of historic sites. Plays, festivals, exhibits. Bicentennial pageant.

FRANKFORT, KENTUCKY
Artists' festival. Historical exhibits. Restoration of historic sites.

treasure trails / page 217